AVID
READER
PRESS

THE HERO NEXT DOOR

Stories of Patriotism and Purpose

MARTHA RADDATZ

AVID READER PRESS

New York Amsterdam/Antwerp London
Toronto Sydney/Melbourne New Delhi

Avid Reader Press
An Imprint of Simon & Schuster, LLC
1230 Avenue of the Americas
New York, NY 10020

First Avid Reader Press hardcover edition May 2026

AVID READER PRESS and colophon are trademarks of Simon & Schuster, LLC

Interior design by Paul Dippolito

Manufactured in the United States of America

5 7 9 10 8 6 4

Library of Congress Control Number: 2025951010

ISBN 978-1-6680-9380-1
ISBN 978-1-6680-9382-5 (ebook)

For our men and women in uniform
and the families who stand with them.

And for my own family. With special love for my
grandchildren, Magnolia, Morgan, Eric, and Gus.

Contents

THE HERO NEXT DOOR

Introduction

IN OCTOBER 2010, JUST BEFORE THE SUN SET OVER THE beaches of Normandy, I walked with a group of veterans, young and old, to the American Cemetery, through rows planted with thousands of white crosses. We moved slowly, lifting umbrellas as a soft rain grew heavier. The weather seemed right for the occasion. Right for us.

I had by then spent more than a decade in combat zones and devoured books about long-ago battles, but I had never been to Normandy. I wasn't the only one. I know all of us were trying to imagine the drama and horror of those days in 1944, when so many men sloshed through the waters of the English Channel, climbed onto the beach, and struggled toward the bluffs to push their way into occupied France. Those lucky enough to make it that far. Standing where we were, we thought mostly of the others, the less fortunate souls who made it to this place only after their bodies were found and they were laid to rest under one of the small crosses that stretched to the horizon.

We proceeded without saying a word. It is a place where you keep your thoughts to yourself. Or that is what we first assumed, until a voice bellowed above the grounds of the hallowed cemetery. Awkward, insistent. An eruption that would startle us all—if only for a few moments—and teach us a profound lesson.

I had come to Normandy on an "Army Staff Ride," an official US military trip in which an Army historian leads military personnel and their guests to famous battlegrounds to share insights about war. I had been invited by General Carter Ham, the commander of US Army forces in Europe. I'd first met General Ham in 2004, during one of my many trips to Iraq, when he served as commander of US forces in Mosul.

The gray light of the day had begun to fade, and General Ham turned our group toward the large American flag that has flown over the cemetery since it was established as a temporary burial ground on June 6, 1944, the day of the D-Day landings. Several members of our group had been asked to help in the lowering of the flag. The cemetery historian explained the procedure.

As we listened to him describe the protocol for this simple ceremony, I spotted an elderly man in the crowd of tourists nearby, wearing a black baseball cap with giant gold letters that read: "Korean War Veteran." He was a big man, stooped and a bit fragile looking. He watched our group intently, although none among the group were in uniform. I learned later that his name was Martin LeMaster and he had served as a corporal in the US Marine Corps. LeMaster may have been elderly, but there was nothing wrong with his hearing; he had listened to every word the historian had uttered about the flag-folding protocol, and his reaction was swift.

His shuffle gained power as he made his way to our group and zeroed in on the young man at my side. LeMaster raised a finger to the young man's chest.

"Don't you know how to fold an American flag?" he asked. There was a bitterness in his voice. It was an accusation.

The young man straightened up. He was small, in his twenties, wearing a checkered cotton shirt and khaki pants, indistinguishable from any number of college students or young professionals back home.

He stood wide-eyed and nearly froze in place as LeMaster hovered over him. "Yes, sir, I do," he answered quietly. Nothing more.

The moment hung there in the rain, the ceremony on hold because an old veteran had challenged a young man in civilian clothes, questioning his knowledge and perhaps his patriotism as well. Neither man seemed inclined to say more. It was only a matter of seconds, but to me it seemed an endless wait.

Mercifully, the leader of our group stepped forward, and with a few words he said what needed to be said.

"Sir," he began, addressing the older Marine, "my name is General Carter Ham and I would like you to meet Staff Sergeant Salvatore

Giunta. Salvatore Giunta, to whom President Obama is going to present the Medal of Honor."

The Medal of Honor. It's hard to overstate what that means. Certainly, US Marine Corps Corporal LeMaster, veteran of the Korean War, needed no explainer. The Medal of Honor is the US Armed Forces' highest military decoration. It's the oldest such award, and of the many millions of Americans who have fought for their country, fewer than four thousand have received it. Most were awarded during the Civil War, and more recently nearly all have been given posthumously. Giunta would be the first living Medal of Honor recipient since the Vietnam War.

If Martin LeMaster's challenge had seemed over-the-top, a small but jarring aggression in the middle of a cemetery, I felt for him now, standing there. He looked at General Ham and turned back to Staff Sergeant Giunta, a young man who knew how to fold his country's flag and who had known things and done things for his country that were hard for those of us who never served to fathom. Even for a veteran of the Korean War.

LeMaster let out a stunned and sober, "Whoa," and took a step backwards. And then, pulling himself upright with all his strength, the old Marine slowly lifted his hand in a salute to the young soldier, a faint tear of gratitude in his eye. Sal Giunta returned the gesture, saluting the veteran who had fought in a war decades before he was born. And then Giunta said, "Your service allows us to live the way we do. We all owe you thanks."

General Ham invited the old veteran to help with the sunset ceremony. As "Taps" played and a small crowd gathered, these veterans, one a Medal of Honor recipient, the other a proud veteran of the Korean War, lowered the flag over the graves of the thousands of service members who had died in World War II.

Martin LeMaster told me later it was the greatest day of his life since his return from Korea. He had also learned a lesson, standing on that hallowed ground—one I had learned in my own way long before: There is no sure way to spot a hero.

How could anyone have known Sal Giunta was a hero? Who would have imagined it, looking at him there, in his ordinary civilian attire? Just a few years prior to that day in Normandy, he had been mopping the floors at a Subway sandwich shop in Iowa. But he had felt a call to duty. He joined the Army and went to war. In October 2007, at twenty-two, in Afghanistan's Korengal Valley, while under withering enemy fire, he exhibited what his Medal of Honor citation calls "unwavering courage, selflessness and decisive leadership." Extraordinary attributes that helped "defeat an enemy ambush and recover a fellow American soldier from the enemy."

On that afternoon in Normandy, after the flag had come down and the last light of the day was gone, we were leaving the cemetery, retracing our steps along a row of the white crosses. It was still raining. Sal Giunta was at my side, quiet as we walked, moved by what had happened with the old Marine.

There among the crosses, he leaned my way and said, in a voice just above a whisper, "I'm nothing compared to any of these men."

That is a sentiment I have heard often during my decades covering the remarkable 9/11 generation of warriors and their families. Whether it is a survivor from a bloody battle, or a spouse back home dealing with loss, none consider what they have done anything other than ordinary. That is true of everyone in this book. They don't believe they deserve to be called heroes. Perhaps there is a lesson in that. The one sure way to spot a hero may be to look for the ones who insist they are not.

People sometimes ask why I am so interested in stories about war and our troops. I understand why they ask. I've had the privilege to cover all kinds of stories, and at this stage of my career I could turn down certain assignments—but I run first to the world's conflict zones. While I've reported on my share of presidential campaigns and natural disasters and other issues that have little or nothing to do with the military, when I get on a plane for ABC News, it's more often than not to go to a battlefield or a warship, a military base or military hospital. I have no military background of my own, no ancestral ties to the military, and I didn't grow up in a family or culture that was tethered to war or the military life. But I have interviewed dozens of American generals and battlefield commanders, hundreds of soldiers and Marines, and I've made sure to meet their families too.

I grew up as a fatherless, scaredy-cat little girl. I tell people this when they wonder why I ever go to dangerous places, as a way of convincing them that I am hardly a thrill seeker, and I certainly don't take long trips to Iraq or Afghanistan or Ukraine for the rush of adrenaline. But perhaps that childhood fear has something to do with why I go. I remember hating the fact that I was so often afraid, and I remember thinking, even at a young age, that I wanted to do something to change that.

Going to a war is an aggressive way to counter one's fears, but the men and women I've met in war zones rarely seem frightened—or at least they seem to have conquered their fears and learned to face them. Or disguise them. It's a quality that can be both awe-inspiring and sometimes terribly sad—I have witnessed countless examples of both—and it has always intrigued me.

Another, simpler answer: You learn in these places how a moment can reveal character, and I have learned valuable lessons from the servicemen and -women I have come to know, life lessons about courage and selflessness, purpose and resilience, that have relevance for us all. I also learned, early on in my time as a war correspondent, that true heroes are rarely the ones you'd imagine. The generals have said this to me too. All too often, the swaggering soldier or Marine who exudes bravado and bluster isn't the one who shines in the moment. And I have been moved by those who aren't battlefield heroes, but who suffer the loss of a father or mother, brother or sister, son or daughter, husband or wife—or whose loved ones return home as shadows of who they were before they went to war. These people serve their country too, in powerful ways.

From the first day I started covering the Pentagon more than thirty years ago, I kept two words in my head like a mantra: "Respect. Remember."

At first, those words were a reminder of how to cover the institution of the military; to hold it accountable, to press for truth, and to do so from a starting point of respect, remembering what it had done for all Americans. I wanted to be worthy of the military's trust, so that I could be the first to report difficult stories as well as covering missions and victories.

Since then, those words have come to characterize how I approach covering stories of individual soldiers and of people touched by the military. I have witnessed the extraordinary courage of young service members and their families and watched from close range—in battlefields and on the home front and in the hospitals in between—as these people show remarkable courage and resilience and conquer unimaginable pain.

Too often their stories are lost or overrun by the broader narratives of the wars they are sent to fight—that's the nature of a busy news cycle. But I find it hard to forget or walk away.

So that's one more answer to that question. One more reason why I keep going. And one reason why I am writing this book.

Few Americans have heard of Captain Rosemary Mariner. Or Dr. Rocco Armonda. Or Specialist Steven Schulz and his mom, Debbie. Fewer still will know Josh Webster, Kevin Mott Jr., Danielle Thiriot, or Mark Little. The list is long, far longer than this book can cover, of men and women who have answered the call, time and again, people whose valor and selflessness know no bounds.

When you spend so much time covering war, you meet men and women at all ranks, people who are not easily forgotten. Some of their stories are unhappy ones—tragic, even—but many are inspiring and uplifting. I feel privileged to have found these people and they have stayed with me. I'm writing this book because I think every American should know their names.

I first met Sergeant Mark Little in an American combat support hospital in Baghdad, on a cloudless day in September 2007. I was watching as a young man was brought in on a stretcher. Even from my vantage point it was clear: Both his legs were gone, or about to be.

The remarkable thing about Mark Little wasn't his injury. It was a tough time in a tough war, and sadly, he was hardly alone. What struck me was that from his very first moments in that setting, under such terrible circumstances, he was smiling. Painkillers, sure, but he had just suffered a grievous, life-altering injury and he was determined to fight his way through it.

I made a mental note: "Whenever I get back home, I'm going to find Mark Little's family." I knew that if my son had gone through anything like what he had suffered, and someone had been with him, I would have wanted to talk to that someone. I would have wanted to know.

I had overheard Mark say he was from Falls Church, Virginia, not far from where I live. Two weeks later, I met his mother at Walter Reed Army Medical Center in Washington, DC. Her son had been brought there to continue his recovery.

She was appreciative and of course she wanted to know everything about that day in Baghdad. We spoke for a long time, at Mark's side. At one point, I asked Mark about the moment he'd realized how bad his injuries were.

"Ma'am, they aren't bad," he said with a smile. "I'm alive."

In this book, I share stories about people I have interviewed over the years who have shaped how I think about service, honor, and war. Individually, their stories are deeply inspiring. Together, they offer something beyond inspiration: insight into what it means to live with a life-defining courage and sense of purpose.

Unlike Sal Giunta, who received the Medal of Honor he so richly deserves, none of the people in this book have received national recognition. They represent the generation that has answered the call to service since 9/11, who collectively serve as powerful antidotes to the corrosive cynicism that prevails in so much of our culture today. In that sense this is a patriotic book.

It is also personal for me. I have known many of these people and their families for decades. These aren't portraits drawn from internet searches; they are people whose stories are in my reporter's notebook, etched in my memory—in my heart. A few of those profiled here have intersected with one another over the years, but I wanted to give each their own separate chapter.

So in these pages you will meet a combat neurosurgeon. A lifesaving pararescueman. A fighter pilot who is also an artist and finds a profound, Zen-like peace in the sky. One soldier who laughs off his injuries and a Marine who became a successful entrepreneur, whose startups help people who have suffered from the same spinal injury that altered his life. They were talented battlefield leaders who were loved and revered by their men.

There are trailblazers here as well. A woman who inspired a generation of combat pilots, and the extraordinary pilot who followed in her "contrails." And there are mothers. Their sons are heroes, no question; but as I have come to know the moms, it's their humanity and selfless service that have stayed with me.

Taken together, these stories remind us of the power of selflessness and commitment to a common purpose. They offer profound lessons in leadership and response to crisis—even, in some cases, at low rungs of an organization—that will be valuable to people in any line of work or human endeavor. They remind us that life can turn on a moment, and that the outcome can be determined by both the hand of fate and the degree or preparation for whatever that moment may bring. They tell us that all the division and cynicism roiling through the nation's bloodstream isn't a given—in fact, in one of our nation's largest and most important institutions, they are hard to find. They remind us that as a nation, we are woefully disconnected from the men and women who are sent to fight our wars.

Visiting Normandy that day, I was deeply moved by the act of remembering the hundreds of thousands of people who shipped out on D-Day, many running toward their deaths to stop Nazi Germany from overtaking Europe. I thought, too, of the mothers and fathers, spouses, children, sisters, and friends whose own courage held up the country, those soldiers left behind. Regardless of our politics or thoughts about any given war, the safety of this country depends on people who give deeply of themselves. I'm not here to judge the wars themselves, or how they were prosecuted. Readers will make up their own minds, or probably already have. It is those who went to war I want to honor. They volunteer and get to work, ready to sacrifice for the greater good. For the person next to them. For the mission. They might have had no idea what shape the sacrifice could take. But they go, and for many, when their moment comes, they are unselfish. Unflinching. They are heroes.

In 2024 I found retired Army neurosurgeon Rocco Armonda in eastern Ukraine, in a hospital near the front lines. He had been working long hours in a crowded surgery ward, his patients among the more than fourteen thousand soldiers and civilians brought during the past year into the triage wing of Dnipro's Mechnikov Hospital. It was nonstop work, awful work, a steady flow of shrapnel wounds and brain injuries and lost limbs and worse. The Ukrainian doctors and nurses were exhausted but determined; many said they considered themselves every bit the fighters that the soldiers were.

"It was a simple call," Rocco Armonda told me. "One of my old Army buddies was helping Ukrainians doing trauma work and said they needed neurosurgeons, and I was there."

"I was there." I have heard that sentiment often from service members. "You have a problem? I'm coming—I'm on my way. . . ." So many veterans feel the tug of mission long after their military service is over. I have seen the power and impact of that devotion up close. In this case, in the tragic yet inspiring setting of a frontline surgery ward.

Rocco Armonda was one of those surgeons who could have practiced his craft anywhere, but he was a West Point grad, and so he took his skills to Afghanistan and then to Iraq, and then to the renowned Bethesda Naval Hospital in Maryland, where he was on duty in 2006 when my colleague Bob Woodruff came in clinging to life by the thinnest of threads.

Dr. Armonda was there. There, for a day and night of lifesaving operations on Bob Woodruff's brain, after he had been gravely wounded by a roadside bomb in Iraq.

Two decades later, I had found Dr. Armonda again, now a volunteer in another war zone, joining the long days and nights on duty at Mechnikov Hospital where he says they have seen ten times the number of traumatic brain injures he saw in Iraq and Afghanistan.

Rosemary Mariner is the oldest member of the group in these pages. "Trailblazer" is an overused term, but that's the word for her. From an early age, growing up in San Diego, Rosemary had a passion for flying. Her mother was a World War II Navy nurse, and her father served in the Army Air Corps and then as an Air Force attack pilot during the Korean War. Rosemary's interest in flying for the military may also have been kindled by tragedy; her father and his copilot were killed in a plane crash in 1956. Rosemary was three years old when she lost her dad—something she and I had in common.

As a young girl, Rosemary had watched planes at Naval Air Station Miramar and worked odd jobs, cleaning houses and washing aircraft, to earn money for flying lessons and flight time. It wasn't long before she began piling up the "firsts."

She was the first woman to graduate from Purdue University's aeronautics program—which she did at age nineteen. She got her pilot's license and was one of the first eight women selected for the Navy's pilot training program. In 1974, Rosemary was among the first six women to earn wings as a US Naval Aviator and was the first woman to fly a frontline tactical strike aircraft.

First. First. First.

Trailblazer.

There would be more glass ceilings to break. 1982: first female aviator assigned to an aircraft carrier. 1987: first woman screened for command of an aviation unit in the US Navy. And in 1990, first woman to command a Navy aviation squadron.

By the time I met her, in 1993, Rosemary was already a superstar pilot; I just hadn't known. She told me her goal was to repeal the laws that forbade women from flying in combat. In the years that followed, I watched her fight for that. I also saw that beyond her own successes,

Rosemary was playing a "Mama Bear" role for many young women in the military, as they faced sexism and abuse on their journeys up a very difficult ladder. She did not want special treatment for women—she wanted equal treatment.

I think about Rosemary Mariner every time I spend time with women in war zones. Even they don't know about her. So I have to assume most Americans don't either.

When she died of cancer at sixty-five, the Navy conducted an all-female pilot flyover over New Loyston Cemetery in Maynardville, Tennessee. Fittingly, this was the first time an all-woman Navy crew had performed the maneuver at a military funeral. The woman who fought to make that flyover happen, Danielle Thiriot, whose bombing missions in Syria helped defeat ISIS, is one of the heroes profiled in this book.

Other hidden heroes? Charles Wickware, the fighter pilot who's also a chronicler of war, a highly decorated aviator who uses his camera and paintbrush to document his time on aircraft carriers and on dangerous bombing runs. Charles does it for the same reason I am writing this book: He wants the world to know.

You will come to know the miracle that is Derek Herrera, a Marine Raider who had made a name for himself in Haiti and the Middle East before the attack in Helmand, Afghanistan, that left him paralyzed, and who since then has channeled his energies and intelligence into the entrepreneurial arena, founding a series of startup companies that design medical devices to improve quality of life for people with spinal cord and other debilitating injuries.

And you will meet Josh Webster, an Army officer who was also a US Air Force pararescueman—a member of an elite division whose missions include perilous helicopter rescues and then providing medical treatment to wounded military personnel, often in the middle of intense combat.

Kevin Shaeffer and Steve Workman exemplify this 9/11 generation perhaps better than anyone. They were both in the Pentagon the day a hijacked plane hit the building. Shaeffer, a young Navy officer, was severely burned in the attack. Sergeant First Class Workman helped save his life. Both men have gone on to do remarkable and, in Shaeffer's case, history-changing work.

When he was younger, my son, Jake, would understandably get upset with me—for heading off in the middle of a weekend or at halftime of one of his football games to go to the ABC News bureau in Washington or to New York or to Baghdad or Kabul or Sana'a or . . .

"I know you feel badly when I leave, Jake," I would tell him. "I feel badly too. Believe me. But it's important that you know that so many of the people in these places, they leave home all the time. And they don't come home after a week or two, like Mom does."

I wouldn't say the rest of it, not to my young son. The bit about how those soldiers on the other side of the world would be gone more than a year, typically—more than a year of no bedtime stories or warm hugs or family dinners. The fact that they don't get to choose where they go or what they do. For sure they don't get to say, "Sorry, my kid's game is today, so I won't be able to be there. . . ."

Or the fact that when they do come home, all too often they are broken, in one way or another. And that some never come home at all.

Along with everything else, this book is an extension of that message to my son, to be shared with all Americans. Another way to make some connections between those who serve and the rest of us. It was a lesson both of my children learned and saw up close.

In 1980, 18 percent of American adults were veterans; by 2022, that had dropped to about 6 percent. Most people, especially those with college degrees, don't know anyone on active duty.

In 2009 I gave the commencement address at Norwich University, America's oldest private military college, which has an unusual blend of military and civilian undergraduates. It seemed a good place and moment to get at that chasm in our culture.

"Today I ask each of you—traditional student and cadet alike—to do your part to build bridges between the military and civilian communities," I said. "I hope that those of you who remain in civilian life maintain friendships that you have made here with cadets, wherever they may be deployed. But just as importantly, I hope that those of you who go off in careers in the military make as real an effort to remain rooted in civilian society. Because we are one nation, and we must remain united if we are to succeed in managing the challenges that await us."

Later that year, at the university's Homecoming Weekend, an actual bridge on the Norwich campus was dedicated, linking South Hall, a civilian dormitory, to the barracks on the Upper Parade Ground. A bronze plaque containing words from my commencement address is part of that structure.

We need more of these bridges. I hope this book can provide some of the bricks and mortar required to build them.

Navy Lieutenant Kevin Shaeffer (right) received the Purple Heart and Army Sergeant First Class Steve Workman the Soldier's Medal for Valor for the events that unfolded at the Pentagon on 9/11.

CHAPTER 1

Sailor, Survivor, Spy

Kevin Shaeffer and Steve Workman

BANDS OF SCAR TISSUE STILL COLOR THE SEARED SKIN on Kevin Shaeffer's hands, arms, and face. The gash in the hollow of his neck has healed into a deep purple thread. Those are the visible wounds, suffered at the Pentagon during the terrorist attacks on September 11, 2001, that left thousands dead, thousands more injured, and a nation mourning, yet resolute. President George W. Bush vowed that America would hunt down the man behind the deadly strikes, Osama bin Laden—however long it took and wherever he was hiding. 9/11 was the deadliest attack on American soil in history. But from that destruction rose a new generation of warriors, intelligence officers, and public servants determined to preserve our values, freedom, and democratic ideals.

I met Kevin Shaeffer at the Pentagon Memorial twenty years after he nearly died from the catastrophic injuries he suffered on that day. And we would meet again years later when he was finally allowed to reveal a mission he had long kept secret. Kevin Shaeffer's link to Osama bin Laden began well before 9/11 and continued for decades afterwards. He was on the ship that fired the first shots at bin Laden's hideout in Afghanistan, and he was watching real-time video at the CIA when bin Laden took his last breath. It is hard to imagine anyone with a stronger connection to the 9/11 generation than Shaeffer.

Kevin Shaeffer's first brush with al-Qaeda came on the night of

August 20, 1998, in the Arabian Sea, where US warships were preparing for battle. Less than three weeks had passed since al-Qaeda terrorists had blown up US embassies in Kenya and Tanzania, ramming massive truck bombs into the embassy grounds that left more than 220 dead. Bin Laden had declared war on America and Shaeffer was on a mission to pay him back.

The sea was relatively calm that night. A steady roll of white froth slapped onto the ship's bow. Nothing out of the ordinary, which was fortunate for the sailors on board the USS *Elliot,* given the launch orders they had received. The destroyer was one of four American warships targeting what intelligence had determined were terrorist training camps in the Khost region of Afghanistan. Bin Laden's camps. Alternately fingering the Naval Academy ring on his right hand and the wedding ring on his left, twenty-six-year-old Lieutenant Shaeffer peered over the bridge of the huge warship. His job as a navigation officer was to ensure that the ship was undetectable. Polished and professional, the junior officer could not hide his excitement as the ship's missiles were readied for launch. Shaeffer had spent plenty of time aboard Navy warships, but this was the first time he would see action up close. It was also the first time the United States would try to take out bin Laden and his al-Qaeda followers.

At approximately 8:30 pm the launch began. A barrage of Tomahawk missiles blasted into the night sky. Seventy-six cruise missiles rose nearly simultaneously from the ships and the submarine that was accompanying them. Lieutenant Shaeffer felt the roar and marveled at the power of the weapons as he watched the bright white trails streak upward and then arc north, to Afghanistan. His pride swelled when he heard that President Clinton had announced to the nation that the "pre-emptive strikes" had targeted "one of the most active terrorist bases in the world," citing "compelling evidence" that Osama bin Laden was planning further attacks. As the ship steamed away from its launch site and back to safety, Shaeffer thought how fortunate he was to be part of this history-making night.

But bin Laden was not at the training camp, nor were any senior al-Qaeda leaders. They had left hours before the strikes. The damage to the camps was largely confined to infrastructure and the mission was widely viewed as a failure. The threat from al-Qaeda was far from over.

Two years after that failed attempt to take out bin Laden, in October 2000, al-Qaeda suicide bombers steered a small boat loaded with a thousand pounds of explosives into the side of the USS *Cole* destroyer during a refueling stop in Yemen. Seventeen sailors were killed and nearly forty wounded. The attack rocked the Navy and prioritized the intelligence community's focus on al-Qaeda.

At the time of the bombing of the *Cole,* Lieutenant Shaeffer was stationed at the Pentagon. He and his wife, Blanca, a Navy officer he had met when they were midshipmen together at the Naval Academy, were working "shore duty" assignments. After months at sea, the two sailors had been "two ships passing in the night, sometimes literally," in Shaeffer's words, so the desk job came as a welcome change. Blanca, also a lieutenant was now at the Strategic Systems program office in Dahlgren, Virginia, part of the Trident Missiles Program. Kevin was working with the strategy and concepts branch for the Chief of Naval Operations. They settled in Fredericksburg, midway between their two workplaces, but still a long commute for both.

Kevin Shaeffer was not an intelligence analyst at the time, but his workspace in the Navy Command Center was next to that of the officers investigating the *Cole* bombing. His interest in counterterrorism had intensified after the failed mission to kill bin Laden.

The Command Center tracked Naval operations around the globe 24-7 and coordinated responses to international events. Big screens monitored ships at sea, while others were tuned to cable news. Offices in the Pentagon form five concentric rings around a large outdoor courtyard, starting with the A ring and ending with the outermost E ring. The rings are connected by ten equally spaced corridors, like a giant five-sided pie divided into slices. Between the B and C ring was an outdoor causeway where maintenance and supply vehicles could make deliveries and carry out repairs. The Command Center where Shaeffer worked was on the first floor of the Pentagon, in the C ring on the westernmost side of the building, between corridors 4 and 5.

Lieutenant Shaeffer's job largely entailed mountains of reading, meetings, and research. Shaeffer found it both stimulating and rewarding. He was contributing to the Navy's future and assessing the strategic challenges it would face worldwide. The three Navy colleagues who shared his cubicle cluster made it even more fulfilling. At twenty-nine on 9/11, he was younger than most and did not have children yet, but he enjoyed hearing stories from his fellow officers who were juggling jobs and parenting.

Commander William Donovan, thirty-seven, had three young children, Lieutenant Commander David Williams, thirty-two, had two young ones at home and was expecting a third, and thirty-nine-year-old Commander Patrick Dunn's wife was two months pregnant with their first child.

On the morning of September 11, 2001, the men were all at work by 7:00 am, a typical start time for most Pentagon employees. Lieutenant Shaeffer had one of the longest commutes. He and Blanca were living about sixty miles south of the Pentagon, so Shaeffer commuted each day by train. Blanca had left the day before for a work assignment in Pittsfield, Massachusetts, in the western part of the state. All told, it usually took him about ninety minutes to get to work. The long commute gave him a chance to catch up on the news and prepare for his regular morning meeting with his department head, Captain Robert Dolan Jr., an affable forty-three-year-old father who, like Shaeffer, was a Naval Academy graduate.

The Command Center was always bustling, and this morning was no different. Shaeffer dropped his lunch at his cubicle, shuffled through some papers, made small talk with the others in the office, and took one last glance at the TV monitors before heading into his morning meeting.

After an hour or so of planning and mapping out assignments for the day, Shaeffer and his strategy team headed back to their cubicles. But no one took their seats. They could see that every eye in the Command Center had suddenly locked onto the TV screens.

At 8:46 am, American Airlines Flight 11 had plunged into the North Tower of the World Trade Center. Shaeffer stood stunned, watching the black smoke rising from the skyscraper, stark against the bright blue sky. And then, at 9:03 am, audible gasps could be heard across the Command Center as United Airlines Flight 175 crashed into the South Tower and erupted in a massive fireball.

The officers in the Command Center were suddenly on full alert. When the first plane hit, there had been talk of an accident, but they knew now it was no accident and began tracking what minimal information was available. One thing was certain: The country was at war. But not for a moment did Kevin Shaeffer and his colleagues feel they were at risk in the Pentagon. The building was a fortress, and a newly reinforced one at that. Some on Shaeffer's team stood quietly watching, absorbing the enormity of the moment. Others began making phone calls to loved ones behind the shoulder-high divides separating the desks. Commander Pat Dunn called his pregnant wife to make sure she knew what was happening. Shaeffer stood transfixed, unable to take his eyes off the screens. He was still standing thirty-four minutes later, at 9:37 am, when American Airlines Flight 77, with seven thousand gallons of jet fuel and fifty-nine innocent souls on board, barreled through the Pentagon's limestone walls and into the first floor with a thunderous roar.

Fire engulfed the Navy Command Center. The plane tore through the outer rings of the Pentagon, incinerating everything and everybody in its path. Shaeffer was instantly blown off his feet and set on fire. Rolling on the floor to put out the flames, he struggled to breathe through the veil of acrid smoke. He felt as if he were melting. His khaki uniform stuck to his arms and torso as if the polyester had been ironed onto his skin. His hands were slick with jet fuel and his lungs burned from inhaling fumes. Mangled wires hung from the collapsed ceiling, the furniture upended and pocked with shrapnel. He could see no one through the blackness, but he heard what he thought were the last gasps of life around him.

In the seconds that followed, there was silence. He sensed he was the only survivor. Blanca filled his panicked thoughts and he imagined that he would never see her again. He needed to stay alive. He needed to find his way out of this hellscape. "Keep moving, keep moving," he said to himself, as he began clawing and climbing through piles of scorching debris, skin peeling as he propelled himself through the rubble. Frayed wires sparked above him as water rained down from broken pipes. It was so dark he could not find his way or know what direction to turn. And then a flicker. As the dust dissipated, he could just make out a faint glow through the haze. Adrenaline pushing him through his pain, Kevin Shaeffer stumbled toward the light. Toward life. Toward forty-one-year-old Army Sergeant First Class Donald "Steve" Workman.

Workman had felt the immense power of the impact in his office—adjacent to the Command Center, but one level below it. Workman had no idea that a plane had hit the building, but he knew everyone had to get out of there. "You need to evacuate. Start moving slowly, no panic," he calmly told his colleagues. The corridors quickly crowded with people fleeing the building, but Workman, an Army paratrooper assigned to the Army's Quadrennial Defense Review, had no intention of leaving the building himself. He climbed the nearest stairway and headed straight toward the impact area, stopping only to soak his shirt in water and grab a small fire extinguisher. Down the hallway, an older man, encrusted in soot, appeared out of a curtain of smoke. Workman rushed and asked if he was OK and if anyone else was behind him. The man looked at Workman solemnly and said, "Hell yes, my entire crew."

Moving forward cautiously through the smoke, the Army sergeant could see only destruction and flames in front of him, nothing that resembled an office space. Wires sizzled as he hollered, "Is anyone here? I will come to you." Again and again, he screamed, "Anyone here? I can help!" Nothing. Heat was now making it impossible to go any farther; the fire was rapidly moving toward him. He had to retreat, had to find another way. Workman headed to the maintenance corridor, hoping the outdoor causeway would be intact. Racing around the corner, he could see the causeway was largely untouched beyond a few piles of bricks next to the crumbling scorched wall of the C ring. He peered inside a large hole that led into the Command Center, briefly entering the flaming space, and once again hollering for survivors. It wasn't until he crept back out that he found Navy Lieutenant Kevin Shaeffer crumpled just outside the hole, smoldering.

"I need help; please help me," Shaeffer pleaded. Workman dropped to the ground beside him and did a quick check. Skin was hanging from Shaeffer's ears and arms. Workman worried that if he touched the flesh, it would fall off. Some of it already had. Shaeffer's face was a mass of blisters, his uniform charred and molded to his body, and his breathing labored. Farther down the causeway, Sergeant First Class Workman spotted a maintenance vehicle. He waved down the driver, but he was unable to get close to Workman. The vehicle, which had a flat surface on the back of it, was blocked by a pile of bricks that had fallen from the building. Workman began tossing the bricks to clear the path. Shaeffer sat motionless until the cart was able to back up next to him. Workman then carefully slid his arms under Shaeffer's shoulders, avoiding the most severe burns, and like a forklift hoisted the young officer onto the cart. Shaeffer, with a desperate intensity, gazed at Workman and said, "Please don't let me die."

Staring right back at him, Steve Workman said, with all the conviction he could muster, "I got you."

One hundred and twenty-five people were killed inside the Pentagon when Flight 77 slammed into the building that morning. Forty-two of them were in the Navy Command Center. Kevin Shaeffer's hunch was right. He was the only survivor on his team, the only person in the area where he worked who was still alive. Among the dead were his cubicle mates, Commander William Donovan, Lieutenant Commander David Williams, and Commander Patrick Dunn, along with their boss, Captain Robert Dolan Jr., the proud father of a fifteen-year-old daughter and nine-year-old son.

Shaeffer had survived the initial blast, but despite his assurances, Steve Workman knew it was far from clear he would make it through the day. He resolved to stay at his side. Given Shaeffer's severe burns and difficulty breathing, Workman knew his lungs were likely damaged. The Army sergeant first class barked orders to the maintenance driver to head to the Pentagon clinic for immediate care. The clinic was a safe distance from the blast area, so Workman assumed triage for the survivors had begun there. He was wrong. When they arrived they found the door locked: The staff had apparently evacuated. Workman pounded on the door, a young nurse finally opened it, and they managed to get Shaeffer into the treatment room and on a gurney. After numerous attempts to find a vein, her hands shaking over the raw flesh, the nurse was finally able to insert an IV. But Shaeffer had to get to a hospital and fast. He was going into shock. Workman had loosened Shaeffer's belt and elevated his legs by placing a small garbage can beneath them while the IV was being inserted. He started rolling him out of the treatment room but then paused. Workman noticed a small oxygen bottle, grabbed it, and put it between Shaeffer's knees as they headed outside.

On the large grassy area on the Pentagon's north side, far from the smoking wedge where Shaeffer had been hit, a few ambulances were lining up. Workman pounded on the outside of the first one he saw and guided the gurney to the rear. The ambulance had come from Walter Reed Army Medical Center, so the driver assumed that was where the wounded man would be taken. Workman pushed Shaeffer in feet first and kneeled beside his head near the door. Someone outside closed the door quickly, wedging Workman's left knee between the door and the gurney.

On a good day it would take at least twenty minutes to drive to Walter Reed. On 9/11, with thousands of Washingtonians evacuating the city in a panic, the gridlock made it nearly impossible to drive those ten miles to the hospital. And the driver was brand-new. "I'm not sure how to get to the hospital," Workman heard her say to the man next to her.

In the back of the ambulance, Workman asked Shaeffer for a family contact and scribbled Blanca's phone number on his hand. The Army sergeant had left his phone, car keys, and wallet in his office when the evacuation had begun. There were no medics in the back of the ambulance, but Workman figured out how to connect an oxygen mask on Shaeffer to the large tank in the vehicle. He kept Shaeffer talking as the ambulance careened over curbs and banged into the bumpers of cars stopped in the road. They were desperate to get to Walter Reed.

Twenty-five minutes into the ride, an alarm began blaring inside the ambulance. Workman had no idea what the alarm meant and hollered, "What's that noise?" The attendant up front shouted back that the oxygen tank was running out. A moment of panic, and then Workman remembered. Still tucked between Shaeffer's knees was the small oxygen bottle he had grabbed before leaving the Pentagon. It would last the rest of the roller-coaster ride to the hospital, until they finally burst through the doors of the emergency room.

A team of doctors and nurses was wheeling Shaeffer down the hallway when Workman heard the Navy lieutenant cry out, "Steve! Steve!" Workman hurried up to the gurney. Shaeffer wanted to know his last name. He was determined never to forget the man who saved him.

Workman left his name with the nurses and gave them Blanca's number before heading back down to the ER entrance. He hopped in the first ambulance he could find and headed back to the Pentagon.

In the ER, scissors sliced through what was left of Shaeffer's uniform and nurses peeled it off his burnt torso. Painkillers were administered through the IV, and a catheter was inserted.

The doctors then began tugging carefully on Shaeffer's raw, swollen fingers to remove his rings. The wedding ring on his charred left finger, the class of '94 Naval Academy ring on his right. They wouldn't budge. The pain was unbearable. A doctor called out for a ring cutter before the swelling got worse.

"Stop! Wait a minute," Shaeffer yelled. He wasn't about to let them cut into his beloved rings. He reached first for his wedding band, grimaced, and with all the strength he could summon he pulled it off. Then he clutched his academy ring, yanking it over his damaged flesh. He handed the rings to a nurse and lay back down, thinking, "Now you can get on with saving my life." Kevin Shaeffer then passed out. Salvaging his rings was his last conscious memory of that horrific September day.

Blanca, still in Massachusetts, had been trying to reach her husband from the moment she saw that the Pentagon had been hit. But cell servers were overwhelmed and none of her calls were going through. She assumed he had been evacuated and she was simply not able to get through. But then the call came: Her husband was badly injured and at Walter Reed. With flights grounded across the country, her colleagues rented an SUV so they could drive her back to Washington. For nine hours, traveling down the dark roads and highways, she could only imagine what kinds of injuries her husband was enduring.

Back at Walter Reed, the doctors were worried most about the skin that remained on Shaeffer's arms. Fluid was building up from the burns and the skin was tightening, constricting the blood flow to his extremities in the same way a tourniquet would. Incisions were made on each arm to relieve the pressure and save his limbs. As soon as he was stable, he was transferred by helicopter for the short flight to Washington Hospital Burn Center, one of the best hospital units for burn victims in the country.

It was 3:00 am on September 12 when Blanca finally arrived at the Burn Center. She found her husband covered in sterile dressing, mummy-like. He was swollen, sedated, and had a trach tube in his neck to keep him breathing and to drain black sludge from his lungs. His hands and arms had been immobilized by his sides. The doctor on duty told Blanca they would do everything possible to keep her husband alive, but his tone was sobering. This would be touch-and-go for a long time to come. Both Kevin and Blanca had faced challenges in their years of service, but what lay ahead for both would be the biggest challenge of all.

When Kevin Shaeffer did wake from his haze of sedation he was slammed with a pain he described to me as "white-hot" and of a "different dimension." A fifty, he said, on a scale of one to ten. Part of his right ear was missing; his face was blackened and blistered, his upper body, arms, and hands a tapestry of trauma. Forty-seven percent of his body had been seared. Some of the burns were nearly bone-deep, and some of the most serious could not be seen from the outside.

Almost immediately he developed an infection in his inflamed lungs. The tube running down his throat was pumping up slime from his lungs, but the infection was getting worse. Within twenty-four hours Shaeffer was moved to a special rotating bed to keep the sludge from accumulating and to clear the lungs more quickly. He was strapped down tightly, which exacerbated the pain, but at least it kept him from falling out as the bed flipped one way and then the other. A burnt man tethered to a mechanical windmill.

He would stay on that rotating bed for weeks, pumped up with antibiotics, his shaved head in a vice, immobilized. The only relief from the constant rotation was another kind of hell as his sterile dressings were peeled from his arms, hands, and torso four times a day. He could not speak because of the tube in his throat, but Blanca soon managed to read his swollen lips and translate for others. One of the few moments of joy in those painful days came when a Navy petty officer arrived in Shaeffer's room bearing his wedding and class rings. Blanca quickly took to wearing the rings on a chain around her neck, fingering them often in the same way her husband had.

During those long days, either Blanca or Shaeffer's parents or sister was always at his side. His Navy family was there too. Prayer circles were formed, meals delivered. Even the Chief of Naval Operations, Admiral Vernon Clark, came regularly to keep the family company while quietly grieving the loss of Navy colleagues who had not survived the attack.

Admiral Clark had been in his office on September 11, on the outer ring of the Pentagon, in a corridor that was some distance from where the plane hit. His office shook violently and the shatterproof glass on the windows flexed as he tried to take stock of what had happened. He likened it to being aboard a Navy destroyer when Tomahawk cruise missiles launched.

Devasted by the loss of forty-two Navy and civilian personnel in the Command Center, he focused on caring for the families and for the survivors. Ten of his sailors had been hospitalized, but none nearly as serious as Shaeffer. The day after the attack, only two remained in the hospital. By the third day there was only one.

When Clark first visited Shaeffer at the Burn Center he was shocked by what he saw. And what he heard. A low-pitched howl generated by the breathing machine pulsed loudly through the room. Shaeffer's bandaged upper body heaved up and flopped down with each mechanical breath. Admiral Clark would come back day after day, week after week, bringing food and comfort to the family. Shaeffer's visitors were restricted during those early days, so the Admiral would stay in the waiting room with family members. He received updates on Shaeffer's condition twice a day, at the top of his daily Navy briefing notes.

The only non-family visitor who was allowed into the room from the beginning was Steve Workman. The day after Shaeffer was transferred to the Burn Center, Blanca was told that someone in uniform was outside asking how her husband was doing. In the hallway was Sergeant First Class Workman, in battle dress, the man who had saved his life. Shaeffer was too heavily sedated for Workman's visit to register, but Workman gave the family all the details he could, ending the visit with a huge embrace. Years later he would still remember how Shaeffer's mother "squeezed the life out of me."

After handing Lieutenant Shaeffer over to the doctors at Walter Reed on September 11, Sergeant First Class Workman had returned to the Pentagon. He was sure others needed help. The ambulance driver who had taken him to the hospital told him she'd heard it was a plane that had hit the Pentagon. When they pulled up to the building, smoke was still whirling above the massive gash in the side of the building. Thirty ambulances waited outside, but so few people in the plane's path had survived that the ambulances sat empty. Workman tried to get back inside, thinking there had to be someone he could help, but no one was allowed in the building. It was still too dangerous. He spotted what he thought was a piece of the aircraft and alerted an FBI agent on the scene.

Looking at the carnage and seeing the news cameras, Workman realized his wife and two sons were likely seeing these images as well. He'd had no chance to think about that, and now, with his phone still in his Pentagon office, he would have to find another way to make contact.

Workman's wife, Angie, an elementary school teacher in nearby Springfield, Virginia, had been home for hours shaking with fear. The staff at the school knew that Angie's husband worked at the Pentagon, so they had her leave as soon as they heard the news about the attack. Word was spreading throughout the Army that the plane had hit very near her husband's office. Her best friend, Darlene Pacheco, had received a call from her husband, Army Master Sergeant Patrick Pacheco, who had seen the images of the Pentagon and the reports of the damage. Master Sergeant Pacheco told her he was almost certain Steve had been killed given where his office was located in the building. Darlene never let on she'd heard this when she talked to Angie, but she was crying uncontrollably, nevertheless.

Angie had sent another friend to pick up her teenage son Adam from class at a nearby high school, but the traffic was now so tangled from people leaving Washington that it was hours before he was home. Angie had no solid information to provide Adam, but given how much time had passed without hearing from her husband, she feared the worst.

Their oldest son, Steven, was at the University of Oklahoma watching the news on television. His fraternity brothers surrounded him as he sat silently. He knew his mother had not yet heard from his dad.

In fact, Steve Workman was lucky to be alive. He had arrived at the Pentagon just before the attack, and just after a ten-mile run. He hadn't even had time to change out of his civilian clothes when he was asked to run upstairs for a quick meeting with Lieutenant Colonel Jerry Dickerson and a few other colleagues. On his way out, he introduced himself to thirty-eight-year-old Staff Sergeant Maudlyn White, whom he met in a hallway. A native of St. Croix, in the Virgin Islands, and the single mother of a seven-year-old daughter, she was on the first day of her Pentagon assignment working with the Army quadrennial review team. "We'll chat later," Workman said, giving her a quick smile and waving goodbye before walking back down to his office. He would soon learn that Dickerson and White and every one of those Army colleagues had died in the attack.

It was close to 2:00 pm when Workman finally got hold of his family. Outside the Pentagon, he found a woman with a cell phone, and after numerous tries on the overtaxed circuits he reached his wife. She sobbed on the other end of the line, saying, "I thought you were dead." Emotional conversations with his sons soon followed, but the most emotional call was with his dad, in Oklahoma. The Army veteran, who Workman says "is the toughest guy I know," was so overcome hearing his son's voice that he was unable to speak.

Steve Workman made his way home that evening on the Metro, Washington's subway system. Covered in soot and sweat, with no wallet or phone, he asked for a free ride, explaining to Metro officers what had happened. The doors opened wide, and Workman headed home, to be safe in the arms of his family.

The Pentagon was soon back to business and planning a war. Sergeant First Class Workman's office space was covered in an inch of water and the smell of fire and smoke permeated everything, but there was plenty of space in the undamaged parts of the sprawling building. He had hardly had time to think about what he'd witnessed, and the friends he had lost, when he learned that the Army had one more difficult assignment for him.

Six days after the plane struck the Pentagon, the remains of Staff Sergeant Maudlyn White, the young woman from the Virgin Islands whom Workman had met briefly in the hallway on September 11, were positively identified. With so many dead, the military was reaching out to soldiers to serve as "CAOs"—casualty assistance officers. Steve Workman was asked to notify Staff Sergeant White's seven-year-old daughter, Vielka, that her mother was dead. The child's father had never been part of her life. Maudlyn had not even listed him on Vielka's birth certificate.

Workman was given a script by the Army Casualty Affairs Office to read to the child. He took one look at it and told them, "There is no way I am reading this." Workman told me it was horribly graphic. The suggested text—"Your mother was burned beyond recognition . . . identified through dental records"—was completely inappropriate for a child to hear. He arranged instead to seek guidance from the Army chaplain and a child psychologist. The chaplain told him to be gentle but clear. Don't leave any room for the girl to think her mother might be coming back. Skip phrases like she "has gone to heaven" or "passed away." The chaplain, a psychologist, and a one-star general were all with Workman when he went to visit Vielka.

The little girl was sitting on the couch, her hair braided in two pigtails. Her mother's close friend from St. Croix and the friend's older children were there as well. After a brief introduction, Sergeant First Class Workman dropped down on a knee. He looked at this tiny child and said, "Sweetheart, I am so sorry to tell you this, but your mama is dead." Vielka stared in disbelief, reached out and wrapped her arms around Sergeant First Class Workman, and cried, "I want my mama, I want my mama." Steve Workman tried not to break down himself, but almost everyone around him, including the general, was weeping.

"I know you want your mama, sweetheart, I know, baby," Workman said. "I know this hurts." A few days later, he escorted the remains of Maudlyn White to Arlington National Cemetery, where a folded American flag was handed to little Vielka White, who would remain in the custody of her mother's close friend. A few hours later, Steve Workman was back at the Burn Center with Kevin Shaeffer.

Workman's primary focus had become the young Navy officer fighting for his life. Shaeffer's words, "Please don't let me die," kept running through his mind. A profound bond had been formed, and a profound sense of responsibility. Kevin Shaeffer wanted to live, and Steve Workman was going to do everything possible to make sure that happened. For Shaeffer's sake and for his own.

In the week that followed the attack, Kevin Shaeffer seemed to be making slight progress. The infection in his lungs had subsided somewhat, but now his arms became an even bigger problem. Burns damage the skin's protective barrier, creating a breeding ground for infection. Dead cells on his damaged skin were being cleaned and removed numerous times a day, but the infection was winning. No amount of antibiotics or exotic drugs seemed to work. The infected cells were amassing so quickly the doctors feared sepsis would set in.

The medical staff at the burn unit was strategizing with experts around the country. They were willing to try anything to save Shaeffer's arms and his life. Anything. The doctors decided to place maggots on Shaeffer's arms, live maggots that would feed on his dead skin.

As horrendous as it sounded, it was an approach that had been used for centuries. The maggots were bred in a sterile laboratory for just this purpose—to eat dead cells and leave the healthy ones alone. As grotesque as the idea sounded, Shaeffer told the doctors, "Go for it." Blanca insisted on only one thing. She was so revolted by the idea that she asked them not to say the word "maggots." Instead, a nurse came up with a more acceptable moniker. The little white worm-like creatures would be called the medicals. For days, these "medicals" feasted on Shaeffer's arms, chomping away at the infected tissue. The treatment helped, but it was not enough.

By early October, the infection from both his arms and his lungs began creeping into the rest of his body. It was the onset of sepsis, and it was spreading fast. His mother had the early-morning visitation duty the morning the infection took hold. Shaeffer asked her to remind Blanca to bring a new toothbrush, and minutes later his heart stopped cold. Splayed out on that hospital bed he flatlined. Doctors and nurses quickly surrounded him. A jolt from the defibrillator revived him, but minutes later, while a doctor was telling his family in the waiting room what had just happened, he flatlined again. The paddles revived him once again. Twice he essentially died, and twice he came back. The danger was not over. Shaeffer was placed in an induced coma.

The moment he heard about the cardiac arrest, Steve Workman headed for the Burn Center to be with Shaeffer's family. At the Pentagon, Admiral Clark's executive officer walked in to give him the bad news. Clark, the head of the Navy, was told Shaeffer might not make it through the night. He pushed his entire staff into action to expedite Shaeffer's medical retirement in case he died that night, a move that would guarantee that Blanca would receive better benefits than if he were still on active duty. And Admiral Clark prayed.

Reverend Dick Foth was a close friend and religious adviser to the Admiral. They had prayed for Shaeffer every day. The Reverend was aware that Admiral Clark did not like the way some people were constantly asking God for things they wanted. So, when he reached out to Foth after hearing about Shaeffer's deteriorating condition, Foth modified his usual approach.

"Dear Lord," said the Reverend. "We know that only you know what will happen to Kevin, but Lord, if it is all the same to you, we would like Kevin around for a while longer."

The next morning, Admiral Clark got a call from an aide: "You won't believe it, sir. Kevin just sat up in bed and said, 'What's going on?'" Shaeffer had no memory of flatlining. None. When he saw Blanca, the first thing he mouthed was, *Did you bring the toothbrush?*

Shaeffer calls it a miracle among miracles. Admiral Clark says he is very careful when talking about the possibility of miracles, but this one was hard to deny.

Miracle or not, in the coming days Shaeffer made undeniable gains. Numerous surgeries followed. Skin grafts and a blood clot in a lung set him back. And there were days when the physical therapy was excruciating. But slowly and surely, he was getting better. By the end of October, just a month and a half after he was injured, he could walk, talk, and start slowly planning for his future.

In the early days of his hospitalization, Shaeffer hadn't wanted to hear about the outside world, needing to concentrate on his recovery. But days after he flatlined, the United States launched its war on al-Qaeda and the Taliban in Afghanistan. Now, whenever he had a visitor from the Navy, he wanted full debriefs on the hunt for bin Laden. The man responsible for the deaths of his friends, and for putting him in this hospital to begin with.

On December 13, 2001, three months, two days, and twenty surgeries after he was nearly killed, Kevin Shaeffer finally went home. His physical therapy would continue for months, but he had beaten tremendous odds. He was medically retired from the Navy because of the damage to his lungs, but he was not done yet. He was set on getting back to work and starting a new chapter in his life. One where he could make a difference, and find purpose. Above all, a future in which he could serve.

The road to recovery for burn victims is a very long one. In the early months of 2002, Kevin Shaeffer faced not only physical recovery but emotional anguish. Nightmares would plague him, his sobbing uncontrollable at times. Though Blanca helped him, counseling was key, as was support from Steve Workman. In April 2002, at a joint ceremony in the Pentagon, Admiral Clark awarded Shaeffer the Purple Heart, and Army Lieutenant General Kevin Byrnes awarded Sergeant First Class Steve Workman the Soldier's Medal for Valor for his efforts to save Kevin Shaeffer. Surviving the catastrophic attack on the Pentagon while losing everyone around him that day took a tremendous toll on Shaeffer, but it also centered him. Sitting on his couch, clutching a golf club to strengthen his grip, he would spend hours watching news reports about the 9/11 attacks and the war on terror. He had been one of the first casualties of that war, and he was ready to fight terror in his own way—or, at the very least, to try to help prevent future attacks.

In June 2002, Pentagon officials came to Shaeffer's home to interview him about his experience on 9/11 and his recovery. He told the officials he had read about the planning for a new government agency—to be called the Department of Homeland Security—and said that was the kind of work he would like to do.

But he still had to deal with the ghosts that haunted him. A month later, while he was driving into Washington on a sun-soaked morning, Shaeffer's heart began pounding, his brow dripping sweat. Frightened and breathing rapidly, he realized he was having a panic attack. He called the one person he knew who could help: Steve Workman, the man who had become like a brother to him.

"Take a deep breath," Workman told him. "You sit right there. There is just too much going on down there, brother." Shaeffer began to relax. "That's good; keep breathing," Workman said, promising he would drive right down to help. His voice alone was enough.

Shaeffer was still in recovery mode at the time—mental and physical recovery both. He wore compression sleeves on his arms and gloves on his hands to minimize the scarring. He had improved enough that he was able to attend a congressional hearing that summer on domestic security, largely out of personal interest. He returned to Capitol Hill that fall to watch the debate about the new department and the accompanying proposal to establish a National Commission on Terrorist Attacks

Upon the United States—what would come to be known as the 9/11 Commission. Its investigative mission resonated deeply with Shaeffer and would give him a new sense of purpose.

"I made it known that I was wanting to contribute," he told me. "I thought it was possibly one of the reasons I had made it through."

By the end of 2002, he shed the burn garments from his arms and hands and was finally able to wear his wedding and Naval Academy rings. Senators John McCain and Joseph Lieberman, who had jointly sponsored the legislation to create the Commission, heard about his desire to join and helped arrange a meeting with the new executive staff.

It got off to a disappointing start. Having spent his entire adult life in the Navy, Shaeffer had never gone through a job interview. He explained to the interviewers why he wanted a spot on the Commission and what he had been through. After thanking him for his service and sacrifice, the staff directors told him that without expertise on counterterrorism or any real experience with intelligence work, he wasn't the right fit for the job. They sent Shaeffer on his way. Or at least they tried.

"I had to turn the table on them," he told me. Pointing out that the Commission had yet to hire a single 9/11 survivor, he told them, "If you bring me on board, you'll have a motivated survivor that will bring and share and spread that motivation to the team, to learn the lessons of 9/11." The appeal worked. The next day, he got a call informing him that he was hired.

Without an intelligence or investigative background, Shaeffer faced a steep learning curve. The Commission staff included former government officials, state investigators, prosecutors, and detectives. What he brought to the table was motivation and his skills as a rising star in the Navy. He was a quick study and a team player with a voracious desire to learn and contribute.

Kevin Shaeffer was assigned to a team tasked with drawing lessons from the crisis management and emergency response actions on 9/11. The work involved a minute-by-minute reconstruction of what had happened on the planes, the actions of the first responders, law enforcement and fire departments, the Federal Aviation Administration, and military agencies, including the North American Aerospace Defense Command or NORAD.

Shaeffer threw himself into the job. Travel by now was much easier. The Commission was in high gear with visits to the World Trade Center site in New York, to CIA and FBI headquarters, and to Capitol Hill. The work kept him busy well into 2003. And then the greatest blessing of all arrived.

On August 17, 2003, Sophia Shaeffer was born. A tiny, beautiful baby, born a bit early, whom the Shaeffers saw as another miracle. Sophia's life, her future, would drive Kevin Shaeffer's every move.

A year later, when the Commission's work concluded and the flaws in the government's intelligence and response had been identified, Shaeffer had to decide what to do next. He could have gone back to work for the Navy as a civilian, but through his work on the Commission he had discovered something important. The drive to understand the broader context had pushed him in a new direction. His heart, he realized, was in the intelligence world.

Though his primary focus at the Commission had been on emergency preparedness, he was intensely interested in the Commission's investigation of Osama bin Laden's network and in terrorism in general. He had met current and former CIA officials during his time on the Commission and attended counterterrorism briefings at CIA headquarters. He had thought often of how his life was unfolding in chapters, and decided that the next one should be at the CIA.

He had learned how to conduct interviews, organize investigations, analyze data, and develop leads in his work with the Commission, all skills that would be essential in intelligence work. And the contacts he had made opened doors for him at Langley. For the CIA, it was a no-brainer. Kevin Shaeffer was hired. Although his desire to hunt down bin Laden would have to wait, there would soon be another remarkable chapter in Kevin Shaeffer's life story.

"You don't really get hired off the street to go find bin Laden," he told me. "I had to prove my merit professionally and prove my worth."

His first assignment was in counterproliferation, with the mission of tracking and halting the international movement of dangerous weapons. Though it was not technically counterterrorism work, the mission was critical and it was an opportunity for him to hone his investigative skills. His work in that department impressed one of his colleagues, and when that official moved to the CIA Counterterrorism Center, Shaeffer was determined to follow him.

Shaeffer's friend was in the unit responsible for tracking "High Value Targets," or HVTs—those key al-Qaeda operatives the Agency wanted to capture or kill. Nothing appealed to Shaeffer more than targeting, working with the detectives who disrupt and dismantle the people and organizations threatening America and its interests. Shaeffer met often with his friend for lunch or coffee, although the two men were in different units at the time. His friend told him he was part of the HVT 2 team, tracking the second most important target, Ayman al-Zawahiri, bin Laden's deputy. His friend was fully aware of Shaeffer's interest, and his past, and one day he reached out to him with exactly the news Kevin Shaeffer had been hoping to hear.

"I think it might be good timing for you to think about coming over here," he told Shaeffer. "Over here" meant the HVT 1 team. The team that was looking for Osama bin Laden.

It was 2009 when Shaeffer joined the HVT 1 team, more than ten years after bin Laden had blown up the US embassies in Africa and Kevin Shaeffer's Navy destroyer had had its sights on his training camps. Nine years since the attack on the USS *Cole*, and eight since 9/11.

Kevin Shaeffer was now one of just a handful of officers dedicated exclusively to the mission of locating bin Laden. Everything they did was secret. Outside of telling Blanca sparse details about his job, he could reveal nothing about what he was up to and who he was hunting.

When Shaeffer joined the HVT 1 team, it was focusing on an individual believed to be a courier for bin Laden. In 2010 the courier was tracked to a large compound in Abbottabad, a city of around two hundred thousand people in northern Pakistan. Inside that compound, round-the-clock satellite surveillance had picked up the image of a tall man who regularly strolled around the top floor of the compound but, unlike those living below, never seemed to leave the compound or its grounds. They called the tall man The Pacer and focused all the resources at their disposal on figuring out exactly who he was. By analyzing the shadows he cast, they estimated his height and compared it to what was known about bin Laden.

Shaeffer's colleagues at the Agency were keenly aware that he was helping to chase down the man responsible for the physical and emotional pain he had endured over the years. In fact, ribbons from the Navy uniform Shaeffer was wearing on 9/11 would be put in the CIA museum. But Shaeffer wanted only to reflect professionalism in his work, not emotion. Not revenge. He said his focus was on adding value, every step of the way.

In time, the targeters grew confident that The Pacer was indeed bin Laden. So did CIA Director Leon Panetta. In March 2011, White House officials and CIA and military leaders considered several COAs or "Courses of Action." The first was a raid conducted by Navy SEALs. The second was a B-2 bomber strike that would have obliterated the compound. The third was a drone strike with smaller explosives. The fourth was a joint operation with the Pakistanis, which seemed the least likely.

After weeks of deliberation, a decision was made. The Navy SEALs would conduct a risky raid to keep the compound intact and preserve the evidence within. Shaeffer took a great deal of pride in the notion that Navy SEALs would take down bin Laden. He couldn't help but think he had brought "a bit of Navy karma" to the decision.

Blanca knew her husband was on the team hunting for bin Laden, though not much else. In April, while the SEALs were rehearsing for the raid, the two of them took a quick break to celebrate Kevin's thirty-ninth birthday. When they returned, he told her the next couple of weeks would feel "like a deployment." As a Navy spouse and officer herself, she instinctively understood what that meant, and nothing else was said.

The raid took place on Sunday, May 1, 2011, long after sundown. A few members of the bin Laden targeting team had flown to Afghanistan to provide direct support to the SEALs for their mission to Pakistan.

Shaeffer and the remaining members set up a small command post at CIA headquarters, following the operations via a direct video feed. A minute-by-minute, real-time view of the mission. Shaeffer was tasked with relaying what he was watching and hearing to the CIA Counterterrorism Center. Every surveillance resource imaginable was at his disposal. Feeds from satellites, and the SEAL team themselves, were projected on large-screen televisions.

As the helicopters entered Pakistani airspace and approached the compound, Shaeffer, calm and steady, said, "Here we go."

The teams began counting down how far the SEALs were from the compound. When the specially equipped Black Hawk helicopters came into the field of view, the room was dead quiet. Then the first helicopter took a sudden, sharp spin over the compound wall and crash-landed inside. Around Shaeffer's room came shouts of, "Oh shit!" followed by a long stretch of silence.

"I think everyone's heart stopped," Shaeffer said. "You could hear a pin drop." But the mission continued. The SEALs crept toward the compound, night vision goggles lighting up the inside. They blasted their way upstairs, and then came face-to-face with the most wanted man in the world. Osama bin Laden, standing near his bed, reached for a weapon, and the SEALs opened fire.

Kevin Shaeffer was anxiously tracking it all with his team. Then he heard the words "Jackpot," followed by "Geronimo." The code words meaning that Osama bin Laden was dead.

For a few seconds, Shaeffer was jubilant. But now the SEALs had to get out of the compound and make it back to Afghanistan without being detected by the Pakistani military. Shaeffer watched closely as the remaining helicopters lifted out of the compound and the explosive charges were set off to destroy the damaged Black Hawk. He was reporting the calls from the aircraft, distances to the Afghan border, a countdown to safety. He wanted to push them to go faster and faster.

When the helicopters crossed the border, the room rejoiced, with hugs and handshakes all round. For Kevin Shaeffer, it was a deeply personal celebration. On the outside he was calm, but inside he was bursting with relief.

Through the incredible work of so many professionals, the hunt for bin Laden was over. Justice had been served for every man, woman, and child killed on 9/11.

For Shaeffer, it was emotionally overwhelming. There were small celebrations at the Agency that night, and he congratulated a few colleagues, but he then packed up his things, and headed home.

Blanca met him at the door, looking at him expectantly. Kevin gave her a big hug and a big smile. "We got him," he finally said. "We got him."

It was late by then, but Shaeffer had one more call to make. He suspected that Steve Workman would be asleep. But the man who saved his life, the man he looked to as a brother, needed to hear the good news.

"Hey, brother, I'm sorry to wake you up, but you need to turn on the TV," he told Workman. "There's some news that's going to be breaking. You're gonna want to hear it."

Shaeffer didn't make Workman wait. He told him the same thing he had told his wife: "We got him." Workman knew Shaeffer was working at the Agency, although he didn't know exactly what he was doing there. Given Shaeffer's history, *their* history, it didn't take long for Workman to figure out what he meant. Kevin Shaeffer would finally have closure. The men reveled in the moment as both awaited the official announcement. The call ended the way every conversation between the two men ended. "I love you, brother," Workman said. "I love you too, brother," Shaeffer replied.

At 11:35 pm, President Obama walked to the entrance of the East Room of the White House and informed the nation that Osama bin Laden was dead. Kevin Shaeffer sat on the bed with Blanca, watching. He placed his ravaged hands over his wife's, and they held on to each other. Neither said a word.

I covered the 9/11 attacks from Washington, DC. Standing on Memorial Bridge, I watched smoke pour from the Pentagon and imagined the horrors inside. I would hear many stories over the years about that day, but I did not meet Kevin Shaeffer until twenty years later, at the Pentagon Memorial anniversary service. I was standing on a riser, broadcasting the event as images of those who had died flashed on a giant screen. Commander William Donovan, Captain Robert Dolan Jr., Lieutenant Commander David Williams, Commander Patrick Dunn, Staff Sergeant Maudlyn White. Chairs were set up for the families facing the large screens. I noticed two men, their backs to me, side by side. When "Taps" began to play, a man with gray cropped hair placed his hand on the shoulder of the younger man beside him. Both were clearly struggling. It was a moment I wanted to remember, an image that said so much about that day. I pulled out my camera and took several pictures. When the service was over, I introduced myself to the men.

"He got me out of the Pentagon that day," Kevin Shaeffer told me, pointing to Steve Workman. The conversation was brief. I didn't want to take away from their time together on such a meaningful day. I got their phone numbers and sent them the picture. I had no idea then what these two men had experienced that day, or what either man had done in the twenty years since.

Three years later, as the twenty-third anniversary of 9/11 approached, I got an unexpected call from CIA officials. Kevin Shaeffer had been keeping a secret for more than a decade, they told me. He wanted to talk to me about his work, and the Agency had helped him to do just that.

A few weeks later, we sat together just outside the new wall of the Pentagon, right where the plane had plunged into the building so many years before. One hundred and eighty-four granite benches have since been placed in a tree-filled memorial there. Fifty-nine benches bear the names of those who were on American Flight 77. One hundred and twenty-five benches have the names of those who died inside the building. Crepe myrtles shaded us as we spoke. Airplanes passed overhead.

The 9/11 anniversaries are never easy for Kevin Shaeffer. He thinks of his friends, his colleagues, the shipmates he lost, and the wives, hus-

Steve Workman (left) with Kevin Shaeffer during the memorial ceremony marking the twentieth anniversary of the 9/11 attacks.

bands, and children they left behind. But he also thinks about the way the nation came together as one. He longs for that now in a country he sees as far more divided.

His bond with Steve Workman, after all these years, is tighter than ever. They talk often. They share emotional pain and family passings. Workman, who subsequently spent years at the Defense Intelligence

Agency, says, "I gave him a promise that I wouldn't let him die. I will do anything for him."

Steve Workman will also do anything for Shaeffers' children. There are three of them now. He is especially close to the Shaeffers' firstborn son, a boy the Shaeffers proudly—and gratefully—named Steven.

US Air Force Pararescueman Josh Webster over Afghanistan, July 2010.

CHAPTER 2

The Man on the Mountain

Josh Webster and Kevin Mott Jr.

IT SEEMED LIKE THE LEAST URGENT RADIO CALL ON A day of unrelenting casualties. After numerous transmissions punctuated by the crack of gunfire this one conveyed a relative calm.

"One of the guys has fallen down the hill. They can't find him."

Staff Sergeant Joshua Webster and his team were on a refueling pad in Asadabad, Afghanistan, when the message reached them via an Apache attack helicopter pilot overhead. Webster, his uniform stained brown by the blood of the soldier he'd just evacuated from a firefight, quickly assessed the level of urgency. "Fallen down," they'd said. As in, the soldier had likely lost his footing on a ridge. He'd slipped, maybe. Nothing about the call suggested mortal danger. It wasn't the kind of message that spiked the adrenaline, or suggested the need for an immediate evacuation. There were other calls coming in, more critical cases out there. Severe traumas. Limbs that might need amputating. This one could wait. It would have to.

Josh Webster was a "Pararescue Jumper" from California's Air National Guard. He had seen combat before, but nothing like this. The PJs, as they are known, are an elite unit of Air Force medics who do search and rescue missions back home—pulling climbers off mountains, hurricane survivors off rooftops. When deployed overseas, PJs evacuate wounded soldiers from active battlefields, often under the most dangerous conditions imaginable.

By the time the call came in at 10:30 am, Webster's six-man team, Pedro 34, and fellow PJ Jake Garel's seven-man team, Pedro 33, had made half a dozen runs in their separate helicopters, picking up badly injured soldiers and ferrying them to a nearby field clinic. The PJs were working in support of Operation Strong Eagle, a mission launched soon after dawn that morning in Kunar Province, and every hour or so the teams had returned to the Asadabad landing zone, or LZ, to refuel and restock. Gas, ammo, medical supplies were all loaded in a quick pit stop before the next call. From the LZ, they could see Apaches circling the firefight, just a few miles away. Throughout the morning they felt the jolt of mortar fire.

The Strong Eagle operation was a bold but risky assault, meant to clear out some three hundred Taliban fighters embedded in the towering mountains between Pakistan and the Afghan village of Daridam below.

The Kunar River runs down from Pakistan's Hindu Kush into northern Kunar Province, flowing roughly parallel to the border for a stretch of one hundred miles. Much of Kunar Province is marked by small villages and overshadowed by sharp peaks reaching as high as sixteen thousand feet. There are few paved roads or bridges to cross the river or its smaller tributaries. Armies from the time of Alexander the Great had come again and again, and none had managed to completely conquer Kunar. Asadabad sits in the heart of Kunar Province, which had seen heavy infiltrations of Taliban and Haqqani militants, who staged deadly cross-border attacks on a regular basis.

Shortly after dawn, American and Afghan troops had been inserted into fighting positions some two thousand feet above the valley. The thirteen men in Pedro 33 and 34 were all waiting at the closest LZ. Medical equipment hung on the back walls of the helicopters, and the choppers' .50-caliber machine guns were bristling with ammo. Josh Webster, kitted in forty pounds of body armor, waited with his team, M4 rifles slung over their shoulders. The PJs all had a sense that things were about to turn ugly.

Just after 7:00 am they received the first report of "troops in contact" or "TIC," a military acronym that in this case meant the unit on the ground was facing ferocious fire and taking casualties. "In contact" hardly did justice to what was happening in the valley.

"*Category Alpha! Category Alpha!*" came the first call of the day. Translation: The patient would die if they didn't get him out of there quickly. Webster and Garel scrambled aboard their respective helicopters, legs dangling out the open doors. The radio transmissions sounded through headphones and they kept coming. As soon as Webster's chopper was airborne, rotors roaring, he heard a one-sentence transmission that stunned him: *"The staff sergeant got hit with an RPG."*

An RPG, a rocket-propelled grenade, is an anti-tank weapon. It can pierce an armored vehicle.

"Like . . . hit?" Webster called back. The answer was brief and direct: *"It hit him in the head."*

The ground troops, still under fire, had pulled the soldier from the battlefield and rushed him to the closest LZ. Within minutes, Webster and his team descended in a swirl of dust and spotted soldiers carrying four stretchers toward the helicopter. The men carrying the first stretcher were openly weeping. On the stretcher was thirty-one-year-old Eric Shaw, a history teacher turned staff sergeant, with a wife and three daughters at home, the youngest only a few weeks old. Shaw was KIA. Killed in Action.

Standing by Shaw's body, the unit's medic spoke evenly and without tears. "This is my buddy and he's dead," he told Webster. "He can go in last because we have three other guys to put on first." The three other guys were Afghan soldiers, wounded in the fight when they were cut off from the squad. Sergeant Shaw had lost his life trying to protect them.

The PJs loaded the four stretchers into the two helicopters—the dead American and the three wounded Afghans. On the short flight back to the small base at Asadabad—no more than five minutes—the PJs went to work on the wounded. Every minute counted. One Afghan soldier had been shot in the head, one in the abdomen, and the last one in the leg.

Once back at the LZ, there was a quick handover and a debrief on the condition of the men. The helicopter floor was cleared—bloody bandages, used intubation tubes, and tourniquets blanketed the chopper floor. The team regrouped and within minutes they were back in the air.

The man who had fallen down the hill would have to wait.

Joshua Maverick Webster had joined the Air Force Pararescue five years prior, after a four-year stint in the Army. He found he was a natural, a six-foot, four-inch kid from Long Beach who took physical fitness and service seriously, and had the added benefit of being a Maverick by birth—a name that had been in the family long before that other Maverick hit Hollywood. Webster had spent most of his years in the Air National Guard. Hikers stranded on mountaintops were his world, that and people flailing in flood waters and fleeing from fires. Men and women in distress in inaccessible terrain. It's what the Pararescue squads did at home and overseas—they went in, landed their helicopters, or dropped a PJ down to help. They plucked people from danger, assessed their needs, did ER-type work on the fly, and then rushed them to clinics and hospitals. When the teams were deployed to war zones, they did the same kind of rescue operations. But these were combat missions, and almost always under fire.

Overseas deployments were nothing new to Webster. In 1999, before he became an Air Force pararescueman, he had enlisted in the Army for a very practical reason—he needed the money for college. He had already completed two years of community college in Long Beach, but he wanted two more. His hardworking parents had made it clear to him and his five siblings at an early age that they'd have to pay their own way. The Websters were never wanting for anything essential, but they were not the family heading out to ski for spring break or splurging on restaurants. The money Webster's parents earned went into putting their kids through Catholic school. "We were like the poorer-kids-in-the-nice-school kind of thing," he said with a grin.

Webster had been a good student in high school. At one point he'd considered pursuing music or sports—a swimming scholarship, maybe.

But none of that panned out, and given the family circumstances, his hopes of paying for an actual university were a bridge too far. "I just had no money even though I was always working outside of class, and taking on that debt seemed a stretch," he said.

So he cooked up a plan: He would join the Army, get his training and funding, then move on to something else. Maybe parlay whatever skills he'd learn in the service into a more interesting career. "Nothing much was going on in the world when I signed up," he said. "So, you know, join the Army. We might be going somewhere cool, I thought. Sure. I'll join. I love a challenge."

When he paid his first visit to the recruiting office in June 1999, Webster was asked what he wanted to do. There were choices, or at least requests he could make. "I said, 'What's the hardest job there is?' And the guy says, 'Airborne Ranger.' And I was like, 'That sounds good.' I'll do that. I'll be a Ranger, whatever that is."

Webster's brother Joe couldn't believe it. "He's like, 'You signed up for *what?* You accidentally picked the Army's version of the Navy SEALs.' But I just thought, 'Awesome, jump out of planes and do stuff.' Joe tells me, 'You idiot! It's going to be so *hard*.'"

Webster's brother didn't doubt he could do it. He just wanted him to know how grueling it would be. "I thought, it'll be fun, four years in and out, you know, what can go wrong? How were we supposed to know what was coming?"

What was coming for Josh Webster and his generation of warriors was 9/11. And for all the shattering, immediate impact of that day, there would be long-term, life-altering consequences for him and for tens of thousands of other freshly minted American servicemen and -women. They had signed up with a plan like his, or just on a whim, never imagining what the commitment would mean after the attacks on the United States on September 11, 2001. 9/11 spiked recruitment in all the services, and made Webster and many others that much more eager to serve. But as the years wore on, the aftermath of that day completely upended the plans and lives of all those young Americans who had enlisted.

As it happened, Webster completed Army Ranger School on September 10, 2001, after passing a grueling three-month field combat test in the woods of Fort Benning, Georgia. On the morning of September 11, Webster and his fellow Rangers woke up early, sore and tired but looking forward to a day of hot dogs and ice cream as a reward for graduation. A long line had formed at the single pay phone on base, the soldiers' only way to communicate with the outside world. Just after 9:00 am Webster got through to his mother to share the news of his graduation. His mother told him that a second plane had just hit the Twin Towers. Word spread quickly among the Rangers. Someone found a small radio, and they all huddled around it. The soldiers were soon told to grab their weapons, and sent to stand guard around Eglin Air Force Base. Like everyone else in the country, Webster spent that morning in shock, trying to figure out what was happening. But unlike the rest of the country, he and his cohort of Rangers were sure of one thing: They were going to war.

The United States invaded Afghanistan and overthrew the Taliban regime that fall. Three months later, Josh Webster and his Ranger battalion arrived on scene. He would spend his deployment on patrol in the freezing January snow, talking to village elders and hunting for al-Qaeda.

"We weren't seen as occupiers yet in '02," Webster recalled. Villagers weren't sure what to make of the Americans. Many had never seen a foreigner—even the Soviets, during their long occupation of Afghanistan, had not come to these far-flung places. "We'd go to these villages, and the people would just stare at us, and the women would scatter, and the kids would run up and tug on our shirts and want to touch our guns."

Josh Webster's Ranger battalion was tasked with helping grow the number of American "FOBs" in Afghanistan—forward operating bases that were springing up across the country in the wake of the Taliban's ouster. They functioned as small military outposts in less-populated parts of Afghanistan, helping with logistics and establishing rapport with local officials. They also facilitated faster, more effective responses to emergencies. The FOB Webster operated out of was in a rugged valley on the Pakistani border—the very same one where he would find himself eight years later.

Webster loved the work of an Army Ranger. It was an adrenaline rush like nothing he had ever known, and he valued seeing, hearing, and learning so much on the job. But as the war dragged on, and a new one began to rage in Iraq, Webster knew he was now likely to be in the service for a very long time. And if that was the case, he wanted a different job. The one that intrigued him most was Air Force Pararescue. "I liked being a Ranger, but I'd worked with Pararescue. They were more like medics, and I thought maybe one day I might become a doctor." Instead of taking lives, he thought, he could save them. "I liked the idea of being in special operations medicine, like a rescue guy. Someone who could help save lives."

Pararescuemen were legendary. Today the Air Force calls PJs "the most highly trained and versatile Personnel Recovery specialists in the world." Within the US military, air rescues date back to the 1920s, the early days of flight. They came into wide use during World War II, as aerial combat became common—along with crashes and the need to search for downed pilots. The Air Force traces its pararescue operations to the China-Burma-India theater, where long flights were common, over territory only loosely held by the enemy, and a pilot who crashed or bailed out of his aircraft had a better chance at survival.

After the war, the military formally created the Air Rescue Service, charged with saving the lives of air crews involved in accidents or crash landings, wherever they might occur.

Pararescue training wasn't easy and it took time. As the Air Force makes clear, "You don't apply. You prove."

During his third year of community college in the winter of 2003, Webster drove to the Pararescue team headquarters and enlisted.

Pararescue training was a three-year commitment from start to finish, though he would complete it in two because he'd done his airborne training in the Army, and his time in boot camp counted too. He soaked it all up—nearly two years of EMT paramedic work and specialized military medicine, woven in with intense physical training. There was free fall parachuting, mountain climbing, scuba diving, a six-week survival school in Washington state.

Finally, in December 2005, at the age of twenty-six, Josh Webster was presented with a maroon beret at a small ceremony at Kirtland Air Force Base, near Albuquerque, New Mexico. He was Pararescueman Joshua Webster now, one of only five hundred who held the title.

Webster's unit was the 131st Rescue Squadron, based at the Moffett Federal Airfield in Mountain View, California, a joint civil-military airfield. The squadron included PJs, combat rescue officers, and flight crews. The cadence was like a fire station's meetings at the start of the shift, a lot of hanging around on most days, and a collection of important routines: workout regimens, maintaining the medicine and scuba shops, checking on the weapons and other military gear, and tending to the helicopters, the workhorses of the team.

The unit ran rescues up and down the West Coast—his squadron's area went from Oregon to Mexico, and included Hawaii, since the PJs had helicopters that could refuel in the air. One of his last missions before deploying overseas had been bizarre even by PJ standards: He'd rescued a Chinese fisherman whose bladder had burst, six hundred miles out in the Pacific Ocean. Webster and another PJ fast-roped down to the boat, hoisted the fisherman into the helicopter, and flew him back to California. Another life saved.

In early March 2010, Josh Webster's team deployed to Afghanistan. They were initially based at the sprawling facility at Bagram Airfield, on the outskirts of Kabul. The tempo was utterly different from back home. Days were broken into two twelve-hour shifts, noon to midnight or midnight to noon. Two-man teams were expected to be ready to load up and fly off within five minutes.

"You would basically just wake up, come to work either at noon or midnight, and read the report of what happened the previous day," Webster said. Sirens sounded to signal a mission, and alerts would pop up on the small Afghan network phones they carried. They'd get in their truck, make their way to the chopper, throw on the kits, and go.

Webster knew the area well from past deployments, but this one was tough from the start. The unit they were replacing—a PJ team from Alaska—had just completed a harrowing search and recovery after a deadly landslide just north of Bagram. Soon after Webster's arrival, he was called to the aftermath of a small plane crash at fifteen thousand feet, for what proved to be a seven-day operation.

Worse than their own experiences was the news that reached them on June 9 from the Pararescue base, in Afghanistan's second-largest city, Kandahar, informing them that Pedro 66 had been shot down by the Taliban in Helmand Province. Five of the seven squadron members on board, all friends, had been killed. They were on an operation to rescue wounded British soldiers when RPGs brought down their helicopter.

It was an emotional blow, and it came with practical implications: A quarter of their squadron was transferred to Kandahar to fill the gap left by the dead men. It was also a stark reminder of the danger of their work in Afghanistan. Soon there would be other reminders. More than once, Webster's bird picked up soldiers hovering between life and death. Sometimes the PJs' quick work and fast flights to the med station weren't enough.

"That's the worst possible thing—going to get someone who's supposed to be alive, and they end up dying in the helicopter," he told me. "It's like what happens in an ER, where doctors and nurses and paramedics can say, 'I *did my best. I did everything I* could; *there was nothing I wouldn't do to help that person.*' And you wonder, *Did I do everything I could? If I had trained harder could I have done something better?* And then you immediately just go start training that thing. You think, *I just need to be faster at triage.* Or *I* need *to be faster at getting IVs* in, *faster at opening airways.*"

One morning they picked up a soldier who'd been shot *and* hit by shrapnel. His eyes had been badly damaged. "We were picking him up, and the doctors were like, 'All right, he's stable, and he should be good for the flight to Kabul. But he can't see, and he can't really talk. So we'll monitor vitals.'"

They laid him in the chopper with great care, but almost immediately his vital signs went south. Blood pressure dropped. Heart rate and breathing spiked. "We're flying, and all of his stats start to go down and we're like, *Oh shit.*"

Webster's partner made a snap decision. "He said we have to put an airway in his throat right now, and we have to paralyze him to do that." It's called a rapid sequence intubation, or RSI—administering an anesthetic and neuromuscular blocking agent that allows for the insertion of a breathing tube. An RSI is the fastest and most effective way to create an emergency airway.

"It's tricky at a hospital," Webster said. "And we're in a helicopter, which also means you can't hear well. So you have your headphones on, you're talking through an intercom, and the pilot can hear you too. And we're like, '*Hey, pilot, we're going to paralyze this guy. Put a tube in his throat. You need to fly really level.*'" This time the procedure worked. They saved him.

When they reached the med station, the attending doctor did a double take. "You did an RSI—in a *helicopter*?" Webster pointed to his fellow PJ, who nodded. The soldier would be OK. The work was done, at least for now.

By 2010, the war in Afghanistan was nearly nine years old. For much of that time, Americans' attention had shifted to the increasingly fraught and deadly US invasion of Iraq. In 2009, President Obama had decided to send thousands of additional troops to Afghanistan after months of public deliberation in an attempt to turn the tide of a war that the US was clearly not winning. But for many it was all too easy to forget that American men and women were still fighting and dying and struggling to make and maintain progress in Afghanistan. The June 9 attack on the Pararescue helicopter had brought the US toll to seventeen killed so far that month, and June wasn't half over. It would be among the deadliest months of the war to that point.

That spring, the 101st Airborne had begun taking over division responsibilities in Afghanistan. In early June they had deployed units to RC East—"RC" for "Regional Center," "East" in this case referring to

US Army Captain Kevin Mott Jr.,
Kunar Province, Afghanistan.

a vast area of eastern Afghanistan covering Jalalabad, Khost, and Asadabad, the capital of Kunar Province, which had been heavily infiltrated by the Taliban.

Captain Kevin Mott Jr. was the battalion scout platoon leader for RC East, in charge of three sniper teams and three recon teams for the Second Battalion, 327th Infantry Regiment, First Brigade Combat Team—the "No Slack" Battalion for short. Mott and his soldiers had been handed the broad and dangerous task of "village clearance"—which, practically speaking, meant doing what they could to identify and drive out members of the Taliban and Haqqani network, who were suspected of smuggling weapons, arms, and people across the Pakistani border.

An ambitious task, for a twenty-five-year-old captain and his battalion. And almost from the day they landed, it was tough going. Mott, a West Point graduate, had been commissioned as an officer in 2007. Like Josh Webster, he had grown up in California and attended Catholic schools, but under very different circumstances. The Mott family lived in an affluent community in Marin County, California. His father was a bond trader for Lehman Brothers, his mother was a teacher, and his twenty-one-year-old sister, Gina, was at college at Sonoma State.

The military was not a calling that had occurred to most of Kevin's friends. But he had been intrigued as a young teenager by war stories from Vietnam, and books about the adventures of Navy SEALs. 9/11 transformed intrigue into action. His father, Kevin Mott Sr., remembers his sixteen-year-old son standing in his school uniform, tan shorts and white polo shirt, watching as he and his wife gasped and cried that morning. He knew many people who'd died inside the World Trade Towers. Kathy, Kevin's mother, immediately understood the implications for her only son; she feared that someday he would be headed to war.

Mott's first deployment wasn't with the Navy SEALs and it wasn't to Afghanistan. He was sent to Samarra, in Iraq, in 2008 with the US Army. A combat zone for sure, but Kevin and his team saw very little combat that summer. The area had been cleared of insurgents (for the time being) before their arrival and a lull in fighting had ensued.

Eighteen months later, Kevin Mott was given a different mission, with a very different outcome. He arrived in Afghanistan's Kunar Province in May 2010. The local population had resisted the Americans more fiercely than most, and the frontier with Pakistan was considered virtually impossible to patrol. Islamic militants representing multiple organizations crossed often and at will. The Taliban, as it turned out, was far from defeated, and al-Qaeda insurgents were known to use Kunar's mountain caves as hideouts. Ambushes against American forces had become common. A US battalion operating in Kunar Province in early 2007 had suffered combat losses accounting for half of those sustained by the entire Third Brigade of the Tenth Mountain Division.

Mott's battalion was part of that Army surge to Afghanistan announced by President Obama in 2009. The strategy involved pouring additional troops into the area, with the hope that more combat power would beat back the Taliban and carve out time and space for a budding Afghan national security force to make its mark. Ideally, small victories in pockets of the province would build momentum—"clear, hold, and build," as General Stanley McChrystal intoned, was the mantra of US counterinsurgency efforts. The hope was that these successes might spread to other areas.

It was early June when Kevin Mott's team received reports that hundreds of Taliban fighters had gathered in the village called Daridam. Operation Strong Eagle aimed to clear them out of Daridam. The preparation was complex, but the mission itself would come with considerable firepower—five hundred to six hundred US soldiers and another two hundred to three hundred Afghans fighting alongside them.

A few weeks later the No Slack Battalion moved in from Forward Operating Base Joyce to begin the assault. The American FOBs in the area were relatively low in the valley, between ground level and four thousand feet. FOB Joyce was at thirty-five hundred feet, but No Slack ran air assaults that reached up to ten thousand or even eleven thousand feet, in terrain marked by sharp rock and limited vegetation, with dramatic drops nearly everywhere you looked.

Before dawn on Sunday, June 27, Mott's platoon was dropped off on a promontory at six thousand feet. They made their way gingerly by foot in the dark to positions overlooking the village. The platoon of twenty-six men split up: Twelve were instructed to stay a safe distance away with equipment and supplies. The soldiers had lugged six hundred pounds of gear—extra ammo, water, everything they imagined they would need for a big fight. The twelve other men, Mott's sniper and recon teams, headed to a small rock outcropping looking down on Daridam. The spot was only about eight feet wide and twenty-five to thirty feet long—"the size of a playground," as Staff Sergeant Brent Schneider would later remember. Boulders were scattered along the ridge. It was still dark when the soldiers took up positions behind them.

Mott and his men believed that if you could hold the dominant terrain, you would be OK—the Taliban couldn't get above you. The platoon spotter was going to "secure and hold," in the vernacular, "overwatching" the place where Mott was waiting with the rest of his platoon.

Mott knew going in that the operation would be tough. And he knew that the PJs would be on alert for the duration to respond to potential catastrophes. The added firepower from the airborne warrior-medics didn't hurt either.

Kevin Mott and his snipers would have a clear view of the Strong Eagle One operation from their vantage point at the outcropping above Daridam. They could radio updates back to the platoon about what was going on below. A good position, and a seemingly solid approach, with a sizable force behind them. Almost as soon as the sun peeked over the mountain, withering explosions ripped through the valley. The Taliban came at Mott's team from almost every direction—a ring of enemy firepower. Rifles, RPGs, and hundreds of Taliban fighters were fanning out from the village below. The mission was exposed.

As the sun lifted over the mountains on that muggy Sunday in June, Jake Garel headed for his helicopter as part of the seven-man Pedro 33 team. Josh Webster and Larry Hiyakumoto's Pedro 34 team had six men.

Pedro 33 and 34 were up in the air from the start, the pair of Black Hawk helicopters ready to turn quickly to any downed aircraft or wounded soldiers. "From the minute we got the first call, it was game on," Webster said. "We were rotors turning nonstop." Nearly every time they did the med station drop-off, the next call was coming in. Grab some ammo. Gas up. Given a few extra minutes, they might scrub down the bloodied chopper floor, but there was little time to rest, or to see how the wounded men would fare.

After the early-morning horror of Sergeant Eric Shaw's death, they picked up others with gunshot wounds, a few with multi-system trauma. They'd fly in and land, or hover while Webster and Hiyakumoto took hold of the men and pulled them on board. "Either I was starting an IV or stopping a bleed," Webster said. "I was opening airways; I was doing CPR, tourniquets, whatever."

Like an ER doc on the roughest shift, Webster thought, *I have to do all these things right now, or else this guy* is *going to die.* He'd done it all before—just never so many cases in such a short time.

Terrain was an issue on nearly every run. The fifth call of the day took them to a soldier who had been shot in the neck. The PJs headed for the closest LZ. But with the extreme slope of the mountain and heavy rocket and mortar fire all around, there was no way to land. Larry Hiyakumoto motioned to the pilot. "We were just like, put one wheel down, just low enough to pull the guy on," Webster said.

Pilot Thad Ronnau executed the one-wheel hover at the pickup site, some seven feet below the ridgeline. With the rotor humming violently just a few feet from the rocky ledge, Webster and Hiyakumoto managed to pull the wounded soldier on board. He was alive but bleeding heavily. "When Larry and I looked at him, we thought, 'Wow, this guy, he's rapping on death's door, if not there already,'" Webster said. "So we just did as much as we could."

They checked his pulse. It was there—and then it was gone. Nothing. "So we started CPR on him in the bird and it was messy and ugly and we did the best we could. He'd already had a tube put in his throat by a combat medic on the ground, and he looked really bad." The man was alive—but barely. "About a two-minute transport, so there's not a whole lot of intervention you can do," Webster said. Again, a quick handoff at the med station. They had to leave before they knew the outcome.

That trauma, the harrowing pickup, the face of the soldier hanging on for life—it was all burned in their minds a few minutes later, when they were finally able to turn their attention to the man on the hill.

Hours had passed since the first call had come about the soldier who had fallen down the mountain. Webster and Hiyakumoto and Garel and his crew hadn't stopped running since dawn. They had put off the mountain rescue in favor of seemingly more urgent calls, partly because they didn't know where to look. But time was moving quickly, and the PJs weren't about to leave a call unanswered.

"Are you actually missing somebody?" Webster asked over the radio. It wasn't long before the answer came in.

"Yes, we're missing an officer. He fell off the cliff."

Webster was taken aback. "We were like, *Holy shit, that's a big deal.*" An *officer*. It was the first time they'd heard that. And it raised alarm bells—not because they would treat an officer any differently than an enlisted soldier, but because, as Josh Webster thought to himself, *The platoon is in the biggest battle of their lives, and their leader isn't there?*

There was also the other part of the message: *He fell off the cliff.* Not a "hill." A "cliff." It was only one word, but it conjured an utterly different picture.

Not long after that, the PJs got another update. The soldiers on the missing man's team thought they spotted their captain in a ravine. They said he had "moved a little bit," and made his way to a nearby tree. He might be OK, but he wasn't responding to calls.

Kevin Mott was the missing officer in question. The guy who had "fallen down the hill." And it was true—he *had* been able to move, and he was by a tree, just as the radio reports had said. But he wasn't anything close to "OK."

Mott had taken a shot to the head. The round had pierced his helmet and circled his skull, taking with it a good deal of skin and bone, before exiting the front, leaving a bloody halo-like wound. He'd been saved from instant death by a matter of millimeters. And then he'd fallen off the narrow shelf and tumbled down the side of the mountain. Somewhere between sixty and one hundred feet, his men estimated. Like a skier, bouncing off a sheer rock face, only there was no snow to cushion the fall.

Those who saw it happen had no idea Mott had been shot. He'd been standing fifteen feet from Staff Sergeant Brent Schneider, the reconnaissance team leader, but in the chaos of combat, it had looked to Schneider like Mott had simply slipped off the ledge. As Mott's body cartwheeled from ridge to ridge, Schneider had lost sight of him. At some point during the fall, Kevin Mott's helmet had come off. His body armor had been torn off. And his weapon had gone flying.

For a time, Kevin Mott lay where he had come to rest, bleeding and drifting in and out of consciousness. The blood eventually acted like a kind of glue, with layers of rock and sticks adhered to his face and chest. Rifle fire crackled around him.

None of his teammates up on that ridge had any idea where their captain had landed. It was as though he had vanished. They shouted his name repeatedly from the overwatch position and heard no reply. Sergeant Schneider was still up on the outcropping taking heavy fire. He had twelve men there with him—a six-member recon team and six snipers. After a brief huddle, Schneider and another soldier decided they would try to make their way down the ridge, to search for their platoon leader. It seemed the only thing to do.

They shed their armor to make it easier to move, keeping only their guns and extra ammo, and started to crawl their way down. They had hardly begun when it became clear it was a suicide mission. They'd never reach Mott that way—and they might lose more men in the process. It was far too steep. Schneider and his men didn't get far before they started getting shot at. Reluctantly, they scrambled back up the mountain, still keeping an eye on the ravine below.

PJ teams are normally routed to specific locations—not asked to search randomly in an active battle zone. "A couple of bullets can take down a helicopter," Webster explained. "You typically don't try to fly right over where they're shooting. Especially when they have RPGs. They can just shoot you down and then you have a whole helicopter crew dead." It's exactly what had happened to their fellow PJs in Kandahar less than three weeks earlier.

But they weren't about to leave a wounded man stranded out there in an operation they'd been tapped to support—a man who they now suspected was in far more serious shape than they'd been led to believe. So they headed for the mountainside, side doors of the chopper open, moving quickly. And thanks to Staff Sergeant Schneider and his team, who were still parked on that small ridge, they found the spot.

It was Schneider who thought he had seen Mott moving through a patch of short shrubs and bushes. He was crawling his way toward small trees, leaving a large smear of blood in his wake. Three or four soldiers were waving and pointing down—a courageous undertaking in an active battle zone. Schneider now understood something else. While the Americans hadn't seen the exact spot where Mott had fallen, the

Taliban had. Afghan allies were telling him that Taliban fighters were making their way to the scene, aiming to take Kevin Mott hostage.

A low-urgency call had morphed into the most urgent mission of the day. A bloodied, battered officer was down there somewhere, barely conscious, and enemy fighters had him in their sights.

All the landings and pickups that day had been precarious enough, given the need to marry speed with care in an open-fire zone. But this one was next-level. To Webster, the mountain looked like one of those steep rock faces in Yosemite National Park. "This was way more dangerous than a regular pickup," Webster said, "because there was no place to land and we were surrounded by rock."

Pedro 34 was vectored in by one of the soldiers on the ridge, crouched on the outcropping, who kept pointing down. Command pilot Thad Ronnau guided the chopper carefully, dipping the bird at a slight angle for a better look. Dust and stones kicked up around them. Ronnau estimated that he was flying a thousand feet above the valley floor, slowly lowering the bird into the valley.

"Down there," Webster said, pointing to the ridgeline. They had seen something. "We think it's a guy, about seventy-five feet down below the rock outcropping." Ronnau guided the bird downward.

Webster saw a faint but sizable splash of color. "But then it turns out as we start descending, to get above the position, that it's just gear. It's just someone's gear that they've come out of. Next to the gear, a piece of armor, and next to that, a whole lot of blood. And I'm looking at this, on comms with the pilot saying, '*This isn't him.* This is just all of his stuff. There is no one there.' We gotta keep going."

Gear. Not the guy. Soldiers are routinely given quick-release packs that they can shed in the event of an emergency, when freedom of movement becomes essential. The things they carried—ammo, radio pouches, water, food—were tethered to a cord mechanism that could be yanked. That cord helped medics in triage situations; one tug and the gear would snap off, and they could get down to business.

They had found evidence of a wounded soldier, but no sign of the soldier himself. "And we're like, *That's not him,*" Webster said. "So we keep going." It was a nightmare, unfolding quickly for the PJs and for the man who had fallen. Wherever he was.

They hovered for what seemed far too long. Josh Webster kept his position, perched on the edge of the bird, peering down. The PJs had trained on maneuvers for such situations: The pilot would hover and turn to one side, almost sideways, so they could look out the open door. A side-slope maneuver, they called it. The chopper dipped to one side, dropping altitude down along the ridge.

"I see this private with a radio and he's got his weapon and he's just pointing down this steep mountain, and again, it kind of looks like Yosemite," Webster said. "Some sparse trees, some big pines, but it's rock mostly, and really steep. And he's like, *Down there. I can see him out in the woods down there.*"

He was pointing to a spot much farther down the mountainside. The chopper side-sloped again, this time making a steep drop. Josh Webster kept craning for a look. "And then I see this little blurry body and I'm like, *I see him.* And the pilots are like, *Yeah, roger that! Let's go!*"

It was clearly a person this time. A body. Curled up on the ground. To Webster it looked like the man was using his hands as a pillow.

Nearly three hours had passed since Kevin Mott had gone tumbling down the mountain. For much of that time, rapid rifle fire and RPGs streaked through the sky nearby.

As the PJs closed in, "getting eyes on this objective," as Webster put it, fresh rounds kicked up around them, sending showers of dirt up from the mountainside. From their vantage point they couldn't determine the source of the fire, and they couldn't tell whether the soldier below them was dead or alive.

Webster or Hiyakumoto would have to rappel down, fighting wind, rotor wash, and enemy fire, and bring the wounded man up onto the chopper. Both were more than willing. Eager, even. It was a willingness to subject oneself to danger that I have seen again and again. If someone is in trouble, nothing will stop a fellow soldier from running into the fray.

With a smile and a shrug, Josh Webster raised his left fist and put it on top of his right palm, suggesting that the "winner" of a "rock-paper-scissor" challenge would carry out one of the most perilous rescues of the day. In the end, the game wasn't necessary. Hiyakumoto knew how badly Webster wanted to do this. The older PJ gave a quick nod and said, "Go ahead, Josh; you've got this." So in this harrowing moment, gunfire blazing, the chopper bent sideways, and the man lying wounded far beneath him, Josh Webster would get the prize of risking his life, to save another.

The fact was that everyone in that helicopter was in serious danger. There were bullets whirring around the valley. No one was sure where the Taliban fighters were. Webster, who always wanted the hardest job, had found it here. Hiyakumoto would take over the minigun—a task he'd always wanted to try in a combat zone.

A typical pararescue involves a PJ hooking up to the chopper's retractable hoist, the extension of a long mechanical arm. The hoist has a cable that can lower a rescuer hundreds of feet and hold up to two thousand pounds. Webster carried a rifle and rescue "strop," a U-shaped device that looks like the foamy thing lifeguards use to rescue swimmers. The strop would tether the wounded man to the hoist. The better his condition, the easier it would be.

Webster fastened himself to the hoist. Flight engineer Scott Lagerveld grabbed the hoist controller, which operates like a big joystick: a handle with down, up, stop, and other buttons to control the line that would lower Webster and bring him back up.

"So the flight engineer is like, *You good?*" Webster remembered. "And I was like, *Let's go.* I've got my rifle on my back. And they lower me onto the side of the mountain."

Lowering Josh Webster was challenging enough, but keeping the helicopter steady was even more perilous. Fighting wind and rotor wash, with a sheer rock face in front of him and cliffs running parallel on either side, Thad Ronnau held a perfect hover, his rotor whirring just twenty-five feet from the cliff face. Twenty-five feet from certain death.

Webster stepped out of the open door, dropped a few feet, and dangled in the air. The chopper blades roared, churning up rocks and dirt on the side of the mountain. The flight engineer pressed the down button, and down he went.

The helicopter was kicking up more earth as the rotors whirred near the stone ledge. Dirt was flying everywhere, caking Webster's goggles. Rocks came at him at what felt like 80 miles an hour, a knock-your-teeth-out kind of speed. "And I'm dropping down, trying to get to this guy."

Well beneath the chopper now but still a good twenty feet from the soldier, Webster grasped for the side of the ridge. It was steep but not vertical. He managed to find his footing and crawl slowly toward the soldier. Soon he was close enough to get a good look at the man they had been searching for.

The cloak of branches and dirt caked to Kevin Mott's body made for a natural camouflage. Webster couldn't tell if he was conscious. The officer looked like he'd been dragged by a rope from a moving car. "He's covered in blood," Webster radioed back. "Not moving." Webster hollered at the man as loud as he could, but Mott said nothing, staring vacantly, seemingly oblivious to the thundering noise of the chopper.

"I crawl up to his face and turn his head a little bit," Webster said. "I'm trying to stabilize this guy's head a little, and I turn his head just straight. I'm trying to be real careful. And then, well, his whole scalp with his hair attached just peels off. And I was like, *Oh, my God.* The soft part of his head, like a baby's, you are just holding his head. His matted brown hair. And I just kind of lay up and just put it back on, like a toupee."

Mott's eyes opened for an instant—and then they fluttered wildly. With his free hand, Webster felt for the rescue strop. He had used it many times before. But the strop and the hoist were meant for people who still had some minimal function, people who could grasp hold of something. Not for someone as battered and broken as the man Webster was now cradling. "The rescue strop is not for unconscious people. It's for rescuing flood victims, people who are on top of their cars, waving."

Webster knew there wasn't much time. He took heart when the man lifted his head, though it was only for a moment. *Good,* he thought. *No serious neck injury.* But nothing else looked good. Not at all. To Webster, it appeared that the soldier had suffered multiple head wounds. He had lacerations and blood splotches across his face and forehead.

And then, as he cradled the man's head and stared at him at close range, the soldier's eyes rolled back, a wild look that made Webster think that for all their efforts, they might be losing him now.

Webster was torn between the needs for speed and for caution, which in this terrifying moment seemed incompatible. He considered calling for the chopper's Stokes basket—a combination stretcher-basket contraption often used in search and rescue operations—to secure him and bring him up that way. But Webster's snap judgment was that there wasn't time for that: "I was like, I'm by myself here. No time. I have maybe thirty seconds, tops, till I figure this out."

An RPG smacked the mountainside, no more than thirty feet from where they were. "Pretty close," Webster said. "I'm like, *Fuck.*"

Up in Pedro 33, Jake Garel felt the reverberation.

"It was big enough that we lost him for a second," Garel said. "We didn't know if he'd gotten blown up. There was an explosion nearby, and it was, '*Where's Webster? Anybody got eyes on Webster?*'"

Webster was all right. Shaken, was all. And Mott, fading as he was, hadn't even registered the hit.

Webster began attaching himself to the wounded soldier in every way he could. He grabbed hold of the long rubber rescue strop, wrapped it around the man's waist, and took his harness and looped it underneath Mott's legs. "Just to make an improvised harness and attach it back to myself," he explained. "I'm tying him to me."

He connected the strop and harness to his own buckles. *Click, click, clip, clip.* One more thing that had to be done meticulously—and as fast as possible. "Had to pick him up, put his arms around me, his arms over my shoulders like a big bro hug, and then put his head on my arm. And then grab the cable."

A *big bro hug*. Another technique they hadn't been taught back at Moffett Airfield. Webster looked up through the dust, the soldier in one arm and his other arm outstretched, signaling to the chopper. More than once he thought, *I could use another arm.*

"I looked up at the bird, and it was all dusty and shit. I could hardly see them. I just gave the big thumbs-up. Like, *I hope you guys can see this,* because I'm not on radio. I can't even touch my radio anymore."

"Just dust and smoke," Garel recalled. "And then there's Webster, coming on up."

Josh looked at the soldier, "just laying on me, like a big dead body. And then I feel the cable start to get tight and I'm like, *Oh, they're picking us up. This is awesome.* And then they hoisted us back up and I'm holding this guy as best I can. I put his legs over my legs. So now we're just like two bodies, chest to chest. And we made it to the helicopter in about fifteen seconds, coming up the hoist."

Together, Hiyakumoto and the flight engineer pulled the two men in—somehow doing so gingerly *and* fast. All the while Webster did his best to cradle Kevin Mott's head. "To keep his scalp on," as he put it.

At last they were on board the chopper. "And then I'm laying on top of him and then we're all of us like, '*Oh God, oh God,*' screaming. '*Just get to the fucking hospital.*'" Captain Ronnau banked left, dipped low to gain speed, and flew out of the fire zone to safety.

Kevin Mott was alive. But his eyes danced, shut one moment, open and rolled back the next. His tongue was bloated and swollen. And he wasn't breathing well. "We didn't know what his breathing state was, and you can't hear anything on a helicopter," Webster said. "It's not like an operating room. And we just hauled ass."

While Webster unclipped himself, Hiyakumoto placed an oxygen mask over Mott's face. "Larry comes in with oxygen, because oxygen's always good for patients," Webster said. "Anyone with a head injury needs oxygen. And he started to open one eye. So I was like, *Not dead,* which is great. And then he hit the oxygen with his hand, knocked it away. And I was like, *OK, this is better than we thought.* At least he's awake enough to know he doesn't want this thing on his face."

They called ahead to the med station. Now they were the ones sending the urgent radio messages.

"Bring a basket. Bring the backboard. Right away. This guy's surgical for sure. Head injury, multi-stage trauma."

At one point Webster said over the radio, *"He's been scalped."* "And someone's like, 'Scalped?' And I was like, 'Yeah, when you get him and go inside you'll know what I'm talking about.'"

The ride seemed to take forever, though it can't have lasted more than two minutes. They landed at the Forward Surgical Team base, dropped off Kevin Mott, and went back to work. It was only later that they discovered that two or three rounds had pierced the bottom and back wall of the helicopter.

On another day, in another place, Webster would have stayed at the med station long enough to learn Kevin Mott's fate. As it was, there was no time. Not even for a proper debrief. They left the officer there, not even knowing the man's name.

"Just like that, we have to refuel, we have to get more gas and more ammo because we're out, and the whole bird is covered in blood too," Webster said. "They have a hose there and we're hosing all this blood, and pushing hair and dirt out and stuff. And then we took off."

There would be two more missions that afternoon. And then finally, a changing of the guard. By the time they'd turned things over to the next crews they had been flying rescue runs for nearly eleven hours. Now it was back to base. All the way back to Bagram.

All the stresses and tensions and gravity of the day hit Josh Webster when he walked into the Bagram mess hall and saw the looks on the faces of his friends. "We're all covered in blood, and our friends were like, 'What happened?'"

Josh could think of nothing to say. It seemed an impossible question to answer.

They had run thirteen pararescue missions that day, bringing nearly twenty wounded soldiers back to the med station. Many would surely have died had they not reached them. One of those was Kevin Mott.

I met Josh Webster less than two weeks after he rescued Kevin Mott. Things had quieted somewhat for the 131st Rescue Squadron and for those who'd been part of Strong Eagle One. That operation would go on for many months. But in the immediate aftermath, Kevin Mott's No Slack Battalion was reassessing its mission and taking stock of the casualties it had suffered on that long day.

I had linked up with Webster's team because I'd heard about Strong Eagle, but at that point I had no idea how bad things had been. I had made numerous trips to Kunar Province over the years, but had never covered the pararescuemen up close. When they agreed to let us ride along with them for several days, it seemed a perfect way to tell the story of what was going on in Afghanistan.

We met at Bagram Airfield and loaded onto a waiting helicopter. I sat on the right side with Webster—the chopper's doors open, our legs dangling in the wind. The specially equipped HH-60 was flying low and fast, gunners manning the powerful .50-caliber machine gun capable of shredding anything in its sights. A safety harness was strapped around my body armor and hooked to the helicopter just in case. For some reason I was never afraid of flying in Black Hawks. I suppose I should have

Joshua Webster and the 131st rescue squadron at Bagram Airfield in July 2010.

been. But the ride was so spectacular through this part of Afghanistan that I usually found myself forgetting about the heavily armed Taliban fighters in the mountains surrounding us. Webster was crouched next to me. "Infidel" was sewn onto a patch on his right shoulder and a "deployment mustache"—so named because many wives wouldn't put up with facial hair—shadowed his upper lip. He wore bright blue latex gloves and clutched his rifle.

Our first call sent us to a FOB not far from Bagram. There had been "an accident"—that was all we knew. In a matter of minutes a young injured soldier was loaded onto the helicopter, in shock and oozing blood through the bandage covering the ring finger of his left hand. Or what was left of it. Webster quickly inserted an IV and gave him some pain medication. It was a gruesome injury and an uncommon one, but not a serious war wound.

The soldier had been "de-gloved." As he jumped down from a truck he'd caught the edge of his wedding band between two metal posts on the tailgate. The ring had stayed on the tailgate, yanking his finger with it. The flesh and muscle of the finger had been stripped away by the force of the jump. For Josh Webster, who twelve days earlier had seen a man's scalp flop from his head, this finger wound was an easy case, a minor trauma. But PJs treated every person the same way, with care and compassion.

As it happened, this de-gloving injury was the most serious issue Webster would tend to in the two days I spent with him. Which meant that on the rides we took together, he and the other PJs had the time to tell me what had happened in the valley, on that long and difficult day. When Webster came to the end of it, all the vivid detail about the drop down that ridge and the rescue of Kevin Mott, and the fact that Mott had been "scalped" by a bullet, I asked him how the soldier he had saved was doing.

He told me that he had gone back to the med station on the day after the rescue to ask about all the soldiers they'd picked up in the valley, "to see and be sure who'd lived and who didn't make it." He didn't know their names—that was the nature of the work—but he knew enough about their circumstances to follow up.

It was here that he first heard the officer's last name and learned a little more about him. He learned that Captain Mott had been transferred on the night of the rescue to a second-level US medical treatment facility in Asadabad, the provincial capital. And that he'd been awake and talking.

"And that was the last thing I heard about that guy, because they shuttled him out pretty quickly to Landstuhl, Germany, where a lot of the patients end up. I did a follow-up the next day, and he'd already gone."

Given Kevin Mott's condition, Webster had taken this as excellent news—the fact that he'd been alert, and in good enough shape to leave the country. "It meant he was getting class A medical treatment at hospitals specifically for these guys. They deal with all the traumatic brain injury and burns and all that stuff."

But he knew very little about the man he had rescued—not even his first name, and nothing about his background, or where he lived. I asked if he wanted to learn more about him.

All too often in these circumstances, even when things end well, the service members involved never have a chance to connect, in the days or months or even years that follow. That's a function of the bureaucracy and sheer size of the military, and the frenetic nature of the battles themselves. Sometimes there just isn't time to chase down a name or number or location.

I figured that if Josh Webster wanted to meet the man he'd rescued, Captain Mott and his family would be even more eager to meet him. I knew only what Webster had told me—the captain's last name. But I also knew it wouldn't take me long to find out more.

I've spent an enormous amount of time with the US Army around the world, and I know soldiers—a *lot* of soldiers. And they trust me. This was a good-news story if there ever was one, and in the summer of 2010 the Army was in need of good news. I went straight to Major General John Campbell, who was commanding the 101st Airborne Division and the Joint Task Force for Regional Command East in Afghanistan—

RC East, the area where Mott had been wounded. Campbell had taken me along on several missions to outposts across his command area, including FOB Joyce. I knew him well.

A few days later, an Army public affairs officer walked into Kevin Mott's hospital room with a request: "Martha Raddatz from ABC News would like to interview you. She has been with the team that rescued you." Kevin's father, Kevin Mott Sr., and his mother, Kathy, were in the room with their son at the hospital in Fort Campbell, Kentucky, where Mott had been transferred after surgery at Bagram.

Only twelve days earlier, at home in Marin County, the Mott family had received the call that brought them to their knees. They were told Kevin "had been shot in the head." For several hours that was all they knew. The family priest had rushed to be with them as they waited for news. Hours later, when Kevin was out of surgery, the hospital called. His mom and dad braced for the worst.

"How far did the bullet penetrate his skull?" Kevin Mott Sr. asked the doctor, clutching his wife's hand as he spoke. "It didn't," was the answer. Their son would recover. The twenty-five-year-old was banged up badly, to put it mildly—with a traumatic brain injury, four fractured vertebrae, and a broken leg. He looked like "he had been dragged through gravel," as his father put it. But Kevin Mott Jr. was talking and alert. And that interview request? His father vividly remembers the moment when his son was asked if he would talk to me.

"A look of horror came over his face." Mott Senior chuckled. Kevin said, "Is that an order?" The public affairs major assured him it was not. And Kevin Mott, groggy and still in a fair amount of pain, answered quickly. "No, ma'am. Tell ABC no thanks." That interview would come much later.

Though Kevin wasn't ready to talk, he did want to know the name of his rescuer. I had passed Webster's name to the public affairs officer. And once Kevin Jr. was out of danger and feeling better, his dad turned to social media and found an email for Josh Webster. He reached out immediately.

From: Kevin Mott
Subject: Yo
To: Joshua Webster
Date: Friday, July 16, 2010, 8:47 PM

I think you picked up a very important package for me on 27 June in Kunar Province. Are you an Air Force PJ?

Webster, on the lookout for phony emails, responded with suspicion. On Friday, July 16, 2010, Joshua Webster wrote:

Hey, what's up man? Kind of a cryptic message . . . anything I need to know about?
Cheers
Joshua

Mott Senior told Webster the family had gotten the name through me.

From: Joshua Webster
Subject: Re: Yo
To: Kevin Mott
Date: Friday, July 16, 2010, 9:57 PM

Kevin,
I am indeed a PJ, and Martha is correct . . . that was me.
Cheers
Joshua

From: Kevin Mott
Subject: Re: Yo
To: Joshua Webster
Date: Friday, July 16, 2010, 10:25 PM

I owe you a debt I can never repay. You saved my son's life. I'm trying to reconstruct what happened and would love to speak with you. We live in Marin County CA, are you from Mtn View?

When are you due back in the USA, I must meet you. You have our family's everlasting thanks and gratitude, I understand you and your teammates undertook the rescue at great risk to yourselves. I salute your bravery and am forever grateful.

Kevin Mott SR.

As it turned out, the Motts' home in California wasn't far from Webster's home. Josh told Kevin Mott's dad that when he returned home in September it would be his "honor" to tell the family what had happened to Kevin. And since they lived near his base, he would be sure to make it happen.

So on a fall day in 2010, while Kevin was still rehabbing at Fort Campbell, and some three months after he'd been carried off the mountain, Josh Webster traveled the hour north to Marin County to meet his parents. Kevin's sister Gina was there too. Each one embraced Webster like they were the oldest of friends.

With tea and snacks on the table and pleasantries exchanged, Kevin Sr. and Kathy asked Josh Webster the question they had been eager to get an answer to for months: *What happened?*

They had spoken to Kevin, tracking his recovery from Afghanistan to Germany to Fort Campbell, but their son could recall almost nothing that had happened on that day. He did remember parts of his journey home, painful memories and his gasping "ugly cry" when he learned his friend Sergeant Eric Shaw had been killed. But he didn't remember the mission itself. Nothing about the planning or launch of Operation Strong Eagle One.

Mott was suffering from retrograde amnesia, a common condition among victims of traumatic brain injury. In most cases, the memories return slowly, creeping back toward the date of the trauma, but rarely as far as the incident itself. Some people never retrieved much memory at all.

In conversations with his parents, Kevin Mott initially had trouble explaining what he'd been doing in Kunar Province. He could summon nothing about the fall down the mountain, or the PJs who'd come for him. His family had been briefed by the medical teams, but even the doctors had only secondhand reports of what had actually happened. So as Kevin Sr. and Kathy poured out tea for Josh Webster on that September day, they weren't just asking a polite question to make conversation. They really didn't know.

Josh Webster started talking. And he didn't stop until long after the sun had gone down.

"I explained to them the whole story," Webster said, a grin breaking across his face. "And his parents were just, '*Oh my God,*' hearing for the first time. '*That's amazing.*' And I was like, 'Yeah, well, that's what we do. That's who we are.'

"And the parents said, 'Well, if you ever need anything.' And I said, 'I think I'm good. I appreciate it.'"

From his hospital bed at Fort Campbell and over the months that followed, Kevin told Josh the same thing—"If you ever need anything . . . ," but his pledges were made via texts and phone calls. It would be a long time before Kevin would meet the man who had lifted him to safety. The man who gave him that "big bro hug" that saved his life. It wasn't for lack of trying.

After Mott's rescue, the surgical teams in Asadabad had stapled fifty sutures into his head to reattach his scalp and treat his extensive wounds. He'd gone on to Bagram, then Germany, ending up at Fort Campbell for months of rehab. And then the young captain did what he had vowed to do as soon as he knew he would recover: got back in the battle. He would do whatever it took, as he put it, to "finagle my way into redeploying to Afghanistan."

"They had kind of put my scalp back together, so my head looked good," Mott said. "You couldn't even tell the difference. It's funny, when I first got my haircut, the barber was like, 'Man, what happened?' And I said, 'Actually, you won't believe this.'

"I was very focused and kind of obsessed about going back to Afghanistan," Kevin Mott told me. "The doctors kind of laughed when I said that I wanted to go back, but it was something that I wanted to do."

I saw that overpowering desire to return to service after an injury time and again in men and women who deployed to Afghanistan and Iraq after 9/11: wounded soldiers who could have recuperated and rested and started new lives, or remained in the military in less dangerous roles—but who wanted back in, for the adrenaline, out of loyalty to fellow troops, or, strange as it may sound to those of us who have never been in the line of fire, because they just enjoyed the work.

Mott got his wish. Just before Christmas in 2010, and less than six months after getting shot in the head and plunging head over heels down an Afghan mountainside, he headed back to the war.

Kevin Mott would do two more tours in Afghanistan—and earn a Silver Star in 2011 for "conspicuous gallantry and intrepidity" by putting himself in the line of fire to call in bomb strikes to protect his men and end the enemy attacks.

He finally ended his Afghan missions in the fall of 2013.

By 2013, Josh Webster had decided to leave the Air Force and Pararescue squad and head back to the Army. He had graduated from UCLA by then, and with his college degree in hand, he hoped to serve as an officer. He was thirty-two, and the age cutoff for officer commissions was thirty-one, but friends told him he could get a waiver. A fellow veteran pushed him. His brother pushed him too: "After all your years in the military, you're still a sergeant. You could be an officer." Webster knew there were more high-level opportunities for him in the Army—Ranger, Delta Force. "You could do any of those things," his brother said. "Maybe you'll retire one day."

"I really did just jump back on the roller coaster," Webster said. "This whole plan started just kind of growing, like a very quickly growing tree. And suddenly, in like a week, it was a fully fleshed-out idea: I could go be an Army officer."

But when Josh Webster submitted his officer packet, he was told not only that he was too old but also that he had a disability claim for a torn labrum in his right hip. And—for good measure—his tattoos were a problem.

"The tattoo policy was really strict in 2012," Webster recalled with a smile. "I guess I had too many. All these problems. Every excuse in the world."

He and Kevin Mott still hadn't met in person since the rescue, but they'd remained in touch via text and email. And Kevin happened to ask, right around this time, how his rescuer was doing. Just checking in.

"I was like, *Not good,*" Webster remembers. He told Kevin about his officer plan and the logjam with his recruiter. He wasn't fishing for help—it was just an answer to the question.

"And Kevin's like, 'Give me a minute. Let me see who I know.'"

It turned out Kevin Mott knew a lot of people. And he wanted badly to make good on the *if-there's-anything-I-can-do* pledge. To pay it forward, as they say. So many people will say that sort of thing and never lift a finger.

Josh hadn't given the Motts' offer a second thought. He believed he'd just been doing his job, same as anyone else did theirs. No return favors expected or required.

Kevin couldn't believe that Josh Webster was having issues with the application. "Webster has all this military training, number one. Army and Air Force, and the PJ training. So he's got all the badges, all the schools, four deployments, you know? Like, why *wouldn't* we have this guy join the Army as an officer? It's ridiculous. This dude checks all the boxes. Why would we *not* let him in?"

Kevin knew Brigadier General Stephen Townsend from his time in Afghanistan. Townsend had been his deputy division commander. He wrote to him.

"I said, 'Hey, sir, my name is Kevin Mott, and here's how we know each other' and all that. 'I'm writing on behalf of a guy named Staff Sergeant Josh Webster.'"

He laid out what he knew of Webster's case. "And to General Townsend's credit, he's like, 'Kevin, have Webster call me tomorrow at this time, at this phone number.'"

As it happened, Webster didn't have to call Townsend. The general made a call to Army Recruiting and told them effectively, *Let that guy in.*

Webster was told to report to the Recruiting Depot in Los Angeles for his officer candidate interview, the final step in the approval process. He put on his only suit and rehearsed answers to questions he imagined the interviewers might ask.

"I went in there, and all the new officer candidates had their best-behavior haircuts, we're all in suits and we had our packets, and they're going to interview us and it's supposed to be really tough," he said. "And they were like, 'Webster, you're going in first.'"

Webster went in and found a row of majors and lieutenant colonels and other officers. An intimidating setting, for what is normally a difficult interview.

"And they were like, 'Sit down, Candidate Webster.' And I sit down and they close the door, and then the vibe completely changed. They were like, 'What do you want to talk about?' I said, 'Excuse me?' And they said, 'Someone up very high has made sure you're getting accepted into OCS.' So this was a formality at this point."

Webster asked about the other candidates, the ones he'd met in the waiting room.

"They go, 'Oh, they'll be rigorously scrutinized.' And me? 'We're just going to sit here and chat for thirty minutes. You're not trying out anymore. You're accepted.'"

And that was that. He was commissioned as Army Officer Joshua Webster in 2013, thanks in no small part to Kevin Mott.

"Not a fair trade," Mott told me—meaning it wasn't as if his call to a general and Webster's lifesaving mission were comparable. "But I thought that was really cool."

Then, just as Kevin Mott had done, Josh Webster went back to Afghanistan. In 2015 and again in 2016. And finally, after those deployments, he would come face-to-face again with the man on the mountain.

Kevin Mott returned to his unit, fully recovered. He was married in 2012 to his girlfriend, Lauren, and they had welcomed a baby girl, Keira, in 2015. He had been accepted to an Army scholarship program at Stanford University. The Downing Scholarship, it was called, a graduate studies program focused on counterterrorism. He was studying the rise and influence of the Islamic State.

Mott still lived in his unit's base housing—which happened to be at Moffett Field. The home of Air Force Pararescue.

"So he moved right onto the base where I used to work," Webster said with a laugh. "We missed each other by two years. If I'd stayed for two more years, he would have moved onto my base."

By then, Josh Webster was at Hunter Army Airfield with the First Ranger Battalion in Savannah, Georgia, but he traveled often, and now he knew where to find Kevin. On a trip to the West Coast, he rented a car and drove to Moffett Field. "I called Kevin; I was like, 'Hey, can I stop by?' And he says, 'Yeah, for sure.'"

They met that afternoon—Josh, Kevin, Lauren, and their baby daughter.

Josh Webster and Kevin Mott, with Kevin's daughter Keira, at Moffett Field in July 2016.

"We hugged it out," Josh said.

"It was really cool, and it was really neat to finally meet face-to-face, give a hug and say thank you," Mott said. "Because, after all he had done for me, you just want to say, 'Thanks,' right?"

"I am super fortunate to be here today because of Josh and Larry and the crew from that aircraft who stuck their necks out for me, for sure," Mott told me later. "It's a pretty amazing thing, and it's to their great credit. Those guys were in direct fire contact with the enemy. The entire time that he was lowered, the one PJ, Webster, it was direct fire the whole time. And he came and grabbed me, and picked me up."

There's a nonchalance in the way Webster describes the reunion. Emotional, sure, but with a shrug and that *this-is-what-we-do* response. It's the same way so many other vets I know react to honors or expressions of gratitude for their courage and heroism. He and Kevin, when they finally met after all those years, had simply "hugged it out."

The way he talked about it—the rescue itself, the reunion, all of it, Josh told me—was simply part of the Pararescue creed: "These things we do, that others may live."

On a bright November day in 2023 in Savannah, Georgia, I watched Josh Webster marry the love of his life, Erin Leverington. They had met in Savannah years earlier, when Erin was a student at the Savannah College of Art and Design. Smart, strong-willed, and stunning, Erin walked confidently through a spray of white flowers lining the aisle of a historic Savannah courtyard. Webster, every bit the "Maverick" in a deep gray velvet tuxedo jacket and bow tie, held back a tear as he caught Erin's eye in her breezy white dress on the arm of her father. It was a wedding I would not have missed. I had kept in touch with Josh, we had formed a strong bond over the years, and when he and Erin moved to Washington, DC, in late 2024 my husband and I would have regular dinners with them. It was also a wedding where I felt right at home, surrounded by military men and women, mostly Special Operations soldiers. The kind of crowd where I can quickly find friends in common.

All these years after that day in the Kunar River Valley, Josh Webster speaks often about his good fortune, and says he struggles sometimes to understand it. He wonders about the vagaries of fate that have left him virtually unscathed, after all he has seen and experienced in the military.

"So damn lucky," he likes to say.

"Some people are in terrible accidents, and they walk away—like Kevin, in the big rescue, right? Kevin was shot in the helmet, fell off a cliff, left for dead. Totally fine in the end."

Webster has lost friends in the Ranger and Pararescue communities to battlefield casualties and to suicide after their return home. Others continue to suffer profound mental health issues—and even his relatively well-adjusted friends from the Army have struggled with the return to civilian life.

Josh Webster married the love of his life, Erin Leverington, in Savannah, Georgia, in November 2023.

"I've had a very fun and nice and easy career," he says. "All this hard stuff I've tried to do and all the tours and combat, I've been extraordinarily lucky with not getting hit with a bullet. Not having any psychological trauma like the trauma other people around me had. I have no way to attribute that to anything other than blind luck. It's like being extraordinarily lucky is like a superpower."

Once a year, Josh Webster gets another reminder of his good fortune—the feeling of a job well done and the blessing of having found a friend who will be close to him forever.

Every June 27, on the anniversary of Mott's injury and the PJ rescue, Kevin Mott's father and mother send Josh Webster an email. They call him Web now. And every year the gist of the message is the same—growing families (Kevin welcomed a son, Ryan, in 2017), deeper bonds, and a gratitude that is never-ending.

Dear Web,

June 27 was the anniversary of your rescue of Kevin Jr. from a mountainside in Kunar, at great risk to your life. Once again, I thank you for your selfless action in rescuing my son. As I've written you many times before, Kathy and I owe you a debt that we can never repay, but which we gladly owe.

Your actions that day saving Kevin proved to be a "force multiplier." As you know, Kevin has 2 kids. I'm admittedly biased, but those kids are the BEST! They bring Kathy and I so much happiness and I know that effect is multiplied for Kevin and Lauren.

I often wonder what those kids will eventually become, but from what I see so far, they will be loving, good people. Your actions that June 27 will have a positive effect for generations to come!

This is a good time to remind you of our eternal gratitude for your bravery in rescuing Kevin. There were many sound reasons why you shouldn't have done that rescue, but you and the crew ignored them. With undisputed courage, you braved enemy fire single handedly on the way down and back up. I can't imagine the fortitude and valor you exhibited that day.

I pray for your happiness, success and safety. Thank you again from the bottom of our hearts.

Kathy and Kevin Mott Sr.

Both Joshua Webster and Kevin Mott remain active-duty officers in the US Army.

Eric Bourquin, Josh York, Ben Hayhurst, Aaron Fowler, and Carl Wild on the Kenai River in Alaska in July 2024.

CHAPTER 3

The Brotherhood

Ben Hayhurst, Eric Bourquin, Carl Wild, and Aaron Fowler

THEY PITCH TENTS WITH PRECISION, BUILD CAMPFIRES with ease, and hike and fish with purpose. For ten days in the Alaskan wilderness in the summer of 2024, these former soldiers are young men again. The men they used to be, imbued with a supreme sense of confidence and invincibility. Towels snap at bare behinds, pranks are planned for nightfall, and competition is constant.

The familiar ribbing began as soon as the men arrived, toting their fishing gear, backpacks, and boots. Towering over the others at six-five, bearded and tattooed, Eric Bourquin was jokingly likened to the mythical Sasquatch. Carl Wild, the smallest at five-eight, is The Hobbit, and, with his ponytail peeking from under his cap, Aaron Fowler was quickly given the moniker The Hippy. The oldest of the group, at forty-six, was Ben Hayhurst, or Grampa, as he would be called, given that he'd just welcomed his first grandchild. Their host, Joshua York was "Jarhead" due to a brief stint in the Marine Corps prior to his career in the Army. York had recently retired from the Army and moved his family to Alaska. He knew his offer of an outdoor retreat would be a welcome relief for the former soldiers.

To an outsider these bearded men in their forties would seem like any band of best buddies moving through life's stages together, but these men are different. While this wilderness adventure is a welcome escape, these soldiers are not the men they used to be. They say they never will be. They are fragile and vulnerable. Combat has changed them all. Physical injuries still plague them, but it is the invisible wounds that can bring them to their knees.

I met Eric Bourquin and Carl Wild in Iraq more than twenty years ago and have known Fowler and Hayhurst for more than a decade. I first reported on the deadly Black Sunday ambush where they fought together in Sadr City, Iraq, back in 2004. But the fight they have been in since is another story altogether. I have watched these men battle some of the worst post-traumatic stress imaginable. Paralyzing self-doubt, guilt, depression, nightmares, and thoughts of suicide still torment them.

Every one of these men will tell you the same thing: They owe their lives to one another. "Hell, yes," said Ben Hayhurst. "If not for these guys I would definitely be dead." He is not talking about what his fellow soldiers did in a long-ago firefight. He means that in the years that followed, he and the others were saved through their friendship: a phone call, a long walk, a conversation prompted by a text that might say: "Bad day. Gimme a call."

For years Hayhurst and the others felt nothing but shame for the post-traumatic stress they suffer, believing others would see them as weak or, worse, cowards. They had almost died together on that day in 2004 during the ferocious urban assault in that Baghdad suburb, one they survived only after shooting an untold number of Iraqis who had come out to kill them. The fighting that day left eight of their fellow soldiers dead and more than sixty wounded, and these four men would spend years dealing with the horror of it all. Slowly at first, sporadically, they had reconnected and opened up, sharing their pain and ultimately forming an unshakable brotherhood. Carl Wild says choosing to reunite with his former teammates was "the most important decision I ever made in my life."

To me, what this tribe of former soldiers has done in the past twenty years to fight the demons that haunt them night and day, while still managing to build families, raise children, is just as courageous, if not more so, as what they did in battle. And they know the fight is far from over.

They were, as Eric Bourquin puts it, "a great team beforehand." Before that Black Sunday battle in Sadr City, where they fought for their lives, watched friends die, and for the first time bore the weight of killing fellow human beings.

The four soldiers, all in their early twenties at the time, were in the same platoon, part of the Army's Second Battalion, Fifth Cavalry Regiment, First Brigade Combat Team, First Cavalry Division, out of Fort Hood, Texas. Bonding during the intense training period just prior to their deployment, Bourquin, Wild, Fowler, and Hayhurst had hit it off right away. They all had team leadership responsibilities that they took seriously and handled naturally, and they recognized the challenges they would face.

They had taken different roads to get to the Army. Ben Hayhurst was born in Bountiful, Utah, to parents who eventually became evangelical Christians and settled in Arizona. Hayhurst saw Page, Arizona, as a stifling small town offering little opportunity for growth. "I didn't fit in," he said. He dropped out of high school in his sophomore year, earned his GED, and then got married. Two years of college followed, with a job as the manager of a local furniture store. It was not the kind of future he wanted. In the back of his mind, his childhood dream gnawed at him. He had always wanted to be an Army infantryman. The nation was not yet at war, and it just seemed to him to be a cool thing to do for a while. So on the spur of the moment, Hayhurst walked into a recruiting office one day in 1999, signed a contract, and went home to give his wife the news. "It probably would have been best if I had told her beforehand," he said.

Hayhurst's plan was to stay in the Army a few years, get a degree with the college money he would receive, and move on from there. He had no real idea what he was getting into. He didn't follow geopolitics or much of anything in the news. He vaguely knew about a US battle in

Somalia that had left Americans dead, recounted in the book and movie *Black Hawk Down*, but that was the extent of his connection to global military events.

What he never expected was how much he would love the Army. "It was a meritocracy," he said. "If you worked hard and did a good job, it was recognized every day. It really does not matter who you are." And for a young man who before the Army had never managed to finish what he started, "because it didn't matter," he found the Army remarkably rewarding. Hayhurst showed up every day on time, his uniform pressed, with a can-do attitude, and he got promoted quickly. His first deployment, however, to South Korea ended his marriage. It wasn't the life his young wife had expected, and that was that. In early 2001, Hayhurst landed at Fort Hood, newly single. An Army medic named Sarah arrived on the very same day, and they got along immediately. Marriage came a few years later.

Aaron Fowler was born in Southern California but grew up "all over the place." He was the child of a single mother who hopped from Colorado to Massachusetts to Arizona, and then back to California, before finally settling in Arizona. A huge reader from an early age, Aaron devoured thrift store history books, biographies, and war stories. Like Ben Hayhurst, however, he dropped out of school in his sophomore year and got his high school degree through the GED test. There were a lot of reasons he left school, but one of them, he says, was gang activity: "I was just getting my ass kicked on a regular basis." By comparison, the US Army would be easy, he figured.

He married his wife, Rebbecca, on Memorial Day, 2001, while stationed at Fort Lewis in Washington state. The 9/11 attacks came a little over three months later. Fowler knew things were about to ramp up for the military, and he was eager to get into the fight. When US troops deployed to Afghanistan that fall, Fowler figured his unit would be part of the push, but it was not. He would spend most of his time on base waiting for his chance. Rebbecca had only one request. She was tired of Seattle's gray skies and wanted to move somewhere warmer. So, Fowler managed to get transferred to Texas, to the First Cavalry Division at

Fort Hood. Fowler had been a light infantry soldier at Fort Lewis and the First Cav is a heavy mechanized unit, so the transfer meant an adjustment. Fowler had never seen a Bradley fighting vehicle before and had to be retrained, but he was a quick study and impressed his commanders with his sensibility and self-assurance.

When Carl Wild's elementary school art teacher asked her class to paint a picture of what they wanted to be when they grew up, he painted a soldier. Wild was just in the second grade then, but he never changed his mind. His parents, both in the Air Force, were stationed on an American base in Britain when Wild was born. They moved to New Mexico, to New Hampshire, to Massachusetts, and finally to Texas, where his family would remain. When Wild was seven years old, his mother was diagnosed with Huntington's disease, a rare degenerative disease that eventually leaves people unable to speak or function. Much of the family's attention went to caring for his mother, and Wild still has vivid childhood memories of helping his mother. By the time he was fourteen, his mother was in such bad shape she had to be moved into full-time care. Despite his mother's illness, Wild did well in school. His family was comfortably middle-class and he had opportunities to go to college. Instead, at age seventeen and still in high school, he signed papers to join the Army. Twenty days after he graduated, he was off to basic training. It was July 2001.

Eric Bourquin's upbringing was the roughest of all. A dysfunctional family prompted Bourquin to leave his Texas home when he was just sixteen. He had no goals and little hope for the future. In the middle of a late-night party, he impulsively decided the Army would be a good choice, perhaps giving him a chance to go to war someday. His teenage imagination had him thinking that a bad guy would take a few wild shots at him and his buddies at some point during a deployment. Then he would be a real soldier. He joined in 1998, at the age of eighteen. Though he enlisted initially in the Army Reserve, he switched to active duty a year later and signed up for the infantry, attracted by the prospect of hardcore service. After advanced training at Fort Benning, Georgia, he was posted to Fort Hood with the First Cavalry Division. He met his future wife, Leslie, at a bar in Austin. They were married in December 2003, just three months before he shipped off to Iraq.

The Iraq war began on March 19, 2003, with a volley of Tomahawk missile strikes on Baghdad—the day Aaron Fowler turned twenty-four. President George W. Bush claimed Iraq was seeking to build a nuclear weapon and was hiding biological weapons and that Iraqi president Saddam Hussein had ties to al-Qaeda, the terrorist group responsible for the 9/11 attacks. The invasion was swift, lasting only six weeks. Statues of Saddam were toppled, and the Iraqi leader went into hiding. On May 1, President George W. Bush donned flight gear and flew out to an aircraft carrier where he announced the end of major combat, backed by a banner proclaiming: "Mission Accomplished."

But there were no weapons of mass destruction, no ties at the time to al-Qaeda, and the mission was far from accomplished. The war was actually just beginning.

At the time, Bourquin, Fowler, Hayhurst, and Wild were all living and training at Fort Hood, in the same platoon, designated Comanche Red One. Near the end of 2003, they learned their platoon and the rest of the First Cavalry Division would be heading to Iraq. All but Carl were married by then, with Hayhurst the father of a new baby daughter, Carey Anne. The military experience these young soldiers had longed for was finally coming; the battles they had imagined themselves fighting were about to get real.

During the briefings the platoon received in Kuwait on their way to Iraq, they were told this would largely be a peacekeeping or civil affairs mission to help the locals and the Iraq Security Forces. The main threat they'd face would be Improvised Explosive Devices (IEDs), the roadside bombs used to great effect by insurgents. The soldiers would be vulnerable, because they would likely be patrolling in Humvees, which are easy IED targets. Ben Hayhurst and another soldier wrote letters to their families to be delivered in case they were killed. They figured the chances they would be riding in the same Humvee were minimal, so they exchanged the letters, with the idea that whoever survived whatever happened would deliver the other one's letter.

Sergeant Ben Hayhurst in the motor pool at Camp War Eagle in Sadr City, Iraq, April 2004. Soon after this picture was taken, he left with his unit on a mission that was ambushed.

By April 1, Comanche Red One was encamped at Camp War Eagle, the 2-5 Cav's new base on the edge of Sadr City, a sprawling Baghdad slum of two and a half million people. Patrolling began immediately. The platoon was assigned four Humvees, each with room for five soldiers. One seat had to be reserved for an interpreter, so only nineteen soldiers could go out on patrol at a time. Since their platoon had thirty soldiers in all, they would take turns. The mission on April 4 was to provide security for an Iraqi unit that was to suck up the raw sewage that ran openly on Sadr City streets.

Aaron Fowler, by then Staff Sergeant Fowler, was one of the odd men out on April 4, so he stayed back at base. Staff Sergeant Josh York got violently ill at the last minute and also stayed back, leaving eighteen soldiers plus an interpreter to do the patrolling that day. Among them were Sergeant Hayhurst, Sergeant Bourquin, and Specialist Wild. The patrols were mostly uneventful, but the men had only been in-country for a matter of days.

Specialist Carl Wild at the gate of Camp War Eagle shortly before the ambush.

On this Sunday, as the convoy passed a mosque on the way home, Carl Wild, riding in the second Humvee, noticed a man holding an AK-47, in violation of rules established by the American military. The American soldiers sensed trouble. A crowd that had been milling in the street quickly dispersed, as if a message had gone out to clear the area. Suddenly the street was empty. Moments later, Eric Bourquin, in the trail Humvee, heard the unmistakable crack of gunfire.

The shots seemed to come from all sides—from behind walls and from the rooftops of buildings along the street. For Bourquin and the others, their Iraq experience changed in that moment. Combat was no longer something to be imagined. Given their military training, the men were accustomed to the sound of gunfire, but they had never had weapons fired directly at them. And they'd never fired live weapons at human beings.

The following minutes were nothing but chaos, with the platoon soldiers and the Iraqi militia fighters exchanging fire. Sergeant Eddie Chen, manning a machine gun in one of the Humvees, started shooting, swiveling back and forth, aiming wildly at the rooftops. A stocky Chinese

American with a boisterous personality, he was screaming profanities over the thunderous racket of his .50-caliber gun.

The shooting was intensifying, with hundreds of Iraqis joining the fight. In addition to their small arms weaponry, some were firing rocket-propelled grenades. Carl Wild saw an Iraqi man emerge from an alleyway and come running toward him, an RPG launcher in his arm. Instinctively Wild raised his machine gun, squeezed the trigger, and shot the man dead. For a moment, he froze, with a dark feeling that would come back to him over and over in the years ahead. Just months beyond his teenage years, he had taken a man's life. He would not forget that feeling, or that image. But looking at the mass of insurgents coming toward him, he did not stop shooting.

The Comanche Red commander ordered his soldiers to evacuate the area, but it was too late. People were now flooding the streets, erecting barricades, setting fire to trash piles, rolling out concertina wire, and stacking furniture in the roadway, making it impossible to pass. And then Chen's machine gun fell silent. He had slipped from the turret and was slumped on the floor, blood streaming from his nose and mouth. An Iraqi bullet had found its way around Chen's ceramic chest armor and into his upper body. He was dead.

There was no time to react. The platoon pulled into a ten-foot-wide alleyway off to the side, where a three-story house offered a possible place to take shelter. The interpreter banged loudly on the door, but no one responded. Eric Bourquin, who had roomed with Chen back at Fort Hood, fired his weapon at the door, blowing off the lock. An Iraqi family was inside, cowering in fear. The soldiers herded them into a back room and secured them. His heart pounding, Bourquin helped carry Chen into the house, grabbed a woman's black abaya from a clothesline, and laid it over Chen's body. With grim determination, he then returned to soldiering.

The house had a rooftop with a four-foot wall along its edges, as decent a place as any to set up a defensive position. The soldiers spaced themselves along the wall, each taking responsibility for a particular firing sector, as they had learned to do in their infantry training. But

Sergeant Eric Bourquin on the roof during the ambush in Sadr City, Iraq, in April 2004.

Comanche Red One was not a platoon of battle-hardened soldiers. They had only arrived in Iraq a few days earlier. Their barracks were not yet ready, and they were still sleeping in their trucks. Bourquin, Wild, and Hayhurst were all young men on their first deployment to a war zone, and they had been expecting a peacekeeping mission, not a combat operation. Just a half hour earlier, they had been safely in their Humvees, heading back to base after what had been a relatively quiet day. Now one of their fellow soldiers was dead, and they were on some Iraqi family's roof, surrounded and under attack from hundreds of heavily armed militiamen. In an instant they were at war.

Barely fifteen minutes after they climbed to the rooftop, Ben Hayhurst was shot in the shoulder, but it didn't seem to register. His left side burning, he moved back into position, peeking over the roof's edge, and resumed fighting. Not for long. His depth perception was off, and he was having trouble focusing. A minute or two later, his left arm popped out of its socket. No longer able to lift his rifle, all he could do was help his fellow soldiers reload their ammo magazines. The men on the roof

Sergeant Ben Hayhurst after being shot in the shoulder during the ambush in Sadr City.

and the soldiers below in the courtyard were firing at any insurgent pointing a weapon their way, but the crowd was growing rapidly.

Hayhurst and the soldier with whom he'd swapped letters in Kuwait now found themselves together on the rooftop. No longer did the exchange make sense; they would either both die or both survive, so they gave the letters back. Carl Wild, the twenty-year-old man who had dreamed of being a soldier since he was in second grade, had his camera with him and started snapping pictures. If they happened to be rescued, that rooftop experience would be something worth remembering. If they all died, their families might at least see them in their last moments.

Aaron Fowler was sitting in a truck back at Camp War Eagle eating an MRE (Meal, Ready to Eat) with Josh York when they heard that Comanche Red One was pinned down and under fire somewhere in Sadr City. It wasn't Fowler's turn to patrol that day and York had been left behind because he was sick, but they knew a rescue mission would be organized, and they instantly raced to join it. York headed off to a

Bradley fighting vehicle. Fowler jumped in the back of one of two open-sided cargo trucks lined up behind the two Humvees that would be leading the response. With no protection whatsoever, the trucks were wholly inappropriate for the mission, but every available vehicle was being used, and every able-bodied soldier was determined to help. Even York, who had been left behind earlier because of a serious bout of food poisoning.

The situation in Sadr City had only gotten worse in the half hour since the ambush, and the rescue attempt itself was turning deadly as well. As soon as the rescue convoy turned toward the center of the city, it came under heavy fire. The driver of one of the Humvees and the gunner in another Humvee were both shot and killed. The two open-sided cargo trucks, each carrying about fifteen soldiers, proved easy targets for the Iraqi fighters, who were now waging all-out war. Two soldiers in one of the trucks were killed within minutes, and between the two vehicles a dozen or more were badly injured. Fowler turned his attention to providing aid to the soldiers in his truck and organized a casualty collection point in a somewhat protected spot along the route. He sent the truck back to the base with the wounded men and squeezed the uninjured soldiers into one of the two Bradley fighting vehicles. Fowler jumped into the Humvee that was leading the rescue effort, positioning himself in the open bed, back-to-back with another soldier, their weapons pointing in opposite directions.

The second attempt to enter the city was even more disastrous. Fowler was sitting behind the driver, his M4 rifle resting on his left knee, when he was shot. The bullet went through that knee and out the other side. In pain, he stretched his left leg out and set his rifle on his right knee, so he could keep firing. And then he got shot again, this time in his right calf. The soldier next to him was also shot, as was the company commander in front. The Humvee by this point had all flat tires and was barely moving. And then Fowler got shot a third time, in his right thigh. Everyone in the Humvee had been hit, and Fowler was barely able to function. The convoy stopped, and everyone with serious wounds, including Fowler, was put in one of the cargo trucks and driven slowly back to the base. Someone gave Fowler an IV, and a chaplain came to pray over him. At first, Fowler thought he was being given last rites, but then he realized it was just a prayer. All he could think about were the soldiers still trapped in Sadr City.

From their perch on the roof Hayhurst, Wild, and Bourquin could see an enormous mob assembled in the alley, waving their weapons in the air and singing and shouting and surging toward the Army platoon on the ground. To the horror of the American soldiers, the mob's leaders had put women and children in the front, fully exposed, and they were moving rapidly toward the house, some of the children toting rifles. The platoon interpreter pleaded with them to go back so as not to get hurt, but they ignored him. When they reached a point about fifty yards away, the soldiers felt they had no choice. The people kept coming. They tried to aim over the heads of the children, but some shots missed the men with the weapons. Desperate and sickened by what they found themselves doing, the soldiers finally fired on the crowd. Within a few minutes, it was over. Dozens of bodies lay strewn across the alley, children among them.

The Iraqi fighters regrouped, more determined than ever to kill the Americans. The situation for the platoon was dire. They had repeatedly radioed the battalion headquarters with their approximate position, but there was no sign of a rescue operation, and their ammunition supply was dwindling. They had no idea what trouble the rescuers had encountered. The men agreed among themselves that surrender was not an option. The images from Somalia of dead American soldiers being dragged through the streets of Mogadishu was clear in their minds.

For the next few hours, the platoon managed to hold its position. But there were few among them who believed they would come out of that house, or off that rooftop, alive. They had gotten word of repeated rescue attempts, but it seemed no one could find them, and more and more men were losing their lives trying. And yet those soldiers on the roof and the men coming to rescue them did not give up, and did not stop fighting.

The platoon would finally be saved hours later with help from the First Armored Division, stationed nearby. Seven tanks were dispatched and set off roaring through the city, over the barricades and through the fires. The tank drivers found the alley when the platoon commander, trapped with his soldiers, ran into the street and waved them down as a final effort to save them. The soldiers crowded into the tanks, as many as could fit. Chen's body was laid on top. Bourquin and some of the other soldiers scrambled up top as well to be with Chen, with Hayhurst holding on to his dead friend to make sure he did not fall. Wild remembers Chen's eyes being wide open before he was loaded onto the tank. They continued to take fire, but they were on their way back.

It had been a devastating day. In addition to Chen, six other First Cav soldiers were killed during the attempts to rescue the pinned-down platoon. A First Armored soldier in the tank battalion also died en route to the alley location. Many of the more than sixty soldiers wounded that

Specialist Carl Wild (left) and Sergeant Eric Bourquin back at Camp War Eagle shortly after their extraction from the alley in Sadr City.

day had serious injuries. Ben Hayhurst and Aaron Fowler both had to be airlifted to the nearby Balad Air Base for emergency surgery. They happened to see each other while their stretchers were being loaded on the same medevac helicopter, which comforted them both. Only then did they learn what each had been through over the previous hours.

For Bourquin, Wild, Hayhurst, and Fowler, the April 4 horror left deep scars. They had lost friends in the battle, and they struggled with the terrifying, unexpected realization that the very people they were supposed to be helping wanted them dead. The nightmarish thought of their own responsibility for the day's carnage would replay again and again. They had never seen themselves as killers, and yet they were, many times over, with some of the dead just children. Someone snapped a picture of Bourquin and Wild shortly after their extraction from the alley. Bourquin, nearly a foot taller than Wild, has his arm around his twenty-year-old friend, holding him tightly. Both men look emotionally broken.

And yet on April 5, just one day after that deadly ambush, Eric Bourquin and Carl Wild were sent back into battle. The First Cavalry's mission had changed abruptly on April 4 from an operation focused on civil affairs to a war against insurgents. The First Cav soldiers had to fight for eighty more days before they were able to retake control of Sadr City.

After their surgeries in Iraq, Fowler and Hayhurst were evacuated for further medical treatment at the US military hospital in Landstuhl, Germany, and then transported back to the hospital at Fort Hood, where they were reunited with their wives. Fowler, whose injuries were more serious, needed more surgery in Texas. But both men were determined to rejoin their fellow soldiers in Iraq as soon as they could, feeling they owed their lives to them. And remarkably, despite their injuries and the emotional trauma they had both experienced, the Army would allow them to return in a matter of months.

Hayhurst was back in Iraq by late June, just ten weeks after he had been evacuated. His wife, Sarah, had assumed that he would not go back to Iraq. Sitting on the porch swing at his parents' house, she remembers Ben gently telling her that he needed to return: "I was shocked and couldn't believe it. He told his doctor that he didn't care what he had to do, but he needed to release him so he could get back to his guys. I was so scared, but I understood. I knew he would never forgive himself if he didn't."

Fowler returned two months later, still troubled by his injuries and now with a medical flag about his injuries attached to his record. Working in the rear detachment unit that summer back at Fort Hood, he was coordinating the redeployment of wounded soldiers like himself, and he figured that if he was going to urge other soldiers to return to Iraq, he should be willing to go as well. Noticing that the paperwork regarding his medical condition was incomplete, Fowler simply entered his own name on the "return to duty" manifest and got himself back to Iraq, in his words, "with a bottle of Percocet" and no reference to his wounds. His wife, Rebbecca, was pregnant at the time, and he knew the chances were slim he would be back in time for the birth of their baby, but he felt he had no choice. Back in Iraq, he was reunited with his platoon, rooming with Carl Wild.

Sergeant Aaron Fowler, on security detail in Sadr City after returning to Iraq following his injury on Black Sunday.

By then, the 2-5 Cav troops were constantly engaged in firefights. It was not long before Hayhurst was wounded again. It was a relatively minor shrapnel injury, but a short time later he suffered a different kind of injury and a far more debilitating one. During a firefight near a school, a child launched an RPG in Hayhurst's direction. It missed, but in that moment something in Ben Hayhurst snapped. The thought of death overwhelmed him. And the image once again of those children in the alley coming after his platoon, and then gunned down. Braced against a wall, Hayhurst suddenly froze, unable to move. "I just fucking fell apart," Hayhurst said. One of his commanders put another soldier in Hayhurst's place, helped him into a Bradley, and sent him back to the base. He was sobbing the entire way and having trouble breathing. A chaplain calmed him down, but then a mortar landed nearby, and he broke down again.

Hayhurst was pulled from combat missions and sent to a combat stress center at the US military's headquarters in Baghdad, where he received mental health counseling and lots of medication and was taught breathing techniques for dealing with anxiety. The Army offered to send him home, but he said he wanted to stay with his fellow soldiers, arguing that he could contribute even if he couldn't fight. He was moved to a noncombat job in a different platoon and worked there until his tour in Iraq ended in March 2005. He spent much of his final months in Iraq on antianxiety and antidepressant medication.

Hayhurst realized too late that he had gone back to combat too soon after his April 4 injury. After a mental health evaluation back at Fort Hood, Army doctors diagnosed him with Post-Traumatic Stress Disorder. He was told he could not stay in an infantry unit but could remain in the Army if he accepted any job the Army picked for him. The alternative was to accept an involuntary medical retirement. He chose to leave the Army, a decision that would come at great cost. The military had not dealt with PTSD for decades and at the time, early in the war, it was looking for causes beyond the battlefield. So the Army decided that Hayhurst's post-traumatic stress was the result of a "personality disorder" unrelated to his military service and thus not deserving of the disability benefits to which he would otherwise have been entitled. It also meant being separated from his fellow soldiers, the support group that had sustained him through his deployment. In the years that followed, Hayhurst sank into isolation and deep depression.

The platoon, in any case, was breaking up. Eric Bourquin, having demonstrated leadership skills in Iraq, shipped off to Missouri to be trained as a drill sergeant. Aaron Fowler returned to Fort Hood for a while, then went back to Iraq two more times, first in Taji, a city north of Baghdad, and then back to Sadr City. He was promoted to sergeant first class, but his medical red flag about his numerous injuries by then had caught up with him. Like Hayhurst, he had to accept a noncombat job in his brigade headquarters.

For Carl Wild and Eric Bourquin, the war fighting would continue. Wild headed back to Iraq in 2007, this time with a ring on his finger after marrying his best friend's younger sister. Bourquin was sent to Afghanistan in 2008 after his stint as a drill sergeant.

Just two months into his deployment, Bourquin would experience horror and profound loss once again. By then, he was a platoon sergeant, meaning he was the senior noncommissioned officer for the platoon, with responsibilities for developing those under his command. He saw great promise in a twenty-nine-year-old soldier from California named Jair Garcia. Bourquin knew that Garcia, with a wife and nine-year-old son at home, was eager to be promoted and wanted as much experience as possible, so he gave him a convoy protection task that involved finding and then blowing up IEDs. Garcia headed out for the mission with his team, but instead of him finding an IED, an IED found him. A hidden cooler full of plastic explosives blew up right near Garcia and three of his soldiers and killed them all.

Three days later, just as troops were preparing for Garcia's memorial service, another tragedy hit Bourquin's platoon. A driver, twenty-three-year-old Private John Mattox, from a small town in Texas, was lying on a cot near a soldier who was cleaning a weapon. The weapon suddenly discharged, and one of the bullets pierced Mattox's femoral artery. Bourquin and another soldier raced to the tent, picked up Mattox on his bloody cot, and ran with him, cot and all, to the aid station. Soldiers lined up to provide blood, but it was no use. Mattox bled out. Hours later, the men would attend Garcia's memorial service and prepare another one for Mattox.

Bourquin was devastated yet again. Mattox's parents had come to see him off to Afghanistan, and Bourquin had told them not to worry. "We'll be back soon," he said. Years later, Bourquin could not talk about Mattox without breaking down. "It really fucked me up," he said. "And it just went downhill after that. Just really, really bad. The worst year of my life professionally, socially, mentally, emotionally." But after the deaths of Garcia and Mattox, Bourquin would remain in Afghanistan another seven months.

Finally, back in Texas in March 2009, Bourquin for the first time in his career sought counseling through the Army. His therapist said he needed to get more help, but Bourquin refused, fearing if he sought more treatment, it would affect his military status. Unbeknownst to the Army, however, he met with an outside therapist. The therapist told Bourquin his PTSD was one of the worst cases he'd ever seen. Bourquin nevertheless returned to Iraq, with an assist from commanders who approved the deployment despite his troubled condition.

Carl Wild, meanwhile, suffered his first serious injury in Afghanistan. By now working in Army intelligence, he and other soldiers had completed a reconnaissance patrol and were back in their motor pool when the Taliban began launching 107-millimeter rockets onto the base. Wild was working on his armored truck, and when the rockets came, he went to jump into the cab. There was no time. A rocket landed about six yards from him, and the blast blew him hard into the truck. Shrapnel tore open his back and lacerated his lung, taking out a big chunk at the bottom. Though he was able to make it to the aid station on his own, he was immediately moved to the base hospital for surgery. The surgeons inserted a tube in his lung to get the blood out, but they were unable to remove a piece of shrapnel embedded in his kidney. Within ten days, Wild was back in the United States at Fort Sam Houston in San Antonio. He spent three months in a "Warrior Transition Unit" at Fort Lewis and by the end of his stay he was headed for medical retirement.

But he wasn't ready to quit. Because he worked intelligence, Wild had a beard and dressed in civilian clothes, and he used his appearance to his advantage. Showing up at the location where troops were being mobilized for deployment, Wild told the officers that he was assigned to do intelligence work and needed to get back to Afghanistan. The officers took him at his word, and two days later he was back with his unit. Inspired by Ben Hayhurst and Aaron Fowler, both of whom had returned to duty despite their serious injuries, Wild had resolved to go back to service no matter what. But after several months the Army finally flagged his previous injuries. He was involuntarily retired in 2012, the same year Fowler left the Army. Like the others, he fought retirement, but it was no use.

Bourquin's mental health struggles finally ended his Army career. Upon his return in 2011 from his deployment in Iraq, he was medically flagged again and was retired honorably with a disability rating. He didn't fight it. "Fuck it. Fine. Let's go get some help," he figured.

The four soldiers who had bonded a decade earlier in Fort Hood saw their military careers end in similar ways, all painfully. But for all that they had endured in the Army, it was the transition to civilian life that nearly destroyed them. "The hardest thing I've ever faced," Bourquin told me.

Not only were they dealing with the trauma of what they'd seen and done; they were now on their own, in an environment none of them had known since their teenage years. They had minimal support and faced a host of challenges for which they were ill-prepared, including more family responsibilities. The skills, values, and instincts that the Army had instilled in them did not necessarily serve them in civilian life. "You're feeling like you've been doing something important, surrounded by guys you care about all day long," said Carl Wild. "And then, they basically tell you, 'You're worthless to us now. Here's the boot. Good luck to you. Hope you find success in the outside world.'"

As frightening and stressful as the Army service could be, it had given them a sense of purpose in life, and it was predictable and manageable. "You become institutionalized," said Fowler. "If you stay in the military that long, you have a different schedule, a different set of experiences, a different language, a different identity. I was a sergeant first class. One day, you've got thirty, forty dudes responding to you, and you're in charge. And then one day it all goes away." They were left with tormenting thoughts from their combat experience, but now with little or nothing to distract or comfort them.

Noncommissioned officers, as these four men were, serve close to the rank-and-file soldiers, managing their morale, responding to their needs, and driving them to excel and accomplish their missions. But when they retire, they become part of the colorless mass of middle-class workers focused on mundane tasks and responsibilities. Eric Bourquin says civilian life brought a change from being Somebody to just being someone. Through his entire adult life, he had gotten used to thinking of himself as the "tip of the spear," making sure that stuff happens the way it is supposed to: "I went from feeling like I was part of this huge worldwide mission, saving lives and helping people. And then, I'm just another dude walking down the street, trying to pay his fucking bills."

Bourquin had been dealing with anger for many years, but in the Army it served a purpose: "It's about being violent and aggressive, because your life depends on it. And then, all of a sudden, 'Put all that aside. Be a nice, sweet guy again.' It's like trying to reprogram how you breathe."

Over and over, Bourquin found himself getting riled up when someone challenged him, even over a minor matter, and it bothered him. "I've definitely ruined some interpersonal relationships, transitioning from the military to being a civilian," he said. "Sometimes I don't feel like a civilian. You know, you can take a tiger out of the jungle and put him in a cage, but he's still a fucking tiger. I feel the same way sometimes." Along the way he struggled with severe depression. Still, he had to find a way to manage his emotions, at least for the sake of his family. Bourquin came out of the military with a newborn, a toddler, and two elementary-school-age kids to father and a wife who was looking for a partner.

Ben Hayhurst, the first of his platoon of friends to leave the Army, found it hard to hold down a job, in part because the civilian work experience seemed so different from what he was used to in the military. "We have this whole idea that our job has to get done, because lives are at stake," he says of his Army experience. "It's hard to break down that mentality of 'live or die,' based on your work. It takes a couple of years to readjust your brain settings to where the people around me don't have to be willing to die for me, and I don't have to be willing to die for them."

Establishing new friendships or renewing old ones proved especially challenging for these men. What do you talk about when you don't have common experiences? You can't necessarily share what's really on your mind, nor is it easy to feign interest in what others care about. Bourquin says he has little interest in professional sports. Hayhurst, who moved to rural Washington state with his wife, says he has only three friends outside his former military circle. Aaron Fowler says he hasn't stayed in close touch with his "pre-combat" friends: "I try to explain that combat changes you. I'm not the same person I was before. I used to be a pretty outgoing, carefree, 'life-is-a-party' guy. I'm just not that guy anymore."

Fowler, Hayhurst, and Wild were all forced to explain to their non-Army acquaintances why they were so eager to return to Iraq after being wounded—in Fowler's case, three more times: "They'd say, 'Are you a war junkie? Are you a killer? Do you get off on the death and destruction?' These were people I'd known for twenty-five or thirty years, and I'd say, 'How could you think that?'" The men had returned to duty in the first place out of a sense of obligation. But it was also an indication of how uncomfortable they felt when they were away from their Army life, with its camaraderie and the certainty of its routine. Once they finally left it behind, they were miserable.

In their early post-military days, they had little contact with one another. Ben Hayhurst spent seven years essentially on his own, believing—as the Army had told him—that his stress was the result of a "personality disorder." Having experienced his panic attack in Iraq, he had many more in his civilian life, sometimes daily. "They're uncontrolled thoughts," he said. "Once they get going, they just keep going. I'm terrible at compartmentalizing." The panic and self-doubt were unrelenting.

He was not alone. Aaron Fowler went through similar episodes, finding it hard to communicate with other people and spiraling deeper and deeper into self-imposed isolation. Carl Wild says his first two years as a civilian were the worst of his life. He was angry at the Army for having forced him out, and he was dealing with serious post-traumatic stress: "I felt like I lost my whole personality. Everything I was and everything I believed in were taken away from me." To make matters worse, he said his wife at the time was not all that understanding. He got the sense that she saw his problems as abnormal and that he shouldn't have the feelings he had. Needless to say, the marriage did not last. Wild knew some of his fears were irrational. After the Army, he trained to be an X-ray technician but soon found it impossible to do his job because of flashbacks to his hospital experience in Afghanistan. When he went to a restaurant, he felt exposed and always chose a seat where he could feel safe.

Memories of the rooftop on April 4 and the gunfire in the alley below plagued the soldiers. Eric Bourquin struggled with a vivid image of a woman in a bright blue headscarf, covered in blood, screaming over the body of a man on her doorstep, probably her husband. "I think about that all the time," he later said. "They were unwilling participants in an ambush."

The men all struggle with the thoughts of the children who were killed in the battle. For Ben Hayhurst it is important that he talk about it. He is haunted by the moment a young boy was directly firing at Hayhurst and the others with an AK-47. Hayhurst shot the boy. A man, perhaps the boy's father, ran up and dragged him away, only to return, pick up the boy's weapon, and resume firing. Hayhurst took him out as well. And then a much older man came running up to get the dead man's body. He likewise turned and picked up the gun and began shooting, and he, too, was killed by Hayhurst. The moment was seared permanently into Hayhurst's brain. "I remember sitting up there thinking, I might have just killed three generations of a family," he said. For years after, Hayhurst avoided parks or playgrounds, any place where he might hear kids yelling, because he couldn't forget the screaming he had heard from the kids in the alley.

For Carl Wild, there are so many moments that torment him, but the enduring image in his nightmares is of a lifeless Eddie Chen propped against the wall of the Iraqi home where they had taken cover, his eyes wide open and his mouth agape.

All of these men were given medication to deal with their depression and anxiety. To Aaron Fowler, it seemed that every troubled soldier was prescribed the same collection of drugs, no matter the diagnosis; the combat cocktail, some called it. It was a combination of antidepressants, painkillers, and sedatives. The side effects hit him hard, as did the withdrawal symptoms when he didn't take the meds on time. Ben Hayhurst recalls the pain meds he was given daily—sixty milligrams of hydrocodone and three thousand milligrams of Tylenol—and how the opioids sometimes made him physically sick and worsened his anxiety and paranoia. Both he and Fowler went through a period where their pain was so all-consuming that they considered taking their own lives, like so many veterans had done. The Veterans Administration at the time found that about twenty veterans were dying by suicide every day. But these men didn't. They found one another.

These damaged soldiers, these men in the depths of darkness, were rescued by friendship, by the unique intimacy that comes with combat, that comes with facing death and tragedy together.

The reconnection between the men happened in 2012 when all of them were out of the Army for good. As a practical matter, reuniting was not hard. A few phone calls, a few messages on social media, were exchanged to catch up on where life had taken them. Since their days at Fort Hood, these soldiers had been leaders in their platoon. "We were always the go-to guys," said Fowler. "We never shirked from responsibility or danger. We kept getting picked for different operations. We were just the dependables, the reliables." And then came April 4, the day that stands out above all others, when their bond hardened into something unbreakable. To his great regret, Fowler did not happen to be on the rooftop on April 4, but he went charging after them that day and kept going even after being shot three times.

The soldiers' first in-person reunion came at Fort Hood in April 2014, on the tenth anniversary of Black Sunday. It was a pivotal meeting for all of them, the occasion when for the first time they realized they were struggling in similar ways, facing the same demons.

"It was hard," said Carl Wild, the youngest of the group by four years. "They were my leaders, the most badass dudes I have known in my life. And to see them being upset and going through the same struggles I was going through was hard. It's like meeting your heroes. I didn't have any idea." But it helped him make sense of his own troubled life.

For Ben Hayhurst, the anniversary meeting was life-changing. After his retirement in 2005, he had come to imagine himself a coward for not being able to fight after his mental breakdown. He had isolated himself, not talking to any of his former soldier friends. "I had told myself that they didn't want me around," he said, "because I had failed and wasn't good enough." But at the anniversary, Eric Bourquin told Hayhurst how impressed he and the rest of the platoon were by his return to combat just weeks after being shot. No words could have relieved him more: "I realized that not only did these guys respect me, but they loved me, and they wanted me to be part of the group." With the soldiers from his platoon, he has experienced a breakthrough of sorts: "The people that you go through those changes with are the people who really know who you are, who you were before, and who you became and why. It's not so much that I feel normal. It's that I feel understood."

Bourquin played a key role in bringing the soldiers together again, initially by reconnecting them on a Facebook group and then following up individually. "Eric has a way of pulling people together," Hayhurst said. "And once you throw in with Eric, you're going to be involved with all of it." Bourquin had taken it upon himself to save some of the items from April 4—the uniform he had been wearing on the rooftop, the mission logs from the first three days patrolling Sadr City, before everything went south, and, with his family's permission, Eddie Chen's pack and name tape. The stuff is still in boxes in the garage of Bourquin's house, which is about forty minutes outside Austin. Aaron Fowler lives just ten minutes away, in a suburb called Georgetown, so it was fairly easy for the two of them to get together.

All of them have been through counseling. They are all believers in the value of therapy and advocate it for others; it has given them the language and the tools they need to process what they went through.

But they will all tell you that therapy alone would never have been enough, because it didn't provide the depth of emotional support they needed to manage their lives, to be responsible husbands and fathers, and to find purpose as civilians.

They also all say they would never have made it this far without the support of their wives. Ben Hayhurst says his wife, Sarah, herself a former Army medic and a First Cav veteran, is "the first reason I'm still here. She helped me deal with medications, alcohol, and violent nightmares and flashbacks, all the while taking care of our kids if they were injured because I fell apart if they got hurt." The wives are all in touch with one another and know when to intervene. "If one of us is struggling," Hayhurst said, "our wives will reach out to one of the other guys and say, 'Hey, why don't you give him a call and see what's going on.'"

Bourquin credits his wife, Leslie, for enduring "all the madness and bullshit that I went through, weathering whatever storms I was bringing into the house while raising our four children."

When Carl Wild is having a panic attack, his new wife, Lela, rubs his legs to calm him down. "When I relay to her that I feel worthless and don't have any purpose anymore," he said, "she reminds me of who I am and the things that I've already accomplished, and that I'm retired and disabled for a reason."

Fowler's wife, Rebbecca, who now works full-time as a doctor of speech pathology, enables him to be, in his words, "the house husband," freed from the need to work outside the home. Instead, he is responsible for cooking and cleaning and running errands, and tending to his hobby farm.

Beyond their family life, what stands out in the men's survival tale is the support they provide one another. The notion of friendship doesn't do it justice. The word they all use is "Brotherhood." For Eric Bourquin, it means he has someone "just making sure that I'm not stagnating, isolating, and being detrimental to myself. Because if they notice that, they're like, 'Hey, where the hell have you been? What's going on with you?'"

It happened to them all, at some point. And each time, the Brotherhood was there. Like suicide SWAT teams, Bourquin called it.

"So wherever the system failed us," he said, "we made our own little system, and now that's available to all of our friends too. We have guys, whenever they're having a hard time, they know . . . they jump in whenever they need to, via Zoom, no matter where they are in the world."

It became a kind of alert system. One member of the group might notice that someone else seemed a bit off. So-and-so was acting strange. Or unusually distant. Or again, it could be one of their wives who sounded the alarm, and made a call to their husband's "brother": "Hey—would you mind checking in on him?"

Bourquin said he used the brothers as a "measuring stick," to gauge if he was headed off in a bad direction. "I use that as a backstop, like, Well, how would these guys view it? Or what would they say if I did it this way or did it that way?"

When Ben Hayhurst was going through a frightening patch of depression in 2017, Aaron Fowler, whose own emotional struggles had made it hard for him to leave his own house at times, booked a flight and was in Spokane a day later. Hayhurst had reached out and Fowler answered the call.

"We do that for each of us," Fowler said, "like when it's my turn to need some help, people come, no matter where they are, and when it's their turn, I'll drop whatever I'm doing. We've been there for, like, everything. So, yeah, they're my brothers."

To Eric, Aaron's trip was the story of a "SWAT team" success. "Ben was going through a pretty rough time, so at the drop of a hat he was able to leave and go up there and handle whatever it is," Eric said of Fowler's trip to Spokane. "It doesn't matter what it is. I could get that from any of those guys if I needed it. And they could all get that too, you know. It's comforting knowing that they're out there.

The men now stay in almost daily touch, texting one another with their latest news and joining in a group therapy session on Zoom once a week. "I think one reason we stay in contact so much is because none of us have much ability to identify with people outside," said Fowler. "We just have so much shared history and language. Once your soul is laid bare to those around you, and they know all of your flaws and all of your strengths, it's a type of friend you can't get anywhere else."

Because they were so young during their combat experience, it shaped their lives. Roughly the same age, they find their life experiences are aligned. "We're going through our major crises together," Fowler said. "Our parents are aging out; we have kids going off to college, getting pregnant. We're dealing with cancer, all this stuff. We talk about our successes, our struggles, our projects. It's where we go to get advice on whatever we're doing."

(From left) Ben Hayhurst, Carl Wild, Josh York, Eric Bourquin, and Aaron Fowler fishing along the Russian River in the Kenai Peninsula of Alaska in July 2024.

Theirs is hardly the only veterans' group that assembles on occasion, but the Brotherhood takes that responsibility especially seriously. "The other veterans I talk to, they don't have that," Hayhurst said. "They may not talk for years, or they only get together and talk around anniversaries, stuff like that. Our ability is to have pretty much a constant dialogue, whether it's sharing stupid jokes or memes, or having someone you trust who can say, 'This is how I did it.'" It was with the support of his old platoon friends that Hayhurst ultimately got the Army to reverse its disability judgment, restoring him to full retirement benefit status and officially recognizing that his disability was due to stress "incurred in the line of combat duty."

April 4 ties them together, but the day rarely comes up in conversation anymore. "We don't really talk about it that much," said Wild. "We just try to enjoy each other's company. We know what we've been through and what we did together, and we know that every day we have is a blessing. We just try to have fun with each other and not make it too emotional."

With his long years of isolation, Hayhurst may have had the most difficult time with severe anxiety and suicidal thoughts. But he feels he is better every day. "We're often too hard on ourselves," he said, "based on what you may have done in the past. You lock in on what you did in some situation, and you have to remember, that's not who you really are. You're not that violent person. You have to remind yourself that you're a good person. Those bad memories never go away, and I still hurt, but slowly you can get past it." Hayhurst says talking to his brothers was just as important as therapy or getting off opioids. "It's not so much that you deal with it as that you learn to live with it," he says.

Despite the progress they have made, the Brotherhood soldiers all recognize they face a long haul, which is one reason why they have become strong advocates for therapy. Carl Wild experienced a setback in 2021, when the Taliban regained control in Afghanistan, wiping out whatever gains the United States and its allies had achieved there and rendering the decades-long war essentially a lost cause. Having been badly hurt in that war during a 2009 deployment, Wild now has to consider the waste of it, and it shakes him deeply.

"It set me back years," he said. "I was doing really good, and not having any real social problems at the time, but Afghanistan broke down, and I broke down, and I don't think I've fully recovered from that. I'm back in the system, trying to get myself better again, doing therapy and taking mental health medication and trying not to lock myself in the house all day long. Some days are harder than others."

Carl Wild says he would never do anything to hurt himself, "because of the guys who died to get me off the rooftop." Remembering them, he says, "helps to motivate me and push me through the day." He actually talks about the soldiers who died on April 4 as if they are a living presence in his life. "None of the guys who died for me to be here today want me to feel this way," he said. "They don't care what I do. I don't have to go out and cure cancer or anything. Those guys just want me to have a happy life." It is what they all want for one another, and for anyone who has experienced trauma.

Fowler echoes the importance of connection: "It doesn't matter who you are, if you're military, if you're a civilian, one of the most basic needs of any living thing is to have people to love and to love them. So when you find people in your life that are worthy of your love, love them while they're in your life wholeheartedly, be there for them. . . . And if you have anybody in your life worth loving, love them with every core of your being, because all of our lives are finite; we're all here for a moment. So love the people in your life when they're there, and be emotionally available."

These men have told their families they need to be prepared for more setbacks along the way. They have acquired the wisdom that comes from dealing with hard times. "I carry around scars," Bourquin said, "from those mistakes I made, to my children, to my wife, to my family. You know, that's just the price I'll have to pay and something that will hopefully guide me into being a better person."

More than twenty years have passed since Black Sunday, and the veterans of that fight have begun sharing the lessons they have learned since then, from one another and from the counseling they have received. And it reaches beyond the tight group they have formed.

Eric Bourquin says it gives him new purpose in his life, to try to help other veterans who are struggling. "I tell them, 'Hey, look, like you, I have these similar problems, and here's what I did. Here are the resources I know about. Let me get you in contact with them.'"

Ben Hayhurst's recovery process has similarly led him to helping others. Within the past three years, he has been teaching kids martial arts, finding it a big help in coping with his own emotional struggles. "I put the time in, and for whatever reason, it just clicked with me," he said. "There are a lot of young people out there who can really use encourage-

Ben Hayhurst at the summit of the Flattop Mountain Trail in Anchorage, Alaska.

ment. It put me back in that position of being able to mentor." Hayhurst enjoyed his service as a noncommissioned officer in the Army, because he was responsible for the training and daily care of younger soldiers. Today he teaches both boys and girls from age five to thirteen. He wants them not only to learn physical confidence but to have the tools to take care of themselves, especially the girls.

The trip to Alaska to link up with Josh York in the summer of 2024 served as something of a reward for the Brotherhood. It came just months after the twentieth anniversary of Black Sunday, which the platoon once again commemorated at Fort Hood. It was an easier reunion than the tenth. I was there for both and saw the difference myself. With more distance from the battle, and from the pain of that day, the soldiers and their families were able to see their experience in a different light.

The memories will never go away. I have learned through my friend-

Carl Wild, Martha Raddatz, Eric Bourquin, and Aaron Fowler in Salado, Texas, April 2024, at the twentieth reunion of the Black Sunday ambush.

ship with these men over the years that they don't want to forget. Those memories are meant to endure. And for all the pain and grief those thoughts have caused them over the years, that day is what makes them who they are today. They are proud fathers, grandfathers, and husbands to their remarkable wives. They are courageous, resilient soldiers who will keep fighting to honor the men who didn't make it, and those who they know will remain by their sides, no matter what the future brings.

Mark Little on the morning of his promotion to first lieutenant in front of the US Marine Corps War Memorial in November 2007.

CHAPTER 4

Warrior 360

Mark Little

Baghdad, Iraq, and Fairfax, Virginia

SECOND LIEUTENANT MARK LITTLE WAS EXACTLY WHERE he wanted to be on Independence Day. Holiday or not, the young platoon leader had a job to do. Bounding into his armored Humvee on this scorching hot morning in 2007, he hollered "Happy Fourth of July!" to his soldiers as he made his way up through the turret. It was not the way any of the men had imagined they would be celebrating America's birthday—rumbling down one of the most dangerous roadways in Iraq. Route Irish, as it was known, was the principal connection between Iraq's main airport and the center of Baghdad; there were few other alternatives.

Swerving around bomb craters, garbage, and the occasional dead animal, the four armored Humvees, with four men in each, advanced in a tight convoy. They were bringing supplies to US forces just outside Baghdad's protected Green Zone, the heavily fortified coalition headquarters where the majority of US civilians and a significant number of troops were housed. The platoon's job was to provide whatever the forward-deployed troops needed—fuel, medical equipment, a pallet truck loaded with sandbags.

The convoy was an inviting target in a tough area at a tough time for the Americans, despite the surge of more than twenty thousand additional troops a few months before. The surge was part of General David Petraeus's plan to send US troops closer to Iraqi neighborhoods to provide security and build trust. Little's Third Platoon, Fox Company, belonged to the First Battalion, Thirtieth Infantry Regiment, Third Infantry Division, out of Fort Stewart, Georgia. While the larger battalion had come under frequent fire, Lieutenant Little's platoon had managed to avoid direct contact in the months since they'd deployed. This July Fourth would shatter that relative calm.

As the convoy approached a soccer field near a burned-out three-story building, Little spotted what he thought was a group of women covered in long abayas watching the convoy. They seemed to turn as one to track the soldiers, their black loose-fitting robes fluttering around them. They were still in his line of sight when they lifted their headscarves to reveal that they weren't women at all; they were men—insurgents armed with AK-47s and they were aiming directly at the convoy.

A fusillade of machine-gun fire ricocheted off the Humvees, quickly followed by sniper fire from the direction of the charred building. "Keep moving, keep moving!" Little shouted over the radio as he clutched the big M240B machine gun on the vehicle's turret. A withering burst of fire from the Americans sent the insurgents running, leaving a pile of disguises behind.

The platoon's first firefight was over. Little's quick check on his soldiers found them rattled but unharmed. Every man in every vehicle was OK. "Yes, *Happy Fourth of July*," he thought with a flush of patriotic pride for his small band of warriors. It would not be the last Fourth of July that held special meaning for Mark Little.

The platoon was based at FOB Falcon—a forward operating base on the outskirts of Baghdad. There were numerous FOBs around Iraq, but this one was especially busy given its proximity to Iraq's capital city. Lieutenant Little was the distribution platoon leader in the brigade support battalion. From that Fourth of July onward, things changed for his platoon. They regularly topped the "SIGACT board"—the data collection hub for "Significant Activity," a catchall term for attacks and other unsettling incidents. Sitting at the top of that board meant they were coming under regular fire.

"We'd leave FOB Falcon, drive from point A to point B, take something or do something, and then drive from point B back to point A," Little explained later. "Most of the time, we were delivering to the most forward outpost that was actively engaged in combat."

On most of their runs, the platoon would try to avoid Route Irish, taking a smaller road that branched off it, one that was just a bit wider than a Humvee. Neither route offered anything in the way of safety. This smaller road had a nickname too. It was called IED Alley.

On August 1, nearly a month after that first firefight, Little was perched in the turret of his Humvee—the position that is most exposed but the one he preferred over the typical command position inside the vehicle. His Humvee hadn't gotten far that morning before the Humvee directly ahead of him called back to say they'd just seen "something weird." Little's vehicle inched forward, but before he could even get eyes on the suspicious object, it detonated. Dirt and steel erupted from

Second Lieutenant Mark Little in the turret of his Humvee in Iraq in July 2007. He led from the gunner's position on most of his missions.

an IED buried deep beneath the road. Little's vehicle shook, its windows shattered.

But Little and his men were lucky once again. Especially Mark. He climbed down from the turret relatively unscathed, with only a few scratches. Those inside the vehicles were not harmed at all.

"A miracle that it wasn't worse," he said of the blast. "All the bulletproof glass around the turret was shattered around me." They didn't call this roadway IED Alley for nothing. And yet the need for supplies was constant, and ways to deliver them limited. Little and his team had no choice but to keep making these runs.

Five days later, on August 6, Little's unit was driving past the same spot, near the crater that the IED had made in the road. Little had a camera out and he was looking over the turret to get an image of the blast hole. He wanted to learn more about how these IEDs were hidden. He didn't get the chance. Less than a week after the initial blast, insurgents had already buried a new bomb near the same spot. The IED detonated just as the convoy approached. Little heard a now familiar thud, but this time the blast did more damage.

For a few minutes, he couldn't see or hear anything. A thin line of blood dripped from one ear, and dust shrouded his face and eyes. The Humvees were able to keep rolling, racing to safety and heading to the base.

Once inside FOB Falcon, Little felt groggy, but he had that same sense of relief and felt he'd once again escaped injury. Or so he thought. It turned out he wasn't just groggy; his brain was badly bruised. Words were coming out in a jumble. His speech was incoherent.

One of his noncommissioned officers looked him in the eye and said, "Hey, sir, you're not OK. You need to go get looked at. You're not making sense." Within minutes Little was medevaced to the US military hospital at Balad, outside Baghdad.

"They were scanning and doing all the MRIs and stuff, and determined I had a big concussive brain injury from the blast, and they wanted to send me home."

Mark Little didn't want to go home. He wanted to stay with his team, and somehow he managed to convince his superiors to keep him in Iraq, with strict orders to remain on base for thirty days and rest. Not an easy thing for Lieutenant Little to do.

On the morning of September 7, the first day he was officially cleared to leave the base, Little gathered his platoon for a mission. There was some backslapping and handshakes before a check-in with the base's intelligence officer, known as the S2. The assistant S2 was a guy Mark knew well—they'd been in high school and ROTC together.

"So when I went in for my convoy briefings, I'm talking to my buddy," Little recalled. "I walk in and jokingly say the same thing I had said every day when we had a mission—'Let me guess, all the roads are black and I shouldn't go, but we're going anyway?'"

The two men had a similar sense of humor—both class clowns, young soldiers who looked for light in the darkness of war. But Little could immediately see that his friend found nothing funny in his attempt at humor on that September morning. With all the seriousness he could muster, the S2 told Little, "I'm disapproving you today. I'm saying your convoy can't go." He told Little they had gathered intelligence suggesting that the insurgents were specifically on the lookout for Little and his platoon. It wasn't a coincidence that his vehicles kept getting hit.

"We have intel that they're actually targeting *you*," he said. "You, Mark Little. You, the human being Mark Little."

The intelligence officer told Little they had learned that the insurgents had given him a street name—The General. Little figured that was because he always got out of the truck, took his helmet and gear off, and talked to the locals like a general would. The deputy S2 continued. "They're sick and tired of you wreaking havoc in their area, so they're coming after you."

Little did not hesitate: "That means we're doing our job. If the bad guys are pissed off at us, we're doing what we're supposed to be doing."

He went to his colonel to ask him to overrule the intel officer. Little's senior officer responded, "It's your convoy. If you want to go, go."

That was exactly what Mark Little wanted to hear. The convoy mission was "a go." At about ten o'clock that morning, Little rallied his troops. He warned his men it was a high-threat movement, that they were being targeted, and that they needed to "keep their eyes and ears open even more than normal, if that's possible."

There would be one more significant detail to that day's supply run. The seating arrangement in Little's Humvee had changed. Earlier that morning, a platoon member had received bad news from home, word that his marriage might be in trouble. The soldier was upset, enough so to share the news with others. Little ordered him to stay put: "I told him, 'By no means are you leaving this FOB. You need to focus on that; this is the last thing you need to worry about.'" The soldier pushed back, but Little was adamant. It was a safety hazard to bring somebody on a mission whose mind was somewhere else.

The soldier's absence didn't just mean one less soldier in the convoy; it changed where Mark Little would be sitting in the Humvee. He preferred to ride in the vehicle's turret, but now he would need to take the place of the absent soldier, in the front passenger seat.

The four Humvees, or gun trucks, as they were called, rolled out of the FOB in a winding serpentine formation—a security precaution—as they drove beyond the compound gates. They had hardly passed the perimeter, not even half a mile, when Little grabbed his radio.

"I want all gun trucks trained on that police vehicle. Something's wrong."

By Little's estimate, his platoon had run 175 missions out of FOB Falcon over the previous four months, and never once had he seen an Iraqi police vehicle south of the checkpoint closest to the base. Now there was one, parked no more than a short sprint from the gates of FOB Falcon. In a high-risk environment, anything out of the ordinary was deemed a threat—and this counted as way out of the ordinary.

Something's wrong.

Little was right. One more bomb was coming. The most powerful bomb of all. And this one was coming straight for Lieutenant Mark Little.

Before he could finish the order "Gun Trucks One, Three, and Four,

I want your guns on that; something seems wro—" a massive projectile ripped through the vehicle's armor. An EFP, or explosively formed penetrator, that almost assured death. A liquid copper molten sphere of destruction that could take out a tank. The Humvee filled with black smoke and metal, a mix that nearly suffocated the soldiers.

At first Mark Little felt no pain. No panic. He was alive. Again. He knew that for certain. His first thought was to stay calm, to wait for the violent motion of the blast to pass. But there was no time to wait. He saw flames leaping from his right arm. Little was *on fire*. The Humvee door was sizzling as well. He tried to pat out the flames and then he did a quick check on his men. He grabbed his driver and got an, "OK." Then "tap backs" from his gunner and the platoon medic.

Flames were now all around. Little tried to bang open the Humvee door, finally wedging it open and then heaving himself against it. The door swung open, but despite all his weight, he could not push himself up or out.

Adrenaline surging, Little was trying to use his feet to springboard out of the truck, but he kept sliding back down, getting nowhere. The harder he would push the faster he collapsed. He glanced down through the haze of dirt and discovered the horrifying reason why. Much of his right leg was gone, and his left leg was barely attached. The rifle that had been wedged between his legs was destroyed.

The shock of it barely registered. Survival mode was driving the young lieutenant. Little grabbed the Humvee's frame, hoisted himself up by his arms, and threw himself out onto the road, rolling to snuff out the fire still smoldering on his arm. When he looked up, he could see the Iraqi police vehicle starting to accelerate, its wheels spinning. Bleeding heavily from his shattered legs, Little grabbed his nine-millimeter side arm and unloaded: "I knew one hundred percent they were the ones that detonated that bomb."

Click, click click. He fired round after round at the car, and when it was clear he was out of ammo Little shook himself into reality, grabbed tourniquets, and started tightening one on his right leg, while the medic who always rode with the platoon placed a tourniquet on the left. The only other serious injury in the attack was a concussion suffered by Little's gunner.

With tourniquets stanching the bleeding, Little sat in the rubble, the remains of his legs covered in dirt, and reached for a radio to call in a medevac. He described the scene, and the blast, and what was needed—all his training kicking in—and then he stopped, catching himself, realizing how close they were to the base. They could drive themselves back to safety faster than any medevac could get there. "Get back in the trucks!" Little told his team. With minimal help, he dragged himself back into the scorched Humvee, and the soldiers gunned it toward the gates.

In a matter of minutes, despite grievous wounds, Mark Little had checked on his soldiers, identified the source of the blast, fired on the Iraqi vehicle, applied a tourniquet to one of his bleeding legs, and made a command decision not to waste time radioing for help but to turn and race back to their base.

At this point Little had no idea whether any part of his legs could be saved. He wasn't sure *he* could be saved either—given the loss of blood.

The Iranian-made EFP, a weapon which would kill countless Americans over the course of the war, had torn through the Humvee's front quarter panel, but the angle meant that it had missed the driver entirely and blown past the front left side of the vehicle. Had that angle been different by just a few degrees, everyone inside the truck would likely have died.

As soon as Mark Little was through the gates, he was loaded onto the medevac helicopter heading for the combat support hospital—the CSH or "CASH," as it was commonly pronounced. He refused morphine in the helicopter at first, pushing the syringe away, worried it might send him out of consciousness and hurt his chances for survival. He asked the flight medic on the helicopter, "Am I stable? Am I going to make it, at least to the CSH?"

Once the medic gave him two thumbs-up, Little took the pain medicine.

At that very moment, inside the combat support hospital in Baghdad's Green Zone, I heard the news about the badly wounded lieutenant. "A traumatic amputation" are the words I remember. I grabbed my ABC News team and we headed out to the nearby landing zone, to wait for the medevac and the soldier I would soon get to know in very dramatic fashion.

I had arrived at Baghdad's Twenty-Eighth Combat Support Hospital in the late morning on that blazing September day, when things were relatively calm. I'd come there with my ABC team because this was normally one of the busiest military trauma centers in the world. We wanted to see the extraordinary work these medical teams were doing with a seemingly never-ending stream of patients. The head nurse, Major William White, told me that morning that the hospital had treated close to nine thousand trauma patients over the last year.

Major White was forty-three, from a small town in northwest Indiana. He'd been with the Army for sixteen years, including a stint running the emergency room at Fort Bragg. He had been at the Baghdad CSH since October 2006, and of those nearly nine thousand cases he'd seen since then, most were Iraqis. Now, however, in the midst of the surge of forces to Iraq, the majority were American soldiers and Marines.

The duty surgeon that day was Dr. Rick Rooney—a young spine specialist from Washington state. Both Rooney and White told me that the pace and intensity of the work, the caseloads that were hitting them, day in and day out, could be overwhelming.

Lost limbs, brain injuries, dangerously heavy bleeding were a constant. "The first time you see it—you have a concept; you get a picture; when the medics give a report on the radio, you have a mental picture of what they're going to look like and you have a mental picture of how you're going to proceed with it," Major White said. "But when your mental picture doesn't match up with the patient you have to take a step back and say, 'OK. Now what do I do?'"

Beyond the daily challenges of treating horrific injuries, the staff were acutely aware that they themselves were in constant danger. There were no faraway front lines in the Iraqi war. Everyone was exposed, wherever they were.

Major White showed me gashes along the wall of the CSH—the marks where mortars had recently struck the facility. They were hit frequently here. When the alerts came and the mortars started falling, the staff would don their body armor and prepare for the onslaught of wounded.

Two months earlier, in July, one of the Army nurse managers, Captain Maria Ortiz, who was getting married in December, was heading back from the nearby gym with another nurse when the CSH and surrounding area were hit by mortar fire. Hit hard—thirty-five mortars blasting around them. In the ER, the staff took cover where they could, pulled on their protective gear, and waited for the casualties—with no idea when the barrage would stop.

The wounded arrived suddenly and relentlessly that day. White was busy in a triage ward when a staffer told him that Captain Ortiz and another nurse were coming in. White was relieved; he needed the help.

But these nurses weren't coming to help. A staffer told White: "No, they're coming in as patients."

Patients? White thought that had to be wrong. He had just been talking to them. Ortiz was going to a workout to get in shape for her wedding. White convinced himself it wasn't serious. Until he saw her. Maria Ortiz, his friend—now his patient—was pale and unresponsive. She had been hit with shrapnel and was bleeding heavily. White rushed her to the OR with a hand on her shoulder and an ache in his heart. No matter how much he tried to deny it, he knew. Captain Ortiz died there soon after. She was the first Army nurse killed in a combat zone since Vietnam.

All of White's coping mechanisms failed that day. He broke down. And yet—like every day in the CSH after that, he picked himself up, straightened up—and hurried to help the wounded pouring through the doors.

While Major White was relaying those painful memories to me

on that September morning, roughly an hour before Mark Little was injured, we heard a commotion down the hospital corridor.

"What have we got coming in?" White asked. "No idea, sir," a nurse replied. Moments later, after a flurry of activity and rapid-fire conversation, we watched the same nurse gently take a young girl from her mother's arms and rush her down the hallway.

The Iraqi mother had waved down American soldiers outside the Green Zone, frantic over the condition of her eight-year-old daughter. The day before, the girl had been stung by a black scorpion; now the child was drifting in and out of consciousness and struggling for breath. The soldiers had hustled the mother and daughter into a vehicle and brought them to the CSH. Doctors and nurses were working to insert a tube to help the girl breathe, and an IV line to deliver fluids and medication.

Not long after, another Iraqi child was carried into the CSH. A two-year-old with severe burns. Her body was blistered; she appeared delirious. Someone had spilled scalding-hot milk on her chest and legs. The mother's wails echoed down the hallways.

And then came alerts of a different kind:

Three minutes out.
Roadside bomb. Soldier's legs blown.
Bomb damage, both legs.
Heavy blood loss.
Helicopter incoming.

The traumatic amputation. Mark Little would be there within minutes.

White and his team notified Dr. Rooney, the duty surgeon, and began prepping an OR. And they waited. I waited too, bracing myself for what I was about to see.

US Army Second Lieutenant Mark Little was twenty-four years old in September 2007. He was a five-ten athlete with hazel eyes and chestnut hair. Hockey and tennis were his sports, but he was also proficient on the oboe, flute, and clarinet. A native of Northern Virginia, Little was the only child of Rahele and Fred Little, but in their home he was the youngest of eight—his widowed father had three children from his first marriage, and his mother had four from hers. There was a close bond between all of the siblings, despite the significant age gap. Fred Little was a veteran who had deployed briefly to Korea after the war. But there was no strong military lineage in his family history. Yet Mark had always felt that serving in the military ran through his blood.

Mark Little attended Norwich University in Vermont, the only private senior military college in the country. When his father's health declined, Mark transferred to George Mason University near his home in Fairfax, where he joined the ROTC—the Reserve Officers' Training Corps. From the beginning, he wanted to be an officer, and ROTC was the path to follow. But an Army colonel who had been a mentor convinced him that the best route would be to enlist in the Army, which would give him side-by-side experience with the lower-ranking soldiers, and ultimately make him a better leader. Little heeded the advice, enlisting in 2002 in the National Guard as a combat engineer.

Four years later, now on active duty, he was made an ordnance officer—ammunition supply and maintenance—not at all what he wanted to do. He wanted an infantry position, and made his preference known. When the time came to head for his first duty station, at Fort Drum, New York, the commander at his training school called Little and told him there was a unit deploying to Iraq soon, from Fort Stewart, Georgia. And given that he had prior enlisted time, he would be eligible to go. He would just need to switch his duty station. Little jumped at the opportunity. He felt strongly that if he was needed in a war zone, that was where he should be.

The unit he joined had already been training for the deployment when he arrived in February 2007. He would be the leader of a maintenance platoon, and he'd have six weeks with them before they headed for Iraq.

During the training, in an exercise that simulated a base coming under attack, Little did well enough to draw the attention of the battalion commander.

"I got all the maintainers, the wrench turners, to grab their gear, and we defended half of the base. And the battalion commander said afterwards, 'You should be infantry, shouldn't you?' I said, 'Yes, sir.' And he goes, 'All right, you're taking this, this other platoon; I'm firing the lieutenant; you're taking this other platoon to war in two weeks.'"

It was what Mark Little wanted—to be, as he put it "on the pointy end of the spear." He would be part of a team that supplied a quick-response infantry battalion. A team that would be a rolling target every time they left the FOB.

One of his closest friends, Jason Ely, drove down to Georgia from South Carolina to see him off. Ely had tried to join the Army as well, but he had issues with color blindness, so he was rejected. It was a huge disappointment, given that he and Mark had always bonded over the notion of service and sacrifice. Jason helped his friend pack. They had a steak dinner at Outback, and Jason took him to the base the next morning. What Jason didn't share with Mark was his concern for his friend. The things he didn't want to think about.

I stood across from the LZ with my crew as the medevac helicopter carrying Mark Little approached. The rotor wash clouded our view as the chopper slowly descended. We had walked the short distance from the hospital with Major White and his team without saying a word, and were mindful to stay out of everyone's way. We had permission to film the soldier's arrival but would not identify him or show his face unless it was cleared. We were determined not to cause this soldier any more trauma than he had already suffered by moving a camera too close to him.

But Mark Little didn't seem to even register that we were there. He was alert, but the pain had finally hit him. All that was left of his legs was a mangled, bloody mess. I concentrated on watching his face, while Major White assessed the damage.

Once inside the hospital ER, away from the roar of the helicopter, Nurse White began asking the young soldier questions—"How are you doing? What's your name?"—less for the answers to those questions, more to get an idea of the officer's condition. I moved in closer to listen and introduced myself. Little was unfazed and gave a quick, "Nice to meet you." Nurse White was intent on keeping Little's spirits up. "We appreciate everything you guys are doing out there," he said. "Ours is the easy job. We just patch you back up." Then he asked Mark Little about his family.

"Your mother and father—I bet they are pretty proud of what you are doing."

That remark—another nod to Little's service, and another way to keep him talking—did not elicit the response any of us expected. Instead, Mark Little looked up at the nurse, smiled, and said, "My mom's gonna kick my ass."

Major White, taken aback, laughed and repeated the line: "Your mom is going to kick your ass?"

CSHs may not seem like places for humor, but it was hard not to smile, when the man at the center of the pain and the blood was making the joke.

Mark Little had "fibbed a bit" when describing his deployment to his mother, who had constantly warned her son of the dangers in Iraq. He'd spun up a tale for her about how he and his team would be spending their time working in a "supersafe warehouse job" moving forklifts around. A humdrum, nothing-special job, he had told his mom. And now here he was catastrophically wounded, knowing he would have to answer for those fibs.

Little was fairly certain he had lost one if not both legs, and now he found himself thinking, "Well, what's the next worst thing that's going to happen to me? That will be my mother, who's going to say, 'I told you so.'"

What mattered to him most at that moment was staying alive. White assured him that despite the damage, doctors would save as much of his legs as possible. He asked him if he had any questions about the treatment. Mark Little had only one.

"So at this point you're pretty fucking certain I'm not going to die, right?"

White smiled again, with a flash of humor of his own. "No worries," he said. White told Little that he had already reached his limit for the month, and that he couldn't afford to have anything go wrong with this latest patient. He gave Little another thumbs-up and told him he'd see him in the ICU, after the surgery was over.

I watched as Lieutenant Little was sedated and wheeled into the OR. Dr. Rooney, the CSH staff surgeon, knew immediately that Little's lower legs could not be saved. The doctor cleaned what remained of the extremities and discarded the rest. Afterwards, Dr. Rooney seemed especially shaken. He told me he had seen his share of difficult cases in the United States, but what he had experienced during this, his first tour in the Baghdad CSH, was something entirely different.

"In the States an amputation can be devastating, but when you see multiple extremities it's just, from a physiological standpoint, it's much more significant," he said. "One of the frustrating things is that as a physician, you're used to succeeding. You're a pretty good student, you go from college to medical school to residency to fellowship, and you're usually doing good things—and here, a lot of times they hand you a patient that's been devastated. There's no win, and so it's loss after loss, even though you do the book answer; you do what's right. You don't feel like you win and that's probably the hardest thing. It's one loss after another. It just sucks."

It was late afternoon when Mark Little emerged from surgery. He was still completely sedated when members of his platoon came to the ICU to visit their leader and friend and to present him a Purple Heart. Little's commanding officer, Lieutenant Colonel Mark Weinerth, was there, and together they approached the bed hesitantly. It was a sober and emotional moment. Weinerth quietly pinned the Purple Heart medal to Little's pillow.

A chaplain came and offered a brief prayer: "We bless this soldier. . . . We thank you, Father, for his family back home. Continue to be with this soldier, continue to bless him, in His holy name we pray. Amen."

Weinerth put on a brave face but acknowledged how hard it was to see his soldier lying there with no legs. "It's extremely difficult. Today Mark woke up, just normal life, going out on another convoy run, and boom, it happens, and his whole life is changed forever."

What the colonel, the doctors, the nurses, and the other members of the platoon couldn't know, any more than anyone else could have known in those early hours, in the frenetic and frightening world of the CSH—was what Lieutenant Mark Little would do next, with the new life, the changed life he would now embrace.

Mark first saw his mother and father on the day he arrived at Walter Reed. It happened to be September 11, the sixth anniversary of the attacks. His parents still lived in nearby Fairfax. The visit was nothing like he had feared when he was lying on a stretcher in Baghdad. Far from "kicking his ass" for getting injured, his father and mother surrounded him with support. "I was still pretty drugged up at the time, but I definitely remember, all happiness, thankfulness that I was alive, and I was going to be OK." He was sure his mom raised plenty of hell outside the hospital room, but when she was with her son by his bedside, "it was all love and family."

I spoke to Rahele Little a few days later. As a mother myself, I instinctively knew that she would want to talk to the person who had been with her son on the day of the injury. She asked endless questions and was amused to hear that her son had worried about her reaction. I visited Little as well during those first weeks at Walter Reed. He was pumped with painkillers but still the funny, engaging soldier I had met in Baghdad.

In South Carolina, Mark's close friend Jason Ely got a message over Myspace from a mutual friend. In its entirety, the message read: *Mark got blown up. He'll be at Walter Reed.*

At first Ely thought it was a prank, some terrible joke. But soon enough he understood. He got in his car and headed for Washington. By the time he reached the hospital, he felt prepared for what he might find. He wasn't.

"I don't know that I've ever tried to put words to it," Ely said. "You walk in the room and you see a friend who you know—"

He had tried at first not to pay attention to his friend's wounds, keeping his gaze turned away from the bottom end of Little's hospital bed, where his legs had once been.

They talked for a while, Jason feeling desperately sorry for his friend. And then at some point Mark grabbed his arm and looked him in the eye with an expression that Jason took as a clear message: *This is just a roadblock. A hurdle. This is a challenge.* Mark Little would overcome this, was how Ely understood the look in his friend's eye, and the grip he held on his arm.

"It was just an honest, very innocent moment between two friends," Ely said, "and I knew as soon as he looked deeply into my eyes and grabbed my arm, that he's gonna be all right."

Wednesday, November 7, 2007, two months to the day after his injury, brought notable milestones for Little. He received news that morning that he would be promoted to first lieutenant on the following Friday. Next came the arrival of a prosthetic for his left leg. The one for the right had been fitted just weeks before. That meant that for the first time in a month he would stand on two legs—not his own, but the prosthetic legs that would carry him for the rest of his life. And Little did not waste a moment getting on with that. Two days later, despite a lack of training on his new legs, and warnings from his physical therapist that it was too soon, Little stood to receive his first lieutenant bars at the Marine Corps Memorial in Arlington, Virginia. Brigadier General John Johnson pinned the bars on him, calling him a "proven leader." His father, Fred, a veteran himself, pinned a silver bar on his son's hat, or cover, as it is called in the Army. He was now First Lieutenant Mark Little.

More milestones would follow. By mid-December, after multiple surgeries, Little headed for Colorado. Walter Reed often arranges special trips for wounded soldiers, and Little, far ahead of the recovery curve, got himself on a trip to Breckenridge. He had been a snowboarder before the injury, and he loved the mountains.

Little spent much of his time in Colorado thinking about his fellow soldiers back in Iraq. With his new prosthetics and those platoon mates in mind, he grabbed a snowboard, strapped his prosthetic legs firmly onto the board, and headed down the mountain. He refused to "sit-ski" but stood tall on that board and made sure there was a photograph to prove it. As much as Little enjoyed snow sports, what he wanted most from this trip was that picture to send to his Army buddies. The soldiers with whom he had bonded in battle. The soldiers who were still at war. Little's message for them was clear: He was going to be OK, and they should understand that if they met the same fate, there was life and joy to be found on the other side. It was a new purpose that Mark Little was wholly embracing.

Mark Little skiing in Jackson Hole, Wyoming, in March 2013.

Little had an old close Army friend named Matt Coyne, whom he'd gotten to know back at Fort Stewart. They'd shown up there on the same day and trained together, and they'd become fast friends as they prepared for their deployments—Little to Iraq, Coyne to Afghanistan. Coyne told his friend, "I'll be home before you, and I'll be waiting with a beer in hand when you get off the plane."

They stayed in touch sporadically from their respective combat zones, and then came a long stretch of radio silence on Little's end. Coyne was worried, and he sent messages asking Little if he was OK. Finally Coyne got an answer.

"I won the game," came the reply from Little. "I got home before you did. I got a little paper cut and they sent me home."

"It's literally what he said," Coyne remembers. "So I sent an email back to him, kidding him that he was weak, so couldn't hang with the rest of us."

Little realized his "paper cut" joke had gone too far, and in his next email he was as blunt as possible:

> *I got my legs blown off.*

Still in Afghanistan, Coyne read the message and burst into tears. And then he raced to the nearest phone bank, sickened that he had made light of the injury before knowing what had happened. Little felt badly too, for worrying his good friend—so he tried a different approach.

"He's like, 'I'm just sitting in the bed trying to grow legs, but it's not working very well,'" Coyne remembers. "And I just, I kind of broke down, and I'm like, 'How are you laughing, and how are you making jokes?' And he said, 'Matt, I should be dead, but I'm not—so why am I going to be upset about it?'"

A year and a half later, in 2009, Coyne was back home, preparing to transfer from Georgia to Fort Leonard Wood in Missouri. He called Mark Little to see whether he would join him for the drive. For the company. Little loved the idea. He was happy to join.

And then Matt Coyne had an even better idea.

The first stop on their trip would be in Atlanta. Matt knew a woman there named Alicia Gheesling, a laid-back person with a good sense of humor and a passion for service. Those traits alone were enough for Matt to think she might be a nice match for his friend.

About a half hour outside Atlanta, the planned "ambush"—as Little would later describe the encounter—began to unfold.

Matt had told Mark that he had a friend in Georgia whom he wanted him to meet. "Her name's Alicia," Matt said. "And you guys would be perfect together."

Mark's first reaction was polite but firm. No. *No way.* "I said, 'I'm so happy, I'm single and living my life.' No thanks."

Romance wasn't anywhere near the front of Mark Little's mind. His focus had been on his own recovery, the hard work of getting himself back into mental and physical shape. Fundraising and volunteer work was taking a lot of his time.

Matt pressed, gently. He told him it wouldn't be a date—they'd all be together. Just a fun stop on their road trip, with a nice woman he happened to know in Atlanta. "Don't worry about it," Matt told him. "Let's just go have dinner and toss a couple beers back, and then we'll head out early in the morning."

And so Mark relented. For his friend. One stop. One meal. And then they would be on their way.

Alicia was twenty-eight, a redhead from a tiny town near Augusta, Georgia, with a degree in international affairs. Both her grandfathers had served in the military—one in the Navy, one in the Air Force—and her first job out of college had been as a contractor at Fort Stewart, the Army base near Savannah. She had military connections for sure, but also a passion for service, doing volunteer work along with her government consulting for the military whenever she could.

Alicia was happy to see Matt on his way to Missouri, but she hadn't given a thought to the buddy who was helping him with the move. Matt hadn't said much about him. Certainly not that he was missing his legs.

So she came to the hotel, and the man who had told his friend that romance was the furthest thing from mind got an arrow through his heart. Once they were introduced, Coyne made an excuse about needing to do something in the car, and he left the two of them alone in the lobby.

"I just, I felt it," Little said. "I believe in energy, right? Not like, I don't have crystals hanging anywhere. But I believe in the concept of energy or feelings. And I absolutely knew that this was just the best, perfect human being on the planet, and I needed to do everything I could to make sure we were together forever."

It wasn't exactly mutual—at least not at first.

Left alone, they grabbed coffee and walked around the city. Mark was moving well on his prosthetics by then—as they walked and talked, Alicia had no inkling of his injury.

Four hours later, Mark made an announcement. "I'm gonna marry you," he told her. "Just want you to know so you're not surprised later, we're getting married." Alicia just laughed, but then Little found a paper clip and fashioned it into a ring and said, "I don't have a ring yet, because I didn't know I was going to meet you today."

Alicia wasn't sure what to think. She found him cute and funny, but he lived in Virginia and she lived in Georgia. She didn't expect it to go anywhere.

But the next morning she came back to the hotel and brought the two men breakfast in their rooms. It was only then that she noticed Little was having difficulty getting up and ready.

"When I first met him, he was wearing long pants. I didn't think anything about it," she said. The next day, at their hotel, she watched as they were getting ready and packing up to go. "And needless to say, he didn't exactly spring out of bed or anything. So that's when I knew. But I had just thought he was a wonderful guy, very nice, and didn't think anything else of it." Neither did Mark Little. He was already smitten; it was the breakfast delivery that sealed it. Thoughtful, kind—and she had been completely nonchalant about his legs.

Matt Coyne saw the look in his friend's eyes. And for the next two days, as the two men made the seventeen-hour drive from Atlanta to Missouri, Coyne realized his "ambush" had been a success. "He wouldn't shut up about her."

A month and a half later, Mark invited Alicia on a sightseeing weekend in the nation's capital. She figured, "Why not?"

What she was not expecting on her tour of DC was a trip to Walter Reed. Mark said he had been asked by hospital staff to stop by.

More and more amputees from the war were landing at Walter Reed, and the hospital called him often, knowing he was nearby and always willing to pay a morale-boosting visit to the new arrivals. Beyond a general hang-in-there, it'll-be-all-right, buck-up message, Little wanted the wounded vets to know that the loss of their arms or legs didn't mean the loss of anything else, in terms of their hopes and dreams for life after war.

For Alicia, it was a first date like no other. "Who does that?" she thought. *"Not only is he a great personality, but here he is wanting to show other people who are coming back—he's already lost his legs for a few years, and he wants to show them it's not the end of the world."* It was a powerful moment for Alicia, with a clear view into Mark Little's big heart.

And it was an opening for Alicia to fill her need to serve as well. In a small way, but a meaningful one.

"I remember one of the moms of the amputees almost more grateful that I was there at Mark's side than anything else," Alicia recalled. "She was, like, *Oh, you-all met after you lost your legs?* And he said, '*Yep, I did not know her.*' And I just remembered that, in this mother's face and eyes. She asked me, '*You met a guy in pieces and parts, and you're OK with it?*' I was like, 'Yeah, absolutely. It's not about that. It's about who they are.' And I remember she just lit up."

The following day, Mark took Alicia to some of the more traditional DC sights. That night, they took a riverboat cruise along the Potomac. Alicia was having a fine time—and then a small gesture made it something more. He took off his jacket and draped it across her shoulders. For Alicia, it somehow said so much about Mark Little.

"We were standing there. He put his jacket over my shoulders, and that was it for me," she said. "I just knew that was what I wanted, forever; that was my definition of perfect. I just knew. It was the bolt of lightning, the magic, the whatever. It was just perfect."

It was during their weekend in DC that Mark explained exactly what

Mark and Alicia Little on their wedding day in February 2011.

had happened to him in Iraq, in graphic detail, with some images to go along with his story. For Alicia, the details were gut-wrenching: "I really wanted to cry, but he was sitting right next to me, so I kind of held it in and didn't cry. But it was very emotional, and I just could not believe what he'd gone through." Mark held Alicia's hands tightly and the two embraced.

A few months later, Alicia moved to DC to be with Mark. And then came an anniversary of sorts. It was July 4, 2010, three years to the day since Mark Little faced his first fusillade of fire in Iraq. That unforgettable Independence Day in 2007, when a band of men with machine guns hiding in women's clothing had attacked him and his platoon. A day he always considered a lucky one. Now he would see if that Fourth of July luck would hold.

The plan was for Alicia to meet his mother and father for the first time during the holiday. The family had rented a condo on the beach in North Carolina. A day in the sun was followed by a big meal and fireworks. And then the finale. As they all walked back to the house from the beach, Mark Little dropped on one knee—slowly and with difficulty—and he proposed. His mother and father were as surprised as Alicia, who blurted "a million yes, yes, yeses!"

They were married the following year in North Carolina in late February of 2011, splitting the difference between DC and Georgia. Mark and his groomsmen wore kilts, a nod to his Scotch-Irish ancestry. Alicia made sure her dress had a short train, so that Mark wouldn't get caught up in it. A big wedding, a quick ceremony, and a very long party. Mark called it the best day of his life.

Remarkably, Mark Little had continued to serve in the Army. This time, he was working in intelligence. He fought medical discharge and proved that he could still contribute. His work was secret but immensely valuable.

Little also found new purpose in his life beyond the Army. A podium for optimism that began when he first got his prosthetics, when he mounted a snowboard, when he first told fellow amputees they would be "OK."

"Very quickly, I realized that I was pretty high-activity, high-functioning for my injuries," he said. "And I used that as an opportunity to bring awareness and raise money."

What he had done, as soon as he was able, was return to peak physical shape. Walking, and then walking faster. Running, and then playing hockey, becoming the captain of the USA Warriors Ice Hockey team—a squad made up of wounded vets—and gym workouts that grew longer and more intense. In 2011, he began entering extreme athletic competitions—the Tough Mudder, Warrior Dash, and CrossFit Games—and here he discovered a blend of service and physical recovery. For each event, he'd ask friends and fellow service members to donate a few dollars per mile he completed. And then he'd donate those funds to organizations that helped veterans. His friend

Jason Ely, who had by now enjoyed some success in business, helped him on the fundraising side, using Little's story "to show other people, don't second-guess a wounded veteran, don't write them off," Jason said. "They can do a whole lot."

After twenty-two Navy SEALs were killed when their helicopter was shot down over Afghanistan in August 2011, Little entered a grueling, full-body-armor CrossFit workout event to raise money for their families.

"We did it in our vests and our full uniform and kit, in memory of

Mark Little participating in a GORUCK Challenge in Washington, DC, on July 4, 2012: a grueling fourteen hours of physical challenges and exercises. Here he is "buddy-carrying" a teammate.

those who fought, who fell, who couldn't be there to work out with us or to push ourselves to learn anymore."

While he pushed himself physically, he also pursued higher education, earning a master's degree in forensic psychology from George Washington University, and later spending a year at the Executive Education Leadership program at Harvard Business School. All of this, while he continued to visit the amputee soldiers who came through Walter Reed.

"I'd get a phone call from a physical therapist or a prosthetist or a doc who knew me, just saying, 'Hey, we've got so-and-so here. It'd be really great if you could visit them.' Well, my first question is, 'How soon?'"

And being Mark Little, he would hunt for the humor, or at least some lighter side, wherever he could find it. Even in the often-dreary hospital rooms at Walter Reed.

He told them jokes, laughed off his own injuries; he had Rollerblade legs made, and if he learned that somebody was a hockey player or skier he would wear those and roll into their room. "Trying to give them that sense of, 'Hey, you know, this is a big speed bump, but that's all it is. We're gonna be OK,'" he said. "And what I found is that the families usually appreciated it way more than the service member, because they're sitting there loopy, getting drugged and in and out of surgeries. The families have all that free time to worry."

Whenever he brought Alicia with him, he would make a point of showing her off, to show the soldiers and their families: There are good things to come in your lives. Things to look forward to.

"What better than to show off that a guy with no legs, post-blast, can find a beautiful hottie and have a happy life?" he said with a laugh. "That was almost a trend, with moms worried that their sons would be single and shunned. And I would say, 'No, I met my wife years after I got hurt, and here we are.'"

Then another challenge came his way. Somewhat out of the blue.

In 2013 a distant friend called Mark Little with a plea. He was close to a combat veteran family that had been struggling financially and had waited too long to seek help—a common problem among members of the military, who, as a point of pride, don't want to ask. Now the family was in danger of having their car repossessed. And if their car was taken, the veteran wouldn't be able to keep his job.

Little told his friend he would help.

"I said, 'OK, how much will it cost to avoid that?' Because they needed to go to work, to go to appointments, just everyday living. And it was something like three thousand dollars. Relatively nominal in the grand scheme of things."

Mark called some of the charities to which he had donated in the past. Might they be able to pitch in? Each one gave essentially the same answer: That's not our mission.

Little learned quickly that rapid-fire, moment-of-crisis assistance of this kind didn't seem to be anyone's mission. None of the organizations seemed to be able to lend help immediately. It all made sense, but it also frustrated him deeply.

"A lot of these organizations, the way their charters are written, they're for very specific things, as they should be—a particular service branch, a particular war, or for certain things that they can do, housing, vehicles, what have you," he said. "They have a whole board that they have to get approval from. What we found is with a lot of veterans, things spiral to the point where it's, 'Oh, I'm going to lose my house tomorrow.' And a lot of organizations weren't set up where they could write a check in two days."

The polite rejections piled up. Ultimately, they moved Mark Little from frustration to action. He called Jason Ely and told him he wanted to start a charity. He asked Ely to join him, because he didn't really know how to go about doing it.

They began by calling around for donations for the family, and they did it quickly. The family was able to keep their car, and the veteran kept his job. And then Little and Ely started a charity based on precisely this moment-of-crisis assistance for veterans.

They called their new organization Warrior 360. The idea was simple: While those other organizations did their own valuable and meaningful work—sticking to their specific missions—Warrior 360 would handle the crisis needs, financial and otherwise, big and small, that risked turning into tipping points for veterans and their families. "360" referred to the fact that the asks could involve anything. Mark Little figured the new organization would function as a financial version of the emergency care he'd been given in the CSH.

"Members of the military have pride in themselves and their work," he told me. They feel "that they're strong, they can take care of things—until they can't." That's where Warrior 360 would come in, to help people through a rough patch: "We're going to pay what you need to keep your car, and then you're going to get back on your feet."

Once a crisis was averted, Warrior 360 would direct people to other organizations that could help with the next phase—a financial management organization, a mental health outfit, and so on. In effect, what Little envisioned was that stopgap, like an ER or CSH, stabilizing the "patients" and moving them to the next level of care.

"I called us the 'quick clot' or 'tourniquet charity,'" Little said, "for things that the service members and their families needed right now that couldn't wait till next quarter, that couldn't wait for a board to approve the payout. We quickly vetted them and just made that problem go away. So I viewed it like the tourniquet on the battlefield."

Within a few years, the organization had brought in a half million dollars in public contributions, 98 percent of which was going directly to veterans and their families for a range of crisis needs.

The organization existed for nearly a decade, sunsetting only in 2022 when the demand fell—a happy outcome, as Mark Little reminded me. The Iraq War was long over; the Afghan war had come to its difficult end. There weren't as many service members coming back with terrible injuries. The requests for immediate help had begun fading away, just like the nation's wars.

Mark Little is in his forties now. After nearly twenty years without them, most days he forgets he is missing his legs. But he knows that things will be harder when he is older. He finally retired from the military in 2021. "I ran the odometer hard post-injury," he said, referring to all those endurance competitions, all those races. He knows that wheelchairs and other forms of assistance will become increasingly important parts of his future: "I understand that that's going to happen probably sooner, sooner than most." Alicia will help him through that.

"He and I have always known whatever comes to us, we'll take it and we'll take it together," Alicia says. "He has a hard day with the legs, then I'm his legs. My grandparents were married for sixty-seven years. They did all the ups and downs. My parents have been married for forty-five years. They will do their ups and downs—it's just the nature of marriage. I married a guy with no legs, but the fact is, we will take the ups and downs because we're a team."

Mark Little is a lucky man in so many ways—for one thing, he has a gift of always seeing the silver lining. It *is* a gift, no question. He knows that. And while Little wouldn't wish an IED blast on anyone, he has told me many times that he is a better person today, and living a better life, because of what happened to him on that September day so long ago. It is simple, he says: "I'm really happy every day when I open my eyes. I get to live another day. I am the happiest I could imagine. Nothing could be better."

US Marine Corps First Lieutenant Derek Herrera during his first deployment to Ramadi, Iraq, 2008.

CHAPTER 5

Spiritus Invictus

Derek Herrera

EVEN UNDER THE HARSH FLUORESCENT LIGHTS OF A drab hotel conference room, Derek Herrera turned heads. Confident, approachable, and leading-man handsome, he was neatly dressed in black twill pants and a light jacket, his dark hair fashionably short. With his six-foot, two-inch frame tucked behind a long open table, he was answering every question thrown at him with precision. He listened carefully and maintained frequent eye contact. Which was a bit challenging at times for those in front of him.

It was what he had on the table that was the distraction. Propped next to a coffee cup and a bottle of water was a large tan-colored mannequin—or part of one. And definitely a *man*nequin, although the part in question was rarely displayed in public. It was just the lower midsection, the slice of the body showing the rear end and male reproductive organs. Where a CPR dummy ended, this one began.

As Derek meticulously explained a new high-tech diagnostic device, he casually pointed to the mannequin's realistic genitalia, with the urinary tract highlighted by a marker. And not once—not for even a fraction of a second—did he display any embarrassment about *what* he was talking about, *how* he was talking about it—or *why* he was talking about it. Nor should he. Derek was explaining his idea for a groundbreaking test for millions of people who suffer from urological problems that could be done without an uncomfortable catheter. "We have better technology," he was saying, "and that's what we're trying to bring to market now."

Derek Herrera had everyone's attention by then. He made you listen and watch. But you might have also noticed something about Derek himself while he was making his pitch—the way his legs shifted or shook slightly under the conference room table. Nothing too dramatic, but it happened sporadically, and it was hard to miss. A kind of subtle spasm in the lower body. A spasm that if you had met him before, as I had, you would quickly forget about and focus on Derek's game-changing invention.

If you were to try to pin down what drives and animates Derek Herrera, you might think he was a medical technician, a science or tech expert, maybe. Or an entrepreneur.

Derek Herrera is all of those things. An entrepreneur, a voracious student of the startup culture and cutting-edge medicine, and a powerful advocate for change. "This test is going to be a much better experience for the patients," he was saying. "More reliable and more accurate for the clinicians."

Derek should know. Like those he is trying to help, he has suffered through what he calls the "archaic, medieval, torturous, uncomfortable, awkward, humiliating, undignified" test many times before. He was determined to change that.

Derek is a former military officer and Naval Academy graduate. A US Marine. A war fighter. A highly decorated special operator. A battlefield survivor. And in one way or another, everything he was saying in front of that plastic mannequin was related to that fact.

That's because the entrepreneur-salesman-warrior is also a paraplegic, with no feeling or control of his body below the chest. A bullet through his spinal cord a dozen years before left this once gifted athlete and natural military leader in a wheelchair.

"It was the worst day of my life," he said, "because something I committed my life to, what I love doing, I can no longer do, and because I have this physical injury, a lifelong injury that I deal with on a daily basis.

"But it was the best day of my life, because it's afforded me opportunities and accelerated the potential good I can do in the world in ways that I never would have had otherwise."

It is that grace and gratitude and his commitment to help others that defines Derek Herrera. It pours forth, in a humble, sweet, and remarkable way. Remarkable, given what life has thrown in his path.

Just before midnight on June 13, 2012, then twenty-eight-year-old Marine Corps Captain Derek Herrera gathered his men in their small camp near Mirmandab, a village in Afghanistan's Helmand Province. He was the commander of a unit of Marine Raiders, a Special Operations Team that went by its company call sign and number—Copperhead 31. Herrera's own call sign was Red Zero One—Red because theirs was the first of three teams (Red, White, and Blue) and One reflecting his top rank within the unit.

The tall, brown-eyed captain was rousing his seven fellow Marines, two Navy medics, and ten Afghan soldiers, for an operation that had been days in the planning. The men moved purposefully around the camp, gathering gear, while clutching paper cups of coffee. The middle-of-the-night start was necessary because Copperhead 31 needed to set up ambush positions before the sun rose at 4:40 am and those ambush spots were a two-hour trek from their small forward operating base.

Derek moved through the base, checking on his men, reviewing the plans one last time. They worked fast, efficiently, and then set off through the dark terrain, arriving well before the first flickers of daylight.

Derek's team had been in Helmand just over a month. Their general mission, like so many American operations in Afghanistan, went by the initials "VSO," for village stability operations. It was a concept that dated to the Vietnam War and a rather clinical term for working with the locals to build their economy, security, and good governance. In Helmand, it involved rooting out Taliban militants. Derek had orders from his battalion commander to pursue the enemy aggressively and to use force when necessary. "The task when we showed up in Helmand was basically just go out there and kill any bad guys you get to, try to train your force, and to be successful," he said. "That was really the primary focus."

The United States had been at war in Afghanistan for nearly eleven years by then and public support was waning. Nearly two-thirds of Americans felt the war was no longer worth fighting. For the seventy-five thousand American troops who remained in the country, those poll numbers meant little. The fight was still very real. While Derek questioned whether there was an overall long-term strategy for success in Afghanistan—"We didn't know what winning was," he said—he also felt that he and the others were sent to Afghanistan to fight. And that is what they were going to do.

Geography gave Captain Herrera and Copperhead 31 a degree of autonomy; the battalion commander was hundreds of miles away, at a Task Force Command center in Herat Province. And Herrera's company commander was at another base some thirty to forty miles away. "So it was just us, and we decided what to do, and people would approve it," Derek said. "In general, we had freedom to do what we thought was best."

Derek Herrera's dad was a career Air Force officer, and Derek had grown up on military bases in different corners of the United States, though he spent most of his time in Delaware. "The military was the family business," as he put it. His grandfathers had served in the Air Force, each for more than twenty-five years. Derek had drawn inspiration from that history, but he had decided on the Naval Academy instead of the Air Force, and made it into the storied institution with ease. Like so many others before him, the lore that surrounded the Navy SEALs had attracted him to the service.

He loved the academy and the Navy from the start, buying completely into the culture and value of service and what he called "the selflessness of being a leader in the military." There was an added bonus to his choice: His high school girlfriend Maura Pierannunzio was an undergrad at Towson University and lived a short hour from Annapolis.

"Very quickly after I got there, I realized that this was my calling, what I wanted to spend the rest of my life doing. I wanted to go and lead men and women in combat."

Derek started at Annapolis in 2002, a year after 9/11 and the US invasion of Afghanistan. Less than a year later, in the spring of his first full year at the academy, the United States invaded Iraq. Herrera saw fellow cadets head for the war, and he heard from some of them about their deployments and resolved to get there: "I doubled down basically on my commitment to try to go and become a combat leader." He felt a conflicting tug like so many young service members at the time: He wanted, as an American citizen, for the war to end. At the same time he hoped, as an ambitious Navy midshipman, that he would get there before it did. It turned out that would not be a problem.

Derek graduated from the US Naval Academy on Friday, May 26, 2006, and just two days later he married Maura in the chapel at Annapolis. She had her college graduation on the previous Thursday. The two would likely have married sooner, but those enrolled at US military academies are not permitted to marry.

Maura and Derek didn't have much time to settle into married life. The wars in Iraq and Afghanistan were still raging and Derek had a five-year service commitment to the Navy as payback for his academy education, and he was intent on joining the SEALs to fulfill the commitment. Derek figured with his confidence, good grades, and powerful build, the SEALs would be proud to have him on the team. He was wrong. "I bombed the interview," he said. What he thought was confidence he later realized came off as "youthful cockiness and immaturity." He did not make the cut.

The rejection left him reeling, but not for long. If he wasn't going to be a Navy SEAL, Derek would select the next best thing: The Marine Corps, which is generally considered the toughest of the services and has been part of the Department of the Navy since 1834. Derek began his Marine Corps career as an infantry officer and thrived in the role. By 2008 he found himself in Iraq. The deployment took him to Ramadi, capital of Anbar Province, which had seen some of the war's deadliest combat. But when Derek got there things were relatively quiet.

"The tribal leaders had decided to stop fighting us for a time," he said. "They'd come to an agreement with some coalition leaders who said, 'We're gonna pay to employ you, and tell your tribe to stop fighting us.'" Suddenly, former insurgents were joining the police, and for a time the daily fighting ebbed. It wasn't completely quiet. There were still high-profile attacks, but little force-on-force combat.

It was still meaningful work for the young Marine Corps officer, but Derek Herrera yearned to be where the action was. He wanted that chance to lead Marines in combat. And there wasn't any combat in Ramadi.

When Derek returned home, he told Maura how much he loved the job and the Marine Corps, but that his goal now was to become a Special Operations Officer, in an elite unit known as the Marine Raiders.

The Raiders had been created during World War II, but the Special Ops unit was new, born of a 2005 directive from Defense Secretary Donald Rumsfeld that had created the Marine Special Operations Command, or MARSOC. The Marine Raiders were designed to operate at the elite level of the Navy SEALs or Army Green Berets, and after the sting of his rejection from the SEALs Derek was even more determined to prove himself. "Of all those specialized units in the Marine Corps," he said, "the Raiders are the only ones in Special Operations that perform similar missions as SEALs." The motto for MARSOC, "Spiritus Invictus"—indomitable spirit—was one that Derek would take to heart. Maura was proud of her husband, although—by her own admission—worried about what the "badass" Marine Raiders did, or what might lie ahead for him.

Maura was a ballet dancer and a dance teacher. "I have all the respect for the military of course, but I came from a different world," she said, by way of explaining her limited interest in getting together with other military spouses, or embracing the military culture. What mattered to her was that she and Derek were happy—happy together and happy in their very different endeavors. She in her world of dance, he in his military service.

When Derek told her he wanted to be a Marine Raider for the foreseeable future, all she could think was, "Great. This is awesome for him. He has found his dream job." He warned her there might be frequent deployments, which could be difficult given both of them wanted a family. But she was reassured they would be able to handle it. "He just protected me so much," Maura said. Derek kept telling her, *"It's not going to be that bad. It's going to be all right."*

By the time Derek's MARSOC team arrived in Mirmandab, most of the locals had left. The Taliban had taken control of Helmand Province, and Derek guessed there were now only about five hundred people left in an area that had been home to some two thousand. It was a deeply poor part of a very poor nation, and some of the benefits that other parts of Afghanistan had seen in the decade since the Taliban's ouster weren't evident here. There was no electricity, no running water, very little infrastructure. Mud huts, no doors, just farmland. The way people there had lived for thousands of years.

Team commander Captain Derek Herrera (left) and Sergeant Prime Hall in Helmand Province, Afghanistan, June 2012.

For decades, the major crop in Helmand had been pomegranates. By the time Derek and his unit arrived, the pomegranate crop had been largely replaced by poppies, the building block for opium and heroin and a lucrative source of funding for the Taliban, whose leaders had been in the Helmand Valley on and off since the early 1990s. The poppy trade had bankrolled much of their operations.

Derek Herrera understood the history of the valley and challenges as well as any newly arrived American service member. Their predeployment training had included cultural and language training with Pashtun speakers. The most helpful preparation had come from the departing unit they were replacing, the Marines with the institutional memory and experience they passed along to Derek and his team. "And so we had a really good level of insight and information," he said, before the mission began.

He would have roughly sixty troops at his disposal. In addition to his twenty-strong unit of Marine Raiders, there was an Army platoon of roughly thirty soldiers and an Afghan Special Forces team of twelve.

The Afghans under his command introduced them to the local elders, and from the beginning, Derek's team lived among the people as much as they could. But for all the cooperation and all the manpower, the dangers of the mission were apparent to Red Zero One on each new morning, when Derek received reports or simply surveyed the landscape. In particular, the goings-on along the other side of the Helmand River. The enemy-held side.

What they watched, nearly every day, were people coming to buy and sell drugs and guns. And if the goal for Derek and his team was to win over the locals in a contest of influence against the Taliban, they were starting with a major disadvantage. The local population may not have embraced the Taliban, but they were historically wary of outsiders. And the Taliban had their own ways of winning them over on their home turf.

"The Taliban, they're on one side, and they're like, 'Here's one hundred bucks,'" Derek said. "'You're going to grow this whole field of poppy, and we're coming back in two months; this is an advance.' And they'd say, 'You're gonna do it, or we're gonna kill your entire family.'"

From their first days, the Marine Raiders were getting attacked with gunfire and underbarrel grenades multiple times a day.

Derek's unit began conducting patrols, channeling the directive of the battalion commander so that they could "find and kill people before they could kill us." The team made the decision to move under the cover of darkness and patrol at night to mitigate the enemy threat, so that Derek and his men could occupy a building and set up an ambush that would launch at first light. It was complex and dangerous work, the risks piling up for what seemed like minimal gains. That lack of a larger overall strategy, as Derek had put it, seemed obvious.

The operation that began on June 13 would take them to the edge of the river, farther than they'd ventured before. Herrera had prepared a plan, gotten the go-ahead from battalion headquarters, and spent the better part of three days practicing and reviewing the operation with his team.

They had tracked the Taliban to a position just across the river from Mirmandab. The operation was aimed at disrupting the flow of Taliban weapons and the fighters themselves. Army Special Forces would move in from the south and flush the Taliban fighters from their positions, in the direction of Derek and his team. Copperhead 31 would secure a position, intercept the enemy, and take them out.

When Derek's Marines arrived at their ambush points in the early hours of June 14, his men surrounded a small farmhouse overlooking the village. They moved the family, who had no advance warning, into a back room and cordoned them off. They told the family members they had to stay put and reassured them the Marines meant them no harm, although the Marines had eyes on the family at all times.

Four Raiders were dispatched to positions in a small grove of trees on the edge of the property. Sergeant Rick Briere, whose family had emigrated from Haiti, and two others took position on the roof. Derek Herrera watched from just inside the house to coordinate and monitor the radios.

Soon after the first bluish tints of daylight came, the Raiders heard the wail of morning prayers across the valley—a clear marker of daybreak throughout the Muslim world. That familiar sound, however, coincided with an ominous sight.

People were streaming out into the fields and along the riverbank as the sun began to rise. It was as if an alarm had sounded or their homes had all caught fire. Women and children were leaving the area. Rick Briere radioed to Derek downstairs and warned him what was happening. They knew that something very bad was about to go down.

Gunnery Sergeant Brian Jacklin, who grew up east of Los Angeles, was on the roof with Briere, eyes trained on a man who was rapidly nearing the farmhouse. Jacklin, a veteran of six deployments to Iraq and Afghanistan, was tracking the armed man as he closed in. It was clear that the Taliban had spotted the Marines and were poised for an attack.

Sergeant Briere fired a burst from his automatic weapon when the Taliban fighter came within 150 yards of the house and watched the man drop. The crack of Briere's weapon brought out more Taliban and a fusillade of firepower.

The initial exchange of fire was intense but brief—not more than ten minutes. A lull followed, and Derek immediately headed up to the roof of the farmhouse to get a better view, switching places with Gunnery Sergeant Jacklin, whom Derek sent down into the house.

Derek and the two other Raiders lay low on the rooftop, weapons drawn, chests down, helmets and armor snug, looking out at positions near the river where the fire had come from. Not three minutes later, after that brief lull, a sharp burst of bullets showered the rooftop.

Derek saw Sergeant Rick Briere lying face down with a hole in his neck. He wasn't moving. A pool of blood was spreading slowly at his side. His thoughts instantly went to what he could do to help Briere, but Derek realized he was in no shape to do that. Captain Herrera, Red Zero One, had been shot in the same volley of bullets that had felled the sergeant. The third Marine on the roof had slid off narrowly missing the wall of fire.

Just outside the farmhouse, with bullets still flying, Staff Sergeant

Hafeez Hussein, an Ohio native on his second deployment to Afghanistan, heard the crackle of his radio. "A call came over the radio, 'I'm hit, Zero One Zero One; this is Zero One; I'm hit.'" Hussein momentarily froze. "At that point, you know, everybody's heart drops." It was Captain Herrera calling in his own injury.

Derek had been struck in his left shoulder, at the edge of his body armor. He felt a pulsing sensation in his back and slumped over. He knew he had been hit with something, but wasn't sure whether it was a grenade or bullet. He tried to pick himself up, but his legs would not move: "I realized nothing below my chest was working, and so I immediately got on the radio, called my team, told them I'd been hit and Briere as well."

The bullet that hit Derek had passed through his shoulder and lodged in his spine. Rick Briere, it was now clear, had been struck in the neck.

Derek kept trying—and failing—to lift himself up. He wanted to tend to his own wounds, so that he could help Briere, but was unable even to get himself into a sitting position.

Within minutes, despite heavy gunfire pointing their way, Marines were scrambling up to the roof, pulling Derek and Briere down. Staff Sergeant Hussein, who had received the radio call, laid Derek down in the house and squatted next to him. His captain was now struggling to breathe. Hussein was not a medic, but he had multiple deployments under his belt and was well trained in combat first aid. So was Derek. Gasping for breath, Derek knew he needed help fast. He assumed he had a collapsed lung and quickly thought of a procedure he had learned in training called a needle decompression, which would allow air to escape from his lung. Hussein was way ahead of him. He pulled off Derek's body armor, jammed the four-inch needle into his thoracic wall, and *whoosh*. The air came out and Derek was able to breathe again. But the captain was starting to fade.

A few feet away, the team medic Petty Officer Jordan Walker and Staff Sergeant Will Simpson worked on Sergeant Briere, who was bleeding heavily from his neck wound. Briere's black skin had turned gray and he was spitting red bubbles. Simpson used clotting agents to stanch the flow of blood. Staff Sergeant Simpson said the entry wound "was like a pinhole," the exit wound "the size of a peach," exposing parts of Briere's spine. But the sergeant was groaning—and that was a good sign. He was alive.

The Marines had immediately called for a medevac helicopter, but with bullets still ripping through the valley they would need to create a landing zone in a way that wouldn't risk more casualties.

The Raiders determined they would blow a hole in the mud wall surrounding the farmhouse where the Afghan family was still huddled. They needed to create enough space for the LZ and a safe pathway for the men who would carry Herrera and Briere to the helicopter. There would still be obvious risks for all the men—they would be exposed to gunfire as they brought the stretchers to the helicopter—but there were no alternatives. As the medevac helicopter neared, they detonated the explosives, blowing out the compound wall, and then formed a cordon around the stretcher-bearers. They would need to carry the wounded Marines into the open field where the bird was to land.

The helicopter swooped in, kicking up a huge swirl of dust near what remained of the compound wall. Eight men—seven Marines and one Afghan interpreter—carried the stretchers, hustling under heavy fire, like pallbearers in a hurry. Brian Jacklin led them to the chopper, out in the open, coordinating counterfire against the attackers until the helicopter could land. Then the stretcher-bearers moved in a steady run given the fragility of their cargo for the helicopter.

It was over quickly. Less than an hour after the first shots had been fired, the wounded men were loaded safely onto the bird. No one else was hit in the hurried evacuation. The chopper lifted and aimed for Lashkar Gah, the capital of Helmand Province and home to a British base, Camp Bastion. The men would be triaged and stabilized there.

Brian Jacklin and the others stayed behind on the edge of the Helmand River to finish the fight, which would continue for two more days. But it was what those Marines did to get Derek Herrera and Rick Briere to safety that would result in five of them receiving the Bronze Star for valor. Gunnery Sergeant Jacklin received the Navy Cross, for what the citation called his "extraordinary heroism" for his actions during that battle and for clearing the way for the medevac helicopter to land.

Even in the mad chaos on that rooftop in Mirmandab, Derek remembers being flooded by a kind of calm, a serenity that came from his confidence that his Raiders would take care of him. That is the one overwhelming sensation he recalls. That feeling of peace before the painkillers kicked in on the helicopter, and he blacked out.

When he woke up at the med station at Camp Bastion, the emotion that came next was jubilation. Extreme gratitude is the way Derek remembers it: "I was just so elated to be alive, just complete joy that I'd experienced this and survived." He had taken a bullet on a rooftop, as a firefight raged around him in a remote and dangerous part of Afghanistan. He had lost his ability to move, lying there hovering in a gauzy state of near consciousness. And he had *lived*. Rick Briere had as well: The bullet that entered his neck had miraculously missed his spinal cord and, despite the size of the exit wound, missed nearly all of the critical anatomy in his neck.

It helped in those early hours that no one told Derek Herrera that he wouldn't recover. Doctors at the medical station simply told him, "*You have a spinal cord injury. It's really serious.*" Which was perfectly accurate, but allowed for a glimmer of hope. Derek thought, *Oh, I'll kick this; forget spinal cord injury. I'm gonna walk out of here in six weeks.* It was a blissful ignorance that would calm him for a brief but important few hours.

The next emotion that came was pride. Derek marveled at the skill and courage of his Marine Raiders. The battle in Mirmandab could have ended very differently, had it not been for those Marines who were willing to risk their lives to save him and Rick Briere. Derek knew they were the only reason he and Briere were alive.

The fourth and final emotion was love. Some six hours after his injury, a nurse came in to see Derek with a gentle but far more blunt prognosis than he had gotten before. The future, the nurse made clear, was not what Derek had convinced himself it would be in those first moments after he'd regained consciousness.

Looking directly into Derek's eyes, the nurse said, "Captain Herrera, you've been shot in the spine. You're paralyzed from the chest down." Derek looked at him with concern—not for himself, but for Maura. "Has anyone called my wife yet?" he said. The nurse shook his head, and Derek said, "Well, give me a phone."

Maura Herrera was home in California when the call came. It was two in the morning. She answered the phone and heard her husband say simply, "I'm sorry."

More than a decade later, Maura Herrera cries as she remembers that night. "I just always get a little emotional," she said. "I don't know why, because it's been so long, but he was just like, 'Maura, it's Derek. I've been shot, and I'm coming home. I need you to call my parents and let them know, and I need you to call your parents as well.' And I was in shock. Like, what does this mean? I didn't know what it meant that he was shot. And I asked him; I said, 'Are you going to make it, are you gonna die?' And he said, 'I'm going to make it. I'm going to be fine. But right now I can't feel my legs.'

"At that moment, I just—I didn't know what to think."

Listening to her husband on the phone, she cried. He wept too—on the other end of the line, half a world away. But in Maura's memory of the call, he kept that remarkable calm: "He was so in control and really trying to make me feel calm, and just doing the best that he could. He hadn't even left Afghanistan yet."

"She was just grateful that I was alive," Derek said. "And I felt the same way."

Maura Herrera was grateful, but there was much she didn't understand, lying there in the middle of the night alone. She replayed the conversation in her head. He'd been *shot.* He was going to be *fine.* But he also *couldn't move his legs?*

In those early hours, she chided herself for having misread the gravity of her husband's mission, the dangers that seemed so obvious in retrospect: "I just didn't know. So it was a shock. I know I could have found out more about the mission, but sometimes you just live in the clouds a little bit just because you're like, *I have to get through it, and you know what? Sitting and worrying doesn't do anything.*"

Derek remained stoic despite the prognosis, somehow still believing he would walk again. But lying in that medical station in Afghanistan, he had one question that was plaguing him: *Would he and Maura be able to have children?* The answer from the doctor was a welcome one. "Not in the traditional way," the doctor said. But yes, he would hopefully be able to have a family.

Three days later, after a stop at Landstuhl, Germany, Derek was cleared to fly to Bethesda Naval Hospital in Maryland, where he would see Maura for the first time. They cried again, together, this time in an embrace. Derek apologized again to Maura, saying he would make it up to her. She stopped him immediately: "We'll be all right. We'll figure this out."

For as long as Maura had known Derek, he had been a protector and a provider, a person who took care of things. It's a reality she shares reluctantly. "I hate that, because it makes me sound like I needed to be coddled and I was a baby, but it's just the way our relationship was, and he was very good at that," she said. "And I think in that moment, he felt like he had let me down, or he had let my parents down, and he certainly hadn't.

"But that's just him, you know? He thought, 'I was doing something that I loved and that I wanted to do, and now look what happened.' But he was doing something heroic and incredible for his country. And I was proud of him."

Within weeks of having the bullet removed from his spine, Derek was transferred to a VA hospital in Tampa, which offered more tailored care for spinal cord injuries. He and Maura went down there together, effectively moving to Florida. Maura was getting her master's in teaching dance—an online degree program with the London-based Royal Academy. She'd been in the midst of her thesis when Derek was injured, and she kept at the work when she could. She told her professors she would need extra time, an extension perhaps. Beyond the obvious time

Captain Derek Herrera seeing sunshine for the first time after his injury in the courtyard at Bethesda Naval Hospital in June 2012.

commitments she now had with her husband, it was not lost on Maura that she was immersed in the world of dance—when her husband had just lost the use of his legs.

What Maura remembers from that time is that her intensely driven husband now had no idea where to direct his ambitions. It had less to do with the injury itself than the hole it had left in his sense of self-worth. Derek had led his men with distinction and sacrificed much, and he had come home with the honors to prove it. But Maura saw the other thing her husband had come home with: a suddenly blank slate for the future. They still had hopes of someday raising a family together, but she had no idea how the injury would change him—and how it might change *them*.

It was in the Tampa hospital that Derek felt things draining away. He knew by then that a cure for his condition was not on the horizon, and that he wasn't going to rehab his way to feeling anything below his waist. But for all the time and effort he was putting in at the Tampa VA hospital, he had imagined or expected powerful, cutting-edge treatments that might lead to some better end.

"I kind of naively thought—spinal cord injury, oh well, they're going to have all these advanced therapies and this and that, and I started doing physical therapy and they're like, 'OK, lift some weights here. Do some stuff.' I'm like, *What else is there?* Turned out, that's pretty much it.

"It was tough, for a few reasons," Derek said. "One was that from day one in the military, you're never alone, ever. You've always got a buddy. That's just ingrained in this culture—you never do anything alone. Even Special Operations units—never alone. It's a buddy system. Everything, everywhere. You're never alone.

"And now, not only did I have this experience, but now I'm in Tampa, Florida, my wife and I, and we don't know anybody there. And I'm just living in the hospital."

He wasn't given to self-pity, but during those long hours alone, in the nights especially, he kept thinking about his men, his teammates back in Afghanistan.

It was all made worse by the news that reached him two months after his injury. On August 10, in the Sangin District of Helmand Province, three Marine Special Operations forces—three Raiders—had been shot and killed in an "insider attack." Afghans within the team had turned fire on their American partners. Derek knew the dead men—the team commander, Captain Matthew Manoukian, Gunnery Sergeant Ryan Jeschke, and Staff Sergeant Sky Mote. He hadn't known the Afghans who shot them. The Afghan soldiers he had worked with had been brave and loyal to the mission. It was a powerful gut punch for Derek.

"I'm sitting there, all this time on my hands," he said. "By myself mostly. I couldn't do anything, couldn't go anywhere, just thinking about all this stuff. It was bad. Up and down, but a lot of down."

As the weeks passed, Derek kept reminding himself that he was a survivor. He had a wife and family who loved him. And he still had the passion to serve, to learn, and to make his life matter. He had also begun to discover new paths—possible outlets for all the energy that was pulsing through him.

He began writing applications for business school from his hospital bed. Just the act of thinking and writing caused the clouds to lift, at least a little. He was *doing* something, never mind that he was unsure that business school was even right for him or that he'd be accepted anywhere. But it was *something*. The mere act of filling out the forms, thinking about new prospects, kept his mind occupied at least temporarily.

His roller coaster of emotions—from calm to elation, pride and love to depression—was less a feeling than a jolt from within that he needed to get out of the hospital bed, to get out of the hospital entirely. He needed to move forward, take risks, and accomplish something. The question he kept asking himself was, *Is there something in the world that only I can do? What is my unique qualification?*

He kept coming back to the one thing he knew well, beyond training soldiers for combat: He knew what it was like to have a spinal cord injury. Not only the trauma, but the daily struggles and indignities. And in that knowledge and experience, Derek Herrera saw not just opportunity. He saw a calling. It was that calling, that reinvention, that brought the young Marine Corps officer who'd been shot and paralyzed on a rooftop in Afghanistan to a Washington, DC, conference room with a mannequin's lower midsection perched on the table, pitching a startup. It would be a bumpy road getting there, but he was ready to begin the ride.

Just before Christmas 2012, he and Maura decided to go home. Derek figured he could lift the weights and do the other rehab work back in California. It was a place they knew, a community they loved, and it would be a fresh start. An acceptance letter from the UCLA business school, which arrived around the same time, sealed the deal.

Not much had changed back home in California. But everything had changed for Derek. The reality of his injury was now inescapable. Here were the trails he had run before his deployment. The stairs he had climbed. The car he had driven. The bed he had shared with his wife. None of that would ever be the same. He was a paraplegic now. It was another wake-up call to prod him into action and immerse himself in all the existing research involving spinal cord injury.

"I'm paralyzed from the chest down and I use a wheelchair to get around," Derek said. "But your body's not designed to be in a chair all day long. I went from being a Special Operations Officer, very fit, athletic person, tall—and now, every time I go around, people look down on you, they look at you because you're different, and that can be a lot to deal with. Having the opportunity to be in a different position, to stand or walk or do these sorts of things could be really psychologically empowering. And make you feel good about your physicality again.

"In the Special Operations community, they kind of teach you to become an expert overnight," he said. "That's just required. You have to become a quick learner and be able to figure things out and adapt. I didn't know anything about spinal cord injury before. So I just tried to read everything there was, meet all the people, find out anything there was to know."

At UCLA business school, Derek threw himself into the work. His research soon led him to ReWalk, which was billed as a bionic walking assistance system. A robotic exoskeleton aimed at enabling paraplegics to stand and walk again.

The device wasn't easy—the system weighed roughly fifty pounds, with a backpack battery, robotic leg attachments, and a remote-control device worn on the wrist. It wasn't cheap either, priced initially at approximately $85,000. ReWalk also required extensive training and was still in the trial phase when Derek Herrera heard about the various models—ReWalk I for patients in medical institutions and under supervision, and ReWalk P for personal use. Both had been designed by an Israeli entrepreneur named Amit Goffer, who had suffered an injury in an ATV accident that left him a quadriplegic. Goffer's devices were in clinical trials outside Philadelphia. There was no commercially available exoskeleton in the United States.

Derek hounded the ReWalk representatives, hoping to try the device himself. They kept telling him the device hadn't yet won approval from the Food and Drug Administration. He finally got himself into the ReWalk clinical trials, which in turn got him one of the first systems when it was approved by the FDA.

Everything Derek learned about ReWalk fired his passion to learn more, about the device itself and, more broadly, about the ecosystem of high-tech possibilities for those with spinal cord injuries. While still at

Captain Derek Herrera stands with the help of a ReWalk exoskeleton during his retirement ceremony at Camp Pendleton, where he was awarded the Bronze Star for valor, in November 2014.

the UCLA business school, he worked for another medical startup for six months. Derek saw firsthand how medical technology could make a profound difference, how startups functioned, and increasingly he came to believe that this was something he could do. A little over a year after the bullet tore through his spine, this man who was so good at setting goals set two new goals for himself: First, he would identify other needs for the spinal-cord-injury community and explore technology to address them; and then, whether with ReWalk or some other new technology, Derek would stand and walk once more. He knew exactly where he wanted to do that.

On November 21, 2014, the Marine Corps held a retirement ceremony for Derek Herrera at Camp Pendleton, the huge Marine base outside San Diego. He would be presented with a Bronze Star with the Combat V for valor, which honors extraordinary acts of heroism under fire.

The ceremony was held outdoors, on a nondescript patch of concrete, with a tent set up for guests. Derek sat and listened to the various preambles, together with a few dozen friends and family who had come for the occasion, along with Marine officers and members of the First Marine Special Operations Battalion. After brief opening remarks from his commander, Derek was called to speak. It was time to test the new device in public. Through the Marine Raider Foundation and a fund raised in his community, Derek had obtained a ReWalk prototype, and he had spent months training and practicing with the system. By now there was a new model, the ReWalk Rehabilitation 2.0, which featured, among other things, improved sizing for taller people like Derek, at six-two.

With the help of crutches, Derek, grimacing slightly, struggled to his feet. That took a few seconds. He wobbled for a moment. Maura watched from her seat next to him as he gripped the crutches tighter and took his first steps. It took him about a minute to make the short walk to the microphone. The audience fell silent. You could hear a light wind and the sound of the crutches as they clopped forward, one small step at a time. Derek moved painstakingly slowly. But he *walked*. He stood *tall.* For everyone watching, and especially those who knew him, it was a long and beautiful minute. No other person had used the ReWalk outside the confines of a medical institution.

Derek steadied himself and began to speak to his fellow Marine Raiders, crediting them for their valor and resilience.

"I've never seen anyone quit, even in the most seemingly insurmountable tasks and experiences and challenges," he said. "I've never ever seen a single Marine Raider quit. That was true of the day I was injured, when our ten-man patrol, of which two of us were critically wounded, with a ragtag bunch of ten Afghans, surrounded on three sides, were able to turn the tide of that battle, call in the medevac to save my life and Ricky's life, and continue to fight throughout the day without suffering any further casualties. Truly incredible things."

His remarks then turned to his own life. He spoke about the path ahead, with some words of counsel for other Marines, for the moment when, as he put it, "you have to take the uniform off."

"I'm not out of the fight," Derek said, standing proud at the microphone. "I'm here for you whenever you need me, whenever any of you need me, and I'm going to continue to struggle and fight to make great changes in the world. I'm just redirecting my path at this point. And so for me, what I've tried to do is find something that I could be as passionate about, as motivated about, something that gets me up in the morning every day to continue to pursue and to move on with my life. And so that's really what it's all about. When you take the uniform off, find *something,* anything that's going to get you up in the morning and get you to accomplishing the goals that you set for yourself."

And then, wearing his Bronze Star and listening to the applause of the crowd, Derek took the short, slow walk back to his seat. When the ceremony was over, he lifted himself once more and headed for his car, flanked by his physical therapist and by Maura, both ready to catch him if he slipped or fell. But there was no need.

Derek Herrera was able to leave the Marine Corps on his own two feet. To stand, walk, salute the flag, do all these things that wouldn't have been possible without innovation in medical technology.

Certainly the exoskeleton had a long way to go. Derek knew that, and he was back in his wheelchair as his primary mode of movement. But even those few minutes of mobility had fired his new mission. He would focus the same energy he'd devoted to his work as a Marine, to improve the lives of others in need.

The loss of mobility is what most people think of when it comes to spinal cord injury, whether you're the patient or the spouse, the parent, or the child of someone who can no longer walk. But Derek decided walking wasn't what he was going to focus on. The greatest challenge for him wasn't the fact that he couldn't walk. It was a more private and urgent need— going to the bathroom. Or, as he puts it, "bladder management." Accidents and incontinence, catheter use, infections, and more. These were the most profound limitations on quality of life—for Derek, and for dozens of other spinal cord patients he had come to know. It was his experience and their complaints that drove him to decide that this would be his focus, his next chapter. He'd caught the bug of medical technology from Amit Goffer and the ReWalk exoskeleton, felt the flash of inspiration and entrepreneurship from watching the people involved in that work. Now he had identified a problem that needed fixing, a way he might help millions of people—and not only wounded soldiers. For Derek Herrera it quickly became a mission every bit as important and inspiring as leading Marines into combat.

Derek would try to find ways to help others like him—for lack of a better way of putting it—to take a piss.

It's something most people take for granted. You feel the urge, head to the bathroom, and relieve yourself. People with no feeling below the waist don't know they need to urinate—and that alone can turn the simple act of urinating into a nightmare. Men must insert a plastic tube into their penises six to eight times a day—an average of fifty times a week—to drain their bladders. For women, of course the path to the urethra is shorter, but for both men and women who are paralyzed, inserting the catheter has to be repeated every time they urinate. Improper use often causes infections.

As Derek put it, "It's not life-threatening, like a heart attack, but it can completely change your life in a negative way."

Maura had seen how difficult it was for her husband to deal with this from the moment they came home from the hospital. Wherever they went, she said, "the first thing was, we would have to know where the bathroom was, because you're just trying to figure out your body." She told stories of being stuck in traffic or other situations when the nearest bathroom wasn't close, and the embarrassment and pain that followed.

Derek described an early lesson learned the hard way—when he guzzled a Diet Coke. Diet Coke is a diuretic, loaded with caffeine, and twenty minutes after finishing it, he'd peed in his pants. It happened with coffee too. After every accident there was the shame and the inconvenience—and if he was out somewhere, an urgent trip back home to wash and change his clothes. "It can become kind of crippling," he said.

In this world of urological nightmares, Derek's first spark of inspiration was a new catheter for paralyzed men. While Maura was now teaching dance, Derek, along with experts in the field, developed and patented a device called the Connected Catheter, which would discreetly but effectively let the wearers know when it was time to urinate. "So basically a smart catheter," Derek said, "that you could remotely control to empty the bladder." The Connected Catheter would be the bedrock product for a company Derek founded called Spinal Singularity—later UroDev Medical. In 2015 he raised millions of dollars to support the product, and in 2018 the Connected Catheter went into clinical trials.

But for all Derek's energy and commitment, and the team he had assembled, the launch of the device stalled. There were delays in clinical research in the wake of the COVID pandemic, but there were bigger problems: "We built it, we put it through multiple clinical studies and got it to work, but we screwed up with the FDA. They wanted a much more rigorous study than we imagined. And that coincided with us running out of cash." Even with his UCLA business degree, Derek was still a novice in that world, and he had learned that the hard way.

Not surprisingly, Derek was undaunted. If the Navy SEALs rejection had been a big setback in the early stages of Derek's military career, Uro-Dev would be the stumbling block on his path to becoming a successful entrepreneur. He had learned as a Marine, and back at the Naval Academy, that initial failure was a key to ultimate success. This was just the entrepreneur's version of the same lesson.

"For me, it was incredibly valuable," Derek reflected, "because I learned everything about how to do all this stuff, and I had firsthand knowledge of what not to do from that experience."

And so it was on to the next mission. Once again, he began by focusing on a problem in which he had a personal and unique perspective. This time it was the standard test that diagnosed and identified serious urological problems. The test that he compared to medieval torture. He calculated that as many as eighty million Americans with overactive bladders, prostate problems, incontinence, or other issues—all of which plagued most patients with severe spinal cord injury—had suffered through the test. The procedure required the patient to be catheterized, tethered to a machine, and subjected to a fast filling of the bladder in the physician's office. It was invasive, awkward, and embarrassing. "It's valuable, but it's a terrible experience," Derek said.

In 2021, Derek founded Bright Uro, a company with a mission to make the testing more accurate for physicians, far more comfortable and less invasive for patients, and more efficient for clinics. Essentially, he would be filling a technological gap that he had discovered the hard way.

In 2022, Derek secured the license to the intellectual property under development by the Cleveland Clinic for a wireless, catheter-free system that allowed the entire testing mechanism to fit inside a person's bladder; no more being tethered to a machine, and no more intense discomfort. The Cleveland Clinic had been working on the technology for some fifteen years, and Derek had met some of their researchers at a conference and built a relationship with them. Ultimately, he said, the technology matured to a point where they were prepared to license it to a partner. Derek had convinced them that his personal experience and business acumen were strong enough to make him and his company the licensee. "It's an academic environment, so it's not the same requirements and incentives as in industry," Derek said. "We basically took it, learned what we could, and then we started from scratch to redevelop, basically, a brand-new device. We rebuilt that device and then an entire ecosystem around it." That "ecosystem" would involve everything from insertion tools to software apps testing regimens.

Sitting in that Washington, DC, conference room in 2024, he ran through his pitch: A miniature computer capable of entering the bladder and providing doctors the insights they need to determine whether the patient is a good candidate for surgery—and if so, an idea of what that surgery might entail: "You can stand up. You're not strapped into the chair. You can walk around. You can void in privacy. You can let your bladder fill naturally, as opposed to forcing it to fill in ten minutes, which is not normal. You can do it anywhere, anytime, and it's easy. Instead of

Derek Herrera founded Bright Uro to fund and develop transformative medical equipment. He is shown here in the lab in Irvine, California, in March 2025.

waiting four months to get your procedure, now it's basically anywhere, anytime."

Listening to Derek, you could see how he had learned through failure. And how he had won over investors—$23 million to be exact, with a $2 million grant from the National Institutes of Health to help develop and launch the product in the United States. "That's the short version of what we're doing," he said with a smile. "I can talk for hours, all day, about the details."

In March 2025, the Bright Uro system—now a product known as Glean—won FDA approval. In a press release, Derek called the FDA's decision "a historic milestone for our company." They manufactured Glean at their headquarters in California, and sold their first units that June.

It had taken four years, but Derek Herrera and his twenty-member team had gone from the germ of an idea to the realization of his post-military, post-injury dream. "Leading the team that helped to accomplish this, from where we started to achieving this milestone, was just unforgettable and amazing," he said. "A really phenomenal experience."

For Marine Corps captain-turned-entrepreneur and CEO Derek Herrera, it was mission accomplished. And it came on the heels of a far more meaningful achievement.

Before any of that business success, before the joy of innovation and technological discovery, came the mission that Derek and Maura launched together. The mission that would give them both the greatest joy of all.

Back in June 2012 in Afghanistan, in the hours after Derek was injured and learned he was paralyzed, he had asked only that one question—would he ever be able to have children? The answer came five years later. In July 2017, twin boys Hunter and Hudson were born with the help of another, far more familiar medical technology: in vitro fertilization. And beyond the obvious gratitude felt by a couple who had wondered if they could ever have children, there followed a deep appreciation of the fact that the boys would have no sense that there was anything different about their dad.

To Hunter and Hudson Herrera, their father is the "cool guy with wheels," says Maura, not a guy with a problem. Hudson, especially, loves to sit on his dad's lap and cruise around. The way he sees it, his father may be different, but he also has more interesting contraptions than Hudson's friends' fathers.

"They see me and know me for who I am, and they have only known me this way," Derek said. "They don't think about what I was."

Derek still gets around primarily in the wheelchair, but he decided to surprise the boys one day. He keeps the ReWalk exoskeleton stashed in his garage and rarely uses it. Revolutionary as it is, it's still a big effort to strap on the leg pieces and fire up the system and go. Certainly he sees no reason to do so around the house. Unless, of course, you want to show it off to your kids. One day a friend helped him set up the system in their garage. The boys ran around, watching, not quite sure what all

Derek and Maura Herrera shortly after the birth of their twins, Hunter and Hudson, in July 2017.

the gadgetry was for and why their dad was putting it on. Hunter's attention was elsewhere, focused on a plastic T. rex. Hudson was making his way through a stack of cardboard boxes in the garage. And then, without fanfare, without saying a word, Derek stood. Strong, staring straight ahead smiling. Hudson was first to gasp in delight.

"Whoa! Daddy, you're *tall*!" Hudson exclaimed. "You're *walking*." And then both boys circled their father, curious and captivated. Derek took a few steps, beaming all the while. And yet moments later back in his wheelchair, the boys saw their father no differently. He was just Daddy, whether standing or sitting.

"I see them as empathetic kids, and I see them as nice and kind and understanding and patient," Maura said. "And how could you not be, when you grow up in a household where you get that lens? Derek and I didn't get that lens until we were older, but now they look at the world like, '*Dad, this way, the ramp's over here.*' They get to see the world differently. And I think they're lucky for it."

Derek himself still has moments when the reality of his physical limitations brings him down. Days when he gets frustrated and angry. But those days and feelings are rare now. Gratitude seems always to prevail. Gratitude, above all, to have Maura, Hunter, and Hudson by his side.

"For a while you think about what's been taken from you, and you have this victim mindset," he said. "*I was a special operator. I was at the pinnacle in my career. I was doing all this stuff, and if only I hadn't been injured.* But maybe if I didn't get injured that day, the next week I would have been killed."

"Nothing has slowed him down," Maura told me. "I mean, he did two startups, and we had twin babies, and I've got to tell you, the reason why, mentally, I am in such a good space is because he is. And with our boys—he can't do everything the same, but he still gets on the ground and wrestles with the boys, doesn't miss out on anything like that, and it's really, really helpful."

Like so many in Derek's life now, I did not know him before the firefight in Helmand Province. But in the decade since we first met I have marveled at his devotion to family, his resilience, and the extraordinary example he and Maura set for others, especially fellow veterans. I watched him along with thousands of others speak before a packed New York City crowd at my friends Lee and Bob Woodruff's annual Stand Up for Heroes fundraiser back in 2014. And "Stand Up" was exactly what Derek wanted to do, once again strapping on the ReWalk exoskeleton. After a brief introduction, Derek emerged from backstage in suit and tie, Maura a step behind. The audience rose in support, with thunderous applause marking Derek's every step. As he looked into the crowd, focusing on the front rows where dozens of wounded vets were sitting, his gratitude and humility were clear.

"I'd like to say that in the company of you all, I'm average," he said. "And I say that because the people in these first rows—all these soldiers, sailors, airmen, and Marines—have sacrificed incredibly and put their lives on the line to protect this country.

"I also say that I'm average in the company of this room, because each and every one of you are dealing with challenges, and you're presented, or will be presented at some point in your life, to deal with trauma and loss, and through that unbearable suffering and incredible pain, you'll confront that obstacle and move forward. And for me, I'm on this stage tonight, I think, because I just have a very visible manifestation of that. But what I'd say is that I truly believe that each and every one of you are no different than me, and that you have the resolve and fortitude to handle those situations honorably and make your family and everyone proud."

He spoke with no notes, and finished with an answer to the question he asked himself so often: How best to live a life that has been so permanently altered?

"Go home and be a beacon of inspiration," he said. "Take action and inspire others into action. It doesn't always have to be money. Organize your community. Volunteer. Coach a Little League team. Do something, anything to show your veterans that you care, and you're vested and you care about seeing this country succeed."

Or, he might have added, *Go start a company that will help millions of people and make their daily lives easier.*

"Because now more than ever, that's what our veterans need," he said. "And this nation needs."

The crowd roared. Again.

Lieutenant Charles Wickware at Lemoore Naval Air Station in March 2019.

CHAPTER 6

Wingnut

Charles Wickware

THERE WAS NO MOONLIGHT BOUNCING OFF THE DARK waters of the Pacific and only a faint glow coming from the massive aircraft carrier when Navy Lieutenant Charles Wickware attempted his first nighttime landing, or "trap," just off the coast of San Diego. Several miles from the ship, Wickware was trying to steady himself as he watched his buddy in the fighter jet in front of him on his final approach or "short final." It was challenging enough to touch down on a moving runway by day, but darkness made it even more difficult, and on this night rough seas were causing the flight deck to heave, pitch, and roll.

Aircraft carriers steam straight ahead, but the 300-foot runway is angled to the left, with only about 140 feet suitable for landing. The angle means that from the pilot's perspective, the runway appears to be shifting to the right, so the approach requires constant correction. Pilots rely on "trapping" one of three or four wires on deck with a tailhook, which brings them to an abrupt halt. They have to increase the throttle to full power on touchdown, in case they miss the wires and have to get airborne again.

Over the radio, Wickware could hear his friend calmly "call the ball," meaning he could see the moving light with its optical landing signals and could line up his "glide slope" to the flight deck. If a pilot is unable to see the ball, a Landing Signal Officer or LSO will guide the pilot to the ship in a move known as a talk down.

Seconds after that reassuring transmission, Wickware heard the LSO's "bloodcurdling" shout over the radio: *"Power!! Power!! Wave off!! Wave off!! Wave off!!"* Stunned, Wickware looked at the ship, fearing he would see a massive ball of fire. Instead, he watched his friend throttle up and roar away from the deck, just moments from a potential catastrophe.

Lieutenant Wickware was up next. The twenty-five-year-old pilot had no time to steady his nerves and shake off the failed attempt he had just witnessed. One mile out from the carrier, he had the ship in sight, its deck, some sixty feet above the surface of the ocean, still rolling in the chop. At three-quarters of a mile, he was told to "call the ball." He checked his fuel and looked to the carrier.

It had completely disappeared. No ball, no boat. Gone. Nothing but darkness. "What the???" he thought. "Why would they turn the lights off? Is this some night vision procedure that I missed in training?" Then he realized what was happening, and it was not good. The carrier had just driven into a fogbank and vanished. The only light Wickware could see was the reflection of his jet off the thick clouds onto the water two hundred feet below.

"*Clara!*" Wickware hollered into his radio. It was the term used by Navy pilots if they can't see the ball. That transmission was quickly followed by Wickware saying, "*Clara ship*," meaning he couldn't see the carrier either. In fact, he couldn't see anything. Nor could anyone on deck see him. Wickware stopped his descent and began leveling his jet to prepare for the wave off. No way were they going to try to talk him down in this fog on his very first attempt at a night landing. "That would be crazy," he thought.

But then, in the next few seconds, a transmission came through from the deck: "Paddles contact—continue." It was the LSO telling him the crew on deck could make out his lights through the fog and planned to talk him down.

"Wait, what?" was all Wickware could think. "They actually expect me to bring this thing down in zero visibility?" Maybe the LSO could see *him*, but he was still flying blind. He had begun to level off his jet, but now the LSO wanted him back on the glide slope. Socked in the clouds, his left hand clutching the throttle, Wickware started nosing the jet back down until he heard the confirmation: "Paddles contact, you're a little high; work it down." A fleeting second to lower the nose, followed by another transmission as he closed in on the ship, the same urgent command his buddy had heard: *"Power!! Power!! Wave off!! Wave off!! Wave off!!"*

Wickware thrust the throttle forward and pushed the jet upward. His descent had been too steep. Climbing through the dense fog, he briefly saw a blur of light from the ship's control tower off his right wingtip. He never saw the deck itself. All he could think was, "This is insane."

But he was not done yet. More to the point, the LSOs—all pilots themselves—were not done with him. They told him to circle back and prepare to land again. Another attempt, another failure. After that, there would be no more tries for Wickware that evening. He was sent back to the North Island Naval Air Station in Coronado, a "divert" where he could easily touch down on the runway. It was the one night in his career when Lieutenant Charles Wickware thought, "I don't know if I'm cut out for this."

Young Charles Wickware with his father, Jared, who also served in the Navy, and his aunt Margaret Noble.

Few would have guessed that Jared and Connie Wickware would raise a fighter pilot. Both were artists, and everyone in their extended family had some connection to the arts. Connie's father was a sculptor and physician, and Jared's mother was in advertising. Jared spent twenty-six years in the Navy, but his career had little to do with war fighting. He served as an illustrator/draftsman on board ship, assigned to paint murals and design newsletters. After the Navy, Jared became an accomplished printmaker and engraver. His wife, Connie, majored in fine art at Berkeley and eventually became a painter and an art teacher. Charles inherited a keen artistic sense of his own. From an early age, he showed an aptitude for drawing, and he became an avid painter and illustrator, though his art would eventually focus on aircraft and flying. "People paint what they're interested in," his mother reflected.

There were no aviators in the family, but in 1969 Jared was aboard the USS *Princeton* when it recovered the Apollo 10 spacecraft from the Pacific Ocean after its moon orbit. The astronauts spent four hours on the ship greeting the crew. Two decades later, he got an assignment that would change his son's life. In 1990, Jared was serving as the illustrator aboard the USS *Enterprise,* an aircraft carrier stationed in Norfolk, Virginia. He brought Connie and seven-year-old Charles to a "Dependents' Cruise," a day when Navy families get an up-close look at what life is like on the carrier, with the bonus of a Naval air show at sea.

Jared, Connie, and little Charles boarded the USS *Enterprise* in Norfolk, alongside dozens of sailors with their spouses and children. The original *Top Gun* movie had hit theaters a few years prior, so the lore of the swaggering pilots in their fighter jets was baked into American culture. Charles was too young to have seen the movie, but he was about to witness the real thing. Huddled together on the flight deck, Jared hoisted his son on his shoulders so he could get a better view. Charles vividly remembers being perched on his father's shoulders and hearing the deep growl of a pair of approaching F-14s. Transfixed, he watched the fighter jets streak over the ship and roar up and away. The deck rumbled, and everyone erupted in a collective shriek.

Charles stared up at the sky long after the jets had passed. What he could not fathom was the idea that human beings were operating those supersonic jets. Leaning down to his father's ear, he asked, "Were there people in there? Is that a job people do?" Jared smiled at his son and said, "Yes, and it is awesome." And that was that. Charles had only one more thing to say to his father: "I want to do that."

Six years later, at thirteen, Charles took his first flight lesson. Connie had tried to talk her only child out of flying, but she soon gave up. Jared's Navy job had taken the family to Hawaii, but Charles had little interest in surfing. He just wanted to fly. From the day he watched those Navy fighter jets, he was obsessed. At the suggestion of a friend of his father's, he joined the Hawaii Civil Air Patrol, a volunteer organization that con-

Charles Wickware, age fourteen, in his Civil Air Patrol flight suit in Honolulu, Hawaii, in 1997. He was already flying gliders and taking powered flight lessons.

ducts search and rescue missions and carries out disaster relief but also promotes STEM and aviation careers for young people.

It was through the Civil Air Patrol that Charles was introduced to gliders, the unpowered aircraft towed by a wire and released into the skies. It would be his first piloting experience. Barely a teenager, with few controls to maneuver and staying aloft by natural forces alone, Charles learned the natural mechanics of flying, floating silently through the clouds over Oahu's North Shore. By fourteen, he was able to fly a glider solo. It seemed to him like art come to life.

The stretch of horizon before him, the blue sky surrounding him, created a sense of serenity he had not experienced before. He was at home in the air. It was where he belonged. Despite his mother's initial apprehension, Charles's parents were supportive of his dreams and paid for his flying lessons. By the time he was sixteen, he had a pilot's license and a plan. He wasn't going to be just *any* Navy pilot. He was going to be "the coolest badass pilot you could be." And he got an unexpected training course to set him on his way.

On a visit to a Macworld Expo, Jared noticed an F-18 Hornet video game for sale. It was the jet that was replacing the F-14. Jared figured it was something Charles might like. *Did he ever.* No gift could have pleased him more. The game was designed by an F-18 pilot, and in Charles's recollection, "It was pretty darn accurate."

Night after night, Charles would switch off the lights in his bedroom and sit in the dark playing fighter pilot. The game allowed him to simulate F-18 carrier landings and air-to-air combat, all with the appropriate symbology from the aircraft, including the radar screen and the sounds a pilot would hear. One tone signaled that his plane's heat-seeking missile locked onto another plane in a dogfight. He was learning a ton about flying an F-18, but to the dismay of his parents, he was learning little about anything else.

"I'd go in there, and he'd have his little controller in his hand when he was supposed to be doing his history homework," Connie remembers. "One time, I grabbed it out of his hand, and he said, 'Mom, you just made me crash the jet!'" Charles tried to convince his parents that playing the F-18 video game would help him someday fly a real jet. Fair enough, but his parents made it very clear he wasn't going to be flying jets *at all* if he didn't start studying. He got the message.

After graduating from Moanalua High School in Honolulu with what his mother described as "OK" grades, he was accepted at Embry-Riddle Aeronautical University in Prescott, Arizona. His application was boosted by the fact that he had his pilot's license and Civil Air Patrol experience. He studied aeronautical science while continuing his flight lessons. On 9/11, he remembers leaving the gym and hearing about the attacks. He spent the rest of the day watching the aftermath. He knew then that a Navy career was likely to involve combat: "Once 9/11 happened, that was part of the deal."

There was no Navy ROTC program available, but through a friend he learned about the Navy's Baccalaureate Degree Completion Program, offering the opportunity of an active-duty enlistment and an implicit guarantee of pilot training after graduation. It was a highly competitive program, but Charles qualified, and he was soon on the way to a career in the Navy. Following college, he went through a ten-week Officer Candidate School (OCS) at the Naval Air Station in Pensacola, Florida, and in January 2006 he was commissioned as a Naval officer.

Normally, a drill sergeant would give the newly commissioned officer a first salute. But standing in uniform beside Charles at the ceremony, a teary-eyed Jared Wickware raised a right hand to salute his now six-four son.

Navy flight training followed, and at each step, Wickware excelled. From water survival to what they jokingly called redneck parasailing, where the trainee straps on a parachute and is hooked onto a truck until the vehicle is moving fast enough to send him airborne. Once the parachute reaches altitude, the trainee is released. The landing is hard, but that is the idea. The students quickly learn the proper way to roll so they don't break a leg.

Wickware, the not-so-studious high school student, consistently ranked at the top of his flight training classes. "I didn't dare tell my classmates that I had already learned a lot from a video game!" he recalls.

But he loved rubbing it in to his parents. "I told them it would pay off!" he joked.

The real payoff was that he graduated at the top of his class in primary flight school, allowing him to pick the aircraft he wanted to fly. Otherwise, like the other young officers, he would only be able to rank his choice of aircraft and hope for the best: "I didn't want to be flying helicopters or cargo planes, so my goal was always to finish first."

There was no question what Wickware would choose. It would be an F-18, the jet he had practiced flying since that video game captivated him as a kid. He opted for the single-seat F/A-18 Super Hornet, the Navy's premier fighter jet at the time. In April 2010, having completed his years of flight training, he was officially attached to one of the Navy's strike fighter squadrons, VFA 137. The patch on his flight suit would bear the logo of the squadron's nickname, The Kestrel, a North American falcon.

Every pilot is given a call sign, and outside of the movies, few of them are flattering. I've met Chimpo and Puff, Shawarma and Johnny Kittens. The call sign is a way to check oversized egos and level the playing field. Wickware received his call sign shortly after joining the squadron. He was a wingman in a large thirty-jet air-to-air combat exercise with the Air Force. He had been assigned to the blue team—the good guys—fighting against the "enemy" red team. Wickware was not familiar with many of the advanced tactics in this war fighting exercise, but he figured aggression was key and he was ready to "shoot down" any red jet he encountered. His F-18 was darting in and out, simulating missile launch after missile launch and claiming kill after kill.

"I was far off the tactical reservation, firing missiles at everyone and flying where no one was expected to be," said Wickware.

Once the exercise was complete, the air-to-air fight was replayed on a huge screen to debrief the pilots so they could learn from the exercise. Wickware's blue jet could be seen all over the place, attacking in and out of the swarm of red jets. A confused senior officer who was conducting the debrief paused the tape and looked around the room. "Whose nutty wingman is this?" she asked. From that day forward, Charles Wickware would forever be known to his fellow aviators as Wingnut.

Over the next few years, he would perfect his carrier landings, including the challenging night traps that had terrified him during his early training. He still had a healthy respect for the danger pilots face when landing on a moving ship.

All pilots are trained to fight nerves, but perhaps it is the artist in Charles Wickware that gives him an extraordinary sense of calm. Even when his adrenaline is peaking, he manages to push fear out of his mind, and "just find the Zen." Aviators succeed by compartmentalizing, artists by immersing themselves in the task. Wickware seemed to do both. Before he'd get into his jet, he'd run his hands over it to "connect and send it good vibes."

"A lot of pilots will say they hate flying hundreds of miles out to sea at night," he muses, "but for me—and maybe there is something wrong with me—I find it quite relaxing." Surrounded by stars and the glow of the ships below, he was completely calm. He would carry that calm with him into war zones.

In 2010 Wickware, now twenty-seven, flew his first combat missions. His deployment to Afghanistan came nine years into the war. By then, the Pentagon was becoming more cautious about air strikes, with an aim to win "hearts and minds" rather than bomb potential hideouts. But the missions Wickware flew were intense and dangerous. He knew what he was doing could mean the difference between life and death for the American service members on the ground. He learned that lesson on day one.

It was late October when Wickware and a second F-18 pilot launched off the USS *Abraham Lincoln* from the Arabian Sea, crossing over Pakistan and into Afghanistan. Fighter jets always fly in pairs, to provide close air support. Meaning that if ground troops are in trouble, if their lives are at stake, the jet fighters can deliver firepower. Moments after the two jets entered Afghanistan, a breathless call came over the radio: *"Troops in contact! Troops in contact!"* It was a US military air controller on the ground, known as a JTAC, or Joint Terminal Attack Controller, letting the pilots know the ground troops were in an active firefight.

The JTAC was not only breathless; he was running for his life. Wickware could hear the crack of gunfire in the background, and frantic voices yelling, "A couple of guys have been hit!" He gave the pilots the coordinates to guide them to the target. Wickware and his wingman made sure they knew exactly where the good guys and the bad guys were located, hyper focusing on the correct coordinates. "The worst possible thing you can imagine as a pilot is possibly killing one of your own guys," Wickware said.

Flying a single-seat fighter jet without a back seat weapons officer, Wickware had to do everything himself, from checking his fuel and weapons to programming the navigation. Once over the target, he switched on his Forward-Looking Infrared (FLIR) camera and readied his targeting pod. He was stunned by the clarity of what he saw. Even from miles away, he could see three Taliban fighters lying prone on the ground, firing heavy machine guns at the Americans. The image was so clear on his cockpit screen he could see the shells pop out, and the grass ripple when the bullets tore through it. The Taliban were so close to the US forces it was far too dangerous for the fighter jets to drop bombs, so Wickware and his wingman rolled in low and fast and strafed the Taliban position with their twenty-millimeter guns, taking out all three of the enemy.

It was the first time Wickware, the artist who loved to fly, had killed anyone. But this was also the first time he said he knew what it was like to "see red." He felt an overwhelming anger that someone was trying to harm the American forces he was there to protect. He knew then that his calling involved much more technical prowess. "I could hear the desperation in their voices," he recalls. "Their lives were depending on us, and there's nothing I wouldn't do to help those guys out."

At times, even strafing was not an option, given the proximity of civilians or friendly forces. The F-18s would be called in for a "show of force"—a violent aerial intimidation meant to send the Taliban running. The pilots would fly as low and fast as possible, popping flares along the way. On one of those missions, with US forces under fire in the dark, Wickware and his wingman donned night vision goggles, streaking just a few hundred feet above a canyon floor—muzzle flashes lighting up the mountains around them. The American ground forces knew the jets were coming, the Taliban did not. Ten miles out, five miles, one mile, and then *boom!* A burst of supersonic thunder as the jets roared over the Taliban position, blowing up dust, rocks, and likely a few enemy eardrums. "They got the message," said Wickware. "'We know exactly where you are.'"

Wickware's squadron was flying missions to Afghanistan off the carrier every day. The USS *Lincoln* was home to more than five thousand sailors and dozens of fighter jets, transport, and surveillance and reconnaissance planes. Given the distance to Afghanistan from the ship and the amount of time the F-18s spent providing air support to the ground troops, every mission meant at least eight hours in the skies.

Fighter jets have small fuel tanks, so the missions always required a midair refueling—one of the most difficult and dangerous maneuvers in aviation next to landing on a carrier. Tens of thousands of feet in the air, moving hundreds of miles an hour, the pilots have to link up with a tanker aircraft, essentially a flying gas station. The F-18 is equipped with a retractable probe near the right side of the cockpit. The tanker dangles a fuel line behind it with a basket at the end to connect to the F-18's probe. The fighter jet has to move in perilously close to the tanker at precisely the same speed and stick the probe directly into the bouncing basket. Once the connection is made, the fueling begins.

While the missions themselves were intense, there were long periods of time when Wickware was just waiting, circling, flying over the rugged mountains, keeping an eye on what was happening below. He was at the upper height limit for a fighter pilot, cramped in his cockpit seat, day after day, with a thermos of cappuccino, a few sandwiches, and a "piddle pack" to relieve himself.

The same high-resolution infrared camera that helped him target the Taliban connected him to the world below: the mud huts, the shepherds tending sheep, the children in schoolyards and families huddled together around small fires for an evening meal. He took note of these things, kept them in his memory. Flying over a patch of southern Afghanistan one evening, Wickware spotted a lone, robed figure in the courtyard of a small home. It was a woman clutching a broom, gently sweeping dried leaves and mud. As he watched, a cat sidled up to her and she crouched down to pet it.

Wickware was struck by the sheer domesticity of the scene. It could have been any house, any woman, anywhere. Outside, under the stars, she had no idea that an American pilot thousands of feet overhead was watching her. In such moments, the artist in Wickware would emerge—the attention to detail, the ability to find beauty in the ordinary. There was another world down there, with people engaged in their everyday lives, even as he orbited overhead. He would think of that moment often as a sort of touchstone during his deployments, determined as he was not to let his missions become so abstract and remote that he forgot why he was there.

He spoke often of the beauty he saw while flying: the blue waters of the Arabian Sea, the dusty towns and busy cities of Pakistan, the forested and rocky terrain of Afghanistan's Hindu Kush mountains. He took in the skies around him, the sun and clouds and stars, the burning reds and yellows of the sunsets, the sharp edges of a clear horizon. He wanted to remember it all. A GoPro camera was tucked into his flight bag, which he began attaching to his jet during flight. He was soon turning the videos into short films to share with fellow aviators and with his family.

That first deployment ended in March 2011, after seven months of combat missions. The USS *Lincoln* would head back to California, with a stop in Hawaii on the way, a stop that would bring a full circle moment

Armed with cameras, Charles Wickware captures his love of flying to inspire others, 2019.

for the family. Many of the five thousand sailors on board the *Lincoln* got off the ship in Honolulu, choosing to spend their post-deployment leave time in Hawaii. That left a lot of unoccupied space for the final leg of the cruise. The Navy allowed Wickware and other sailors and pilots to invite family members to join them for the four-day journey to California. Jared and Connie jumped at the chance.

In 1990, when Charles had boarded the USS *Enterprise* with his parents for "Dependents' Cruise," he was the dependent. Two decades later, he was returning the favor—his parents were the dependents on a Navy cruise where their son would be a star attraction.

When Charles first headed to Afghanistan, Connie had erected a small shrine at home dedicated to their son. "It was more of an artsy thing," she said. While she described herself as not particularly religious, the shrine consisted of figurines of Jesus with a child on his shoulders, winged angels, prayer cards, and a tiny glass seahorse near a dark amber votive where she kept a candle burning. The light from the flame illuminated a nearby photograph of Charles standing next to his fighter jet.

"He was in God's hands." Charles Wickware's mother, Connie, made a shrine to help her get through his deployments. She still keeps it today.

No F-18 had been shot down in combat since 1991, but the shrine helped her stay strong: "He had a dangerous job, but I eventually got to the point where I was not going to ruin my life worrying. I just have to trust. He was in God's hands. Somehow that little shrine helped me."

The "Tiger Cruise," a much-extended version of the Dependents' Day cruise, would take place over four days at sea. Charles showed his parents everything he could on the ship. The first day, on the flight deck, he helped them don the safety vests, earplugs, and helmets required to watch the flight operations. "He got us access to spots to watch the jets where you normally couldn't go," Connie said. "He's an officer with an attitude and he likes to push boundaries."

Geared up in his flight suit, Charles escorted his parents to the end of the carrier, where the F-18s were launching and landing just yards away. The power of those jets is so great that flight deck personnel are in danger of being blown overboard. For the first time, Connie and Jared were

Lieutenant Charles Wickware hosting his parents, Jared and Connie, for a "Tiger Cruise" on board the USS Abraham Lincoln *as it transited from Honolulu, Hawaii, to California in March 2011. They are standing in front of the jet he flew in combat.*

able to watch their son launch from a ship. When Charles did a low-level flyby a few minutes later, just like those pilots who had inspired him as a boy, his parents hugged each other and smiled.

Once they were back in California, it wasn't long before Wickware began to prepare for a second combat deployment aboard the same carrier running similar close air support missions over Afghanistan. Like the first tour, the missions this time were mostly defensive. Earlier that year, Osama bin Laden had been located and killed in Pakistan. The United States was now trying to scale back offensive operations. If US or allied ground troops in Afghanistan were in trouble, Wickware and his fellow pilots brought in the firepower to help them out. But they avoided targeting the Taliban or its leaders unless they were actively attacking US or allied forces. This meant that to an even greater extent than on his first mission, Wickware and his fellow pilots spent a good deal of time waiting.

2011 was the year the last US forces pulled out of Iraq. "After nearly nine years," President Barack Obama declared in a White House address, "America's war in Iraq will be over." It turned out that was wishful thinking. The war was not over, and Charles Wickware would soon see some of the fiercest fighting he had ever witnessed.

The Islamic State in Iraq and Syria, or ISIS, as it was known, launched a major offensive from Syria into Iraq in June 2014, after the withdrawal of US troops. Horrific images of beheadings—including of Americans—and public hangings were flooding the news. Shiites, Christians, and Yazidis were being slaughtered, the Iraqi Army was suffering massive casualties, and a Jordanian fighter pilot who was forced to eject from his F-16 over Syria was caged and burned alive by ISIS while their cameras recorded video. Some 40 percent of Iraq was occupied by ISIS, stretching from the Syrian border to the outskirts of Baghdad. Terrorist groups in the Middle East and Africa were declaring their allegiance, and ISIS operatives were murderously intent on hitting Western countries.

By August 2014, President Obama was ready to send troops back into the fight, ordering US air strikes on Iraq and sending military advisers to Baghdad. In October, the US military launched Operation Inherent Resolve, aimed squarely at the destruction of ISIS. US forces were back in combat.

Lieutenant Wickware was tracking all of this from the Naval Air Station in Lemoore, California. Since returning from Afghanistan, he had been given "shore duty" and was working as an F/A-18 instructor, passing on lessons from his time in Afghanistan. But he was well aware the fight against ISIS was expanding.

He was halfway through a three-year assignment when the commanding officer from one of the strike fighter squadrons based at Lemoore gave him a call. "Hey," he said, "would you like to come out on a deployment with us?" Wickware did not hesitate. He would head back to the Persian Gulf, this time to patrol the skies over Iraq and Syria in what would be some of the most active flying of his career. US pilots were now on the offensive.

The stakes in this fight and the importance of the mission were even higher than in Afghanistan. While Wickware was on his way to the Gulf, in November 2015, ISIS terrorists launched coordinated attacks in Paris, killing more than 130 people, including 90 at a concert venue. ISIS was expanding its scope, and the United States and the rest of the Western world were trying to stop them.

The operations against ISIS were more strategic by design, aimed at weakening the group's capabilities. In Afghanistan, Wickware and his fellow pilots were acutely aware of the need to avoid civilian casualties, given the importance of winning "hearts and minds." The fight against ISIS was different. While still wary of hitting civilians, Wickware was soon dropping two-thousand-pound bombs on a regular basis.

The largest share of the missions were pre-planned, directed at targets identified through aerial surveillance or intelligence gathered from headquarters or troops on the ground. Among the targets were ISIS supply lines, ISIS fighters, and factories where Improvised Explosive Devices—the deadly IEDs—were being built. Wickware felt for the first time that he was "at the tip of the nation's spear."

He was flying five or six days a week, up to eight hours a day, and waiting to be "cleared hot" to hit a target almost every day he was launched off the ship.

US drones piloted from a secret command center were in the skies constantly looking for ISIS hideouts. The drones would track suspected fighters for days at a time, and when they were certain the targets were ISIS they would call in the F-18 pilots to blow them up.

Wickware was well aware that the ordnance he was dropping was killing people. From the moment he watched the World Trade Towers crumble in college, he knew that "killing bad guys" would be part of the job. He felt that the Taliban in Afghanistan and ISIS fighters in Iraq and Syria were legitimate targets, and he never hesitated to take out anyone attacking Americans. But he always sought to keep a perspective on his missions: "As a pilot, there's a level of detachment from what you're doing. But I've tried to treat it with reverence. You have some military guys with a warhead-on-forehead mentality, and they're all about that. I've always thought it's a serious matter. That's someone's kid; that's someone's parent. While perhaps a necessary evil, it's never something to celebrate, no matter who they are."

It was on this third deployment, in March of 2016, aboard the aircraft carrier USS *Harry S. Truman,* that I first met Lieutenant Charles Wickware. I had been on the ground in Baghdad in June of 2014 when ISIS first stormed into Iraq. For days we could hear gunfire outside our hotel and feared that the city would be overrun. ISIS flyers were dropped throughout Baghdad warning that the terror group was on its way. I watched Iraqi men of all ages crowd into open trucks and head north to try to stop the advance. They had no weapons and no training. I couldn't imagine many of them would made it back alive. But in recent months, it was clear that US airstrikes against ISIS had made a significant difference. I returned frequently to the region to report on the terror group, but I wanted to see the air operations up close. I flew with my crew on a Navy Sea Stallion helicopter out of Bahrain to the *Truman* to get a firsthand look at Operation Inherent Resolve. By then, nearly two years into the fight, US and allied aircraft had carried out close to eleven thousand air strikes, 80 percent of them by US pilots. But the fight was far from over.

The flight out to the ship, crossing the blue waters of the Persian Gulf, took well over an hour. I had done tailhook landings on aircraft carriers numerous times. Landing in a helicopter was far less dramatic. But once on the flight deck, we saw F-18s and surveillance aircraft launching and landing nonstop.

Commanders on the *Truman* had asked for volunteers to be interviewed on the ship, and Wickware and Lieutenant Commander John Hiltz both raised their hands. Hiltz, a seasoned fighter pilot and former member of the Blue Angels, the Navy's famed demonstration squadron, was naturally outgoing and naturally competitive, like Wickware. When I walked into the ready room to meet the two towering pilots, Hiltz pointed out that at six-five, he was taller than Wickware and outranked him. "Not by much and not by much," Wickware quickly shot back with a smile. Both were eager to talk about their missions against ISIS.

On the day we met, the plan was for Hiltz and Wickware to launch

Martha Raddatz with Lieutenant Charles Wickware on board the USS Harry S. Truman *in the Persian Gulf as the United States targeted the terrorist group ISIS, March 2016.*

from the ship, fly to Syria, and strike a critical oil pipeline in ISIS-controlled territory. A disruption of the oil pipeline would have a significant impact on ISIS's financial capability. US intelligence officials at that point were estimating that ISIS was earning as much as $2 million per day in an illegal oil trade, siphoning from fields in Iraq and Syria and selling at below market rates.

It was supposed to be a daytime strike, and we had planned to place a GoPro camera inside the cockpit to record what we could of the mission. Wickware was way ahead of us. His passion for shooting video and producing short films had only grown since he first started carrying a camera on his missions in Afghanistan. He was determined to record the mission from start to finish—the launch off the ship, the refueling, the moment the bombs were dropped, and the landing on the carrier when they returned. A true pilot's eye view of an air strike. There was only one problem: The day mission turned into a night mission. That is when his creative streak saved the story.

Since my team didn't have the equipment to shoot night video in the jet, Wickware grabbed an extra pair of night vision goggles and fashioned what he called Frankenstein goggles, duct-taping two GoPro cameras to the lenses, one focused outside the jet and the other focused tightly inside the cockpit.

For all the last-minute preparation, there was one more challenging element—the weather. Seconds apart, Hiltz and Wickware launched off the carrier. The shuttle connected to the jet's nose gear yanked the F-18s down the track and accelerated the aircraft from 0 to 165 mph in just three seconds. One by one, the jets disappeared into the darkness on the way to Syria, no moonlight or stars above.

What *was* above them were heavy storms across their planned route. Sheets of lightning came down all around the jets as they climbed through the clouds, rising to more than forty-three thousand feet. Given the distance from the ship to the targets, both jets needed to refuel before they could launch their weapons. Midair refueling is hard enough in the daylight in good weather. Refueling in poor conditions over hostile territory is one of the hardest things a pilot can do. It's even harder when one hand is flying the jet and the other holding a pair of night vision goggles rigged with cameras.

Hiltz was up first to refuel. The basket to which he needed to connect was bouncing wildly in the weather. Wickware was just behind him, taping the dramatic scene as Hiltz fought the turbulence while trying to attach his probe. Sharp bolts of lightning flashed dangerously close. Every minute spent trying to connect meant the fuel was running lower. Hiltz finally managed to connect his probe to the basket. As soon as his tank was topped off, Wickware approached, his jet bobbing through the choppy air as the basket whirled erratically. He could sense the ticking in his brain: "You're behind the tanker, and it's like the movies where they are trying to disarm a bomb, but in this case coming down to seconds before you could run out of gas and have to dump your aircraft in a war zone and try to find your way out of there alive." Like Hiltz, Wickware channeled all his energy into getting that lifeline of fuel, and in a matter of minutes he was on his way.

I waited on the carrier, getting updates whenever possible throughout the mission. Six long hours would pass before the pilots returned after successfully striking the ISIS pipeline. Hiltz and Wickware were able to dip below the clouds, locate and identify a gas flame at a pressure relief point in the pipeline, and drop their bombs simultaneously. "We got the results we wanted," Hiltz told me. And Wickware had the video to prove it. It was all there, from the moment the F-18 hurled off the carrier, to the perilous midair refueling, to the bombing and finally the landing. And it was all extraordinary. Wickware had aimed the GoPro at the "pickle"—the red button that releases the ordnance—as he counted down, "Three, two, one, pickle," to the weapons launch. This was far beyond gimmicky shots from a fighter jet to show off in a bar over a few beers. He had a deep desire to share all the things he saw, day in and day out, things most people would never see or experience. And for me, it provided perfect images to tell the story.

Between his near-daily missions over Syria and Iraq and his previous deployments to Afghanistan, Wickware had accrued hundreds of combat hours, experienced those sudden jolts of bad weather over hostile territory, and managed the delicate and crucial work of aerial refueling. But the mission that turned out to be the most harrowing had little to do with the enemy below.

Nearing the end of his 2016 deployment on the USS *Harry S. Truman*, Wickware and his wingman were again launching nighttime strikes on ISIS, this time targeting a hideout in northern Syria. Both fighter jets were loaded with a two-thousand-pound bomb on each wing, the largest bombs the F-18 can carry. Bombs that size cause catastrophic destruction, flattening buildings and leaving craters forty feet in diameter. The wingman released his bombs first, hurling them into the target. Wickware double-checked his coordinates and launched as well. But a message immediately flashed in the cockpit, warning that one of Wickware's bombs was "hung and unlocked." One of his bombs had hit the target, but the second live bomb was still under the wing of his jet, not yet released, and not fully attached. Hoping the message was an error, Wickware tried to peer out the cockpit to see for himself. But it was too dark, and he couldn't get a clear view under his wing.

Then he felt the thudding and heard the clanking with each movement of the aircraft. The bomb with which he had intended to blow up a building was now banging on the side of his jet.

Guiding the F-18 into a slow turn south, Wickware was headed back to the ship. With the sun now reaching for the horizon, he radioed ahead for an airborne inspection from a tanker that was circling near the carrier. The tanker pilot, a Texas native with the call sign Yokel, moved closer to Wickware's fighter jet to inspect the wing, and then quickly broke away. "Dude," he said to Wickware with an unmistakable southern drawl. "You got a bomb hanging off your wing."

Bombs connect to a jet with two lugs, or connection points, in the front and back. The front connection point had released, but the back one had jammed. The bomb was half off, half on. Landing on the carrier was out of the question. The violence of a tailhook landing risked blowing up not only the plane and its pilot but a chunk of the carrier and hundreds of sailors on board. Wickware talked to the ship's officers about how to get the bomb off the wing or "emergency jettison" the weapon. He was told to go out over open water and try to release the bomb into the ocean.

Wickware climbed back up through the clouds, far from the carrier to a safe spot over water to drop. He tried each procedure, followed all the instructions, but the bomb did not budge.

Since there was no way he could attempt a carrier landing, he diverted to Kuwait, the nearest airfield where he could try to land without blowing himself up.

"Focus. Focus," was all he could think. He wiggled his toes and fingers to keep calm. Steady on the throttle, soaring over the deserts to avoid populated areas, in case the bomb suddenly unlocked, he radioed the air traffic control tower in Kuwait to tell them he was heading their way and alert them to the emergency.

"Hey, I'm coming in," Wickware said. "I've got partially released ordnance that's hanging off my wing. I'm not sure about the status." Every alarm bell went off in the mind of the controller. "You've got what?" he said. "You've got a bomb off your wing?"

The airport controller cleared a runway and called in an explosives team. Commanders on the carrier were also dispatching a bomb squad from the ship to be in place when Wickware arrived.

As he neared the airport, he could see the bright lights of the sirens on the emergency vehicles dotting the runway. Slowing the fighter jet down on final approach, he could see the bomb was drooping even farther as his airspeed decreased. By now it was hanging so far down he feared it would hit the runway and rip off. If that happened, his plan was to go "full afterburner," to roar away from the airfield and get as far away from the bomb as possible. That is, if he even survived the initial touchdown.

Taking a deep breath as the clanking of the errant ordnance grew louder, Wickware lowered his landing gear, set the jet down as gently as possible, and rolled down the runway. By the time he eased the F-18 to a stop, the loose bomb was just two inches from hitting the ground. Two inches from a potentially devastating explosion.

The explosive ordnance disposal (EOD) teams rushed out in their heavily padded suits to begin dismantling the live bomb. All Wickware could think, sitting in his cockpit, was, *Those suits aren't going to do anything if this blows up. It's a two-thousand-pounder.*

Together with an ordnance team that had flown in from the *Truman,* the bomb squad carefully disarmed the bomb by deactivating its igniter. Then a message came in from the ship, in what Wickware described as typical Navy fashion—"Hey, Wingnut, can you bring the jet back to the ship now?"

He had not slept in thirty-six hours. He had launched into the night, performed a midair refueling, helped destroy an ISIS hideout, flown back to the carrier to have the hanging bomb inspected, flown to Kuwait, and skillfully set down his F-18 with a live bomb on the wing without killing himself or anyone else. But he knew he had no choice but to follow orders. He headed back to the carrier exhausted yet exhilarated. "When you pull it off, there's an incredible rush of satisfaction," he said. "That's what I love."

By the time Charles Wickware finished his deployment for Operation Inherent Resolve, he had flown more than 350 combat hours and received numerous decorations for meritorious service. He was proud of his Navy service, but after returning to California, he had enormous decisions to make about his future. There was no way he was going to give up flying, but those carrier cruises had meant being away from his family and friends for eight or nine months at a time, and the prospect of finding a long-term relationship under those circumstances was daunting. He had to decide whether to make the Navy a lifelong career, or to find something else that would give his flying purpose while allowing him to find a partner and start the family he had always wanted.

In 2019, at thirty-six, Lieutenant Commander Charles Wickware made the difficult decision to leave active duty. He had served thirteen years in the Navy, flown more than two thousand hours in the F/A-18 Super Hornet, and completed 430 carrier landings. His next challenge was to somehow combine flying with family.

I have met a lot of pilots over the years—but I have never met a pilot who loves flying more than Charles Wickware. He is more at home cloud surfing than anywhere on land. It is not only the thrill of being airborne, but the love of what he sees and is sensing.

Some former military pilots take jobs with commercial airlines, but that wasn't for Wickware. "Pay-wise, it's great," he says. "The schedule is great. But as far as job satisfaction, that wasn't for me." What he wanted was to find some way of flying that would provide, in his words, "a pretty direct translation" of his experience as a fighter pilot. He found what he was looking for working as a military contractor flying foreign jets simulating "enemy" aircraft in training exercises with US military pilots. The exercises allow the military pilots to gain experience in simulated dogfights. Wickware had no trouble mastering Russian or Chinese aircraft, acting as an adversary pilot, and challenging Navy, Marine, and Air Force pilots flying modern US jets in air-to-air combat. It wasn't far off from the exercise that had earned him his call sign—Wingnut. But this time, instead of being on the home team, Wickware was flying as the "bandit" jet.

One of his favorite jets is the Hawker Hunter, a British fighter developed in the late 1940s and early 1950s, before computer-assisted systems simplified aviation. It has to be flown manually. "I feel like I should have a white scarf around my neck," he says. "When you're flying the Hunter, you're actually flying. It can be out of control in a matter of seconds if you don't constantly pay attention. You have to use every aspect of the flight controls."

Though he was now a civilian, many of the people with whom he flew were former fighter pilots like himself, including some he knew from his Navy days. He worked only about half the month, leaving him plenty of time to pursue other activities.

One of those was working with a company called Boom Supersonic at the Mojave Air and Space Port in California. Boom is developing the next supersonic airliner—a modern, more affordable successor to the Concorde. The company was testing a single-seat demonstration aircraft known as the XB-1, basically a way of showing that it had a prototype with the potential to be a full-fledged supersonic aircraft. Wickware's former commanding officer was one of the project's chief test pilots, and he asked him whether he'd be willing to be the LSO (Landing Signal Officer) for the X-B1 tests. So Wickware had been helping them develop landing and emergency procedures—important work for an aircraft that lands at such a high angle the pilot can't see the runway.

"I'm on the ground talking it down, like what happens on the carrier when the pilot can't see the ship," Wickware said. "You're trying to land this relatively, supersonic, slick aircraft with no peripheral or visuals. You really needed someone to talk the pilot down, give them height calls and give them direction if needed."

Later still, he worked as the test pilot for a company working to build hybrid electric aircraft. That job was particularly challenging, even for an aviator of his experience, simply because of the nature of test piloting: It meant that the aircraft hadn't been put through the wringer. That's what Wickware was doing.

"So there is a level of cautiousness and a level of danger, of unknown that exists with flying in the test world," he said. "You do what you can to mitigate that, and then also get yourself out if something does go wrong."

Even in his downtime, Wickware was all about flying. Once he settled in Fresno, he bought an RV-8, a two-seat aerobatic plane that he used to commute to his various jobs in Southern California. He picked it for the pure pleasure of flight.

Wickware's personal life also picked up after he left the Navy—and that wound up involving flying too. Becca Davenport, a clinical specialist in cardiology who lived near him in Fresno, was also a pilot. They spent weekends together in his RV-8, taking mini trips around the state.

He also found time to pursue his artistic interests, and began creating intricate and highly accurate drawings and paintings of planes for friends and people in his flying community. And he continued to produce jaw-dropping flight videos he would post on social media. "One of the greatest things was having guys who were younger and watched my videos," he said. "I've met a handful of people who said, '*Your videos inspired me to get in the Navy.*' Or if they were having a rough time going to flight school, they'd watch it to keep them going . . . and so I really love that.

"Or little kids—you know, *'my son wants to be a pilot,' 'my daughter wants to be a pilot from watching your stuff,'* hearing that is awesome."

In the fall of 2020 Charles helped Becca fulfill one of her own dreams. While she could pilot a single-engine propeller plane and joined him in his acrobatic flying, she had always wanted to fly in a fighter jet. At the time Wickware had also been flying for a private owner of several fighter jets and he gave Wickware the OK for Becca to join him on a quick flight. So on a gloriously sunny day in Southern California, Becca Davenport donned a flight suit, helmet, and oxygen mask and climbed in the back of an F-5. Wickware blasted off from the legendary Mojave Air and Space Port and, within minutes, hit Mach 1—supersonic speed. The thunderous crack of a sonic boom echoed through the valley as the jet shattered the sound barrier. For Becca, it was an indescribable thrill. A few weeks later, Charles and Becca learned that someone else had been along for that ride of a lifetime. Fittingly, little Margo Wickware experienced supersonic flight long before she was born.

Eight months later, on June 15, 2021, Margo Mae Wickware came into the world. On the day of her birth, Charles Wickware penned a letter to his baby girl, harkening back to his own childhood.

"When I was a child," he wrote, "there were two things I wished for—to be a fighter pilot, and to be a father. I can now say all my childhood dreams have come true. I have been through many chapters, seasons and adventures in my life but that true adventure is really just about to start. All my past failures and successes will pale in comparison to how I do as a father. Baby Margo—I promise to do my best for you and your mom—Love Dad."

That "best," of course, included flying. A "family plane" would soon be added—an RV-10 four-seater. Barely a few weeks old, Margo would regularly be strapped in a car seat behind her parents in the family plane. Pink headphones over her ears to protect her hearing, gazing out the window for hours.

"This is what we do," he says. "We fly everywhere." There were trips to the beach, last-minute lunch plans, or just a day of flight.

Becca and Charles never married. Both ended up finding happiness with new partners—but they remained close, committed to jointly par-

Charles Wickware with his three-year-old daughter Margo on board his RV-10 aircraft, flying to a camping spot with a runway in November 2023. They call it "flamping."

enting Margo. She is a bright, funny girl—the spitting image of her dad. Tall, intensely curious, and adventuresome. And, of course, she loves to draw and loves to fly.

On a spring day in 2024 at just three years old, Margo climbed into the back of her father's small two-seat aerobatic plane. Charles strapped her in tightly, her pink headphones now connected to the radio.

"Hey," he said. "Do you want to try and go upside down?" His daughter paused for just a moment and then said, "Yeah." So Wickware put his hand on the controls and did an acrobatic roll in the small plane, spinning the two of them upside down. Margo was quiet for a moment after the aerial spin. Once the plane was level, her dad asked, "How was that?"

He should have known what she would say. A moment later Wickware's little girl hollered, "*Again!*"

Charles Wickware was on cloud nine.

Navy pilot Danielle Thiriot in the cockpit of her F/A-18 Super Hornet on board the USS Carl Vinson *during its 2014–15 deployment in the fight against ISIS.*

CHAPTER 7

Trailblazers

Rosemary Mariner, Danielle Thiriot

THE RUMBLE OF THE JETS COMES BEFORE YOU SEE AND feel their power. Distant specks grow larger on approach, the roar builds, the earth seems to shake, and then they are there, four sleek aircraft thundering overhead—for a moment only—and gone. Three scream past in formation; the fourth veers sharply skyward. All in a matter of seconds.

In a war zone, flyovers get nods of gratitude from the troops they protect. When they come in over a stadium, the crowd might burst into cheers. But on a February day in 2019, we stood quietly as the F/A-18 Super Hornets neared, and watched solemnly as that single aircraft broke away, in what's known as a Missing Man formation, the aerial salute to honor a fallen comrade.

In this case, there were no missing men being honored, and no men doing the honoring. This aerial salute, in a quiet rural corner of Tennessee, was flown for Captain Rosemary Bryant Mariner, one of the Navy's first female tactical jet pilots, who had died at age sixty-five of ovarian cancer. The young aviators in the formation were her legacy. Up there in the winter sky, the Navy was performing its first-ever all-female flyover—eight women in four jets, streaking past a small cemetery as a color guard snapped to attention. It was a powerful tribute to the woman who had helped launch their careers. At the controls of that

Missing Man aircraft was thirty-four-year-old Lieutenant Commander Danielle Thiriot, the perfect steward of Rosemary's legacy.

Thiriot had met Rosemary only once but saw her as a mentor and an icon. I had known Rosemary for decades. In fact, she was one of the first women in the military I met when I began covering the Pentagon in the early 1990s. I am embarrassed to say that when I first saw her, pregnant and standing alone at a social gathering for Navy officers, I assumed she was the *wife* of an officer, and not an officer herself. I introduced myself and asked, "What's your connection to the military?" Her answer stunned me. "I am a Navy attack pilot," she said—with only the slightest of smiles. *Lesson learned.*

Rosemary had spent her life shattering stereotypes and preconceptions, and her story opened my eyes to the challenges women in the military were facing. We stayed in touch and became fast friends. When her daughter was born she was just a few years younger than my son, and Rosemary and I would often spend weekends together with the kids, whether at a neighborhood pool or wandering the Smithsonian's National Air and Space Museum.

Rosemary's career had been one of firsts. First woman to receive a degree in aeronautics from Purdue University. The first woman to fly a frontline tactical strike aircraft. First woman aviator assigned to an aircraft carrier—the USS *Lexington*. First woman to command a Navy aviation squadron. But the only "firsts" that mattered to her were those that opened doors for others, and the one door—the one opportunity she wanted for her fellow female aviators—was to fly in combat.

Back then, women were forbidden from flying combat missions or, in the Navy, from even being assigned to ships at sea. Female officers were not even allowed *on* a ship unless they were on leave, in civilian clothing, and were accompanied by a male officer. That left them unable to prove they could be equal to their male colleagues, and unable to advance in the Navy in the same way men could. Rosemary was one of six graduates of the Navy's first female flight training classes. They all earned their Wings of Gold, but they were grounded when it came to combat. Tammie Jo Shults, who gained prominence in 2018 after safely landing a crippled Southwest jet, with a passenger partially sucked out of a damaged window, earned her wings in 1987. She became a training officer under Rosemary's command in 1991 at Naval Air Station Lemoore. Shults told a reporter at the time, "I joined the military because I wanted to be a warrior and getting to fly what we have been trained to fly would be great."

Rosemary and the others were not seeking special treatment for women; they sought *equal* treatment and *equal* opportunity. It was Rosemary's belief that if women "cannot share the equal risks and hazards in arduous duty, then you are not equal."

Through tireless advocacy, countless appearances on Capitol Hill, and her own skill and relentless determination, she became a leading

Rosemary Mariner as an ensign preparing for a flight at Naval Air Station Oceana in 1975.

voice for change and was instrumental in striking down the laws that held women back.

The combat restriction on women flying in combat was finally lifted in 1993 thanks in large measure to Rosemary's efforts. The ability to accrue combat hours meant that female pilots would now have the same opportunity for advancement afforded to male pilots. It was too late for Rosemary Mariner, but thanks to her dogged persistence, young women would have opportunities she had only dreamed of.

It was this history that made the flyover in Tennessee so profoundly meaningful for me and for Rosemary's contemporaries watching from below. We knew how proud she would have been of these seasoned combat pilots—and how proud they were to be flying in her contrails. What we didn't know then was how hard they had had to fight to make that flyover possible.

Following the funeral services, all eight female aviators, still in their flight suits, gathered at the Mariner family farm. Rosemary's husband, Tommy, a retired Naval aviator himself, and their twenty-four-year-old daughter, Emmalee, crowded around them. This was where I met Lieutenant Commander Danielle Thiriot, who stood in the center of the group—five-nine, wearing a broad, confident smile. She'd been the catalyst for making the flyover happen. Thiriot, who regularly launched off aircraft carriers and bombed ISIS terrorists, seemed as proud of the flyover as anything she had done in her career. "I was the missing lady," she beamed, "and I made damn sure this flyover happened." For as much as Rosemary Mariner paved the way for women like Danielle Thiriot to succeed, there was no question they earned it.

Danielle Thiriot, like me, was raised in Salt Lake City, Utah, a non-Mormon in the Mormon heartland, just as I was. Despite the fact that she was Greek Orthodox, she had a Mormon-style upbringing: "We went out for ice-cream dates, and I don't think I drank or smoked, ever." What she loved was sports and school—excelling in soccer, basketball, academics, and like most of us raised in the Rocky Mountains she loved to ski. Her father, Paul, would plop her in a backpack as a baby and race down the mountains. She was doing it on her own by the time she was three years old.

Thiriot had just begun her junior year of high school on September 11, 2001. In the weeks after the attacks, she felt powerful tugs of emotion and patriotism, and goose bumps when the national anthem was played at high school games. She saw military service as a noble calling—her grandfather had been shot down over German-occupied Belgium just before D-Day—but she had never really thought about joining herself. And becoming a pilot? That had never entered her mind—ever. She was not that kid who stared skyward or longed for supersonic flight. Her eyes were on sports and academics.

In fact, it's hard to imagine that anyone has a how-I-became-a-Navy-pilot story to compare with Danielle Thiriot's—a journey that took her from Utah to Harvard to Wall Street and the South China Sea, and then on to the Persian Gulf and the war against ISIS.

The first step on her path began randomly. In the summer of 2002 she attended a seminar and rowing camp at the Naval Academy in Annapolis, Maryland, and was blown away by the quality of the instructors. "I thought they were Navy officers," she said. "I had no clue that they were actually college students." Thiriot also learned about ROTC and the notion that she could sign up for the Navy and get a scholarship for another school. She had her eyes on Harvard. *Wait—they'll pay you? To study somewhere else?* It seemed too good to be true.

The following September, she walked through the gates of Harvard on an ROTC scholarship. After graduation, she would be commissioned a Naval officer with a service commitment of three to five years. Danielle Thiriot entered Harvard in 2003, two years after the US invasion of Afghanistan and just a few months into the war in Iraq. She figured the wars would be over by the time she was done with college.

"I remember my mom having some hesitation," she said. "But I also remember thinking, *Well, I'll be in college while this is going on.* Little did we know that we would be fighting the same war twenty years later."

At Harvard, she plunged into academics and majored in government, with a year at the Divinity School. She was also a varsity rower for all four years. "I was all over the place," she said. "But I loved doing a lot of different things." As a junior, thinking about the summer ahead, she noticed that many classmates were interviewing for summer internships at Wall Street investment banks. She hadn't considered investment banking—she didn't really know what that entailed. But she decided to apply for a few of the internships. Never mind that she hadn't studied economics and knew almost nothing about finance.

Her first two interviews "were absolutely abysmal," she remembers. "They asked me to do math problems; they asked me things about financial markets. I was like, *I have no idea.* I read the *Wall Street Journal* yesterday, and that's about the extent of my knowledge on finance."

But then came interviewer number three, who happened to have been a soccer player. The conversation started there and went well thereafter. They talked soccer, not finance, which Thiriot acknowledged she knew nothing about, but the interviewer was confident that she was a fast learner and offered her the internship. And not just any internship. It was with Lehman Brothers, on the bank's subprime mortgage–backed securities trading desk. "Quite a mouthful!" she said with a smile. (This was at a time, before the 2008 financial crisis, when such trading was still profitable.)

She quickly learned the basics of finance, and worked hard at Lehman. But she still had an obligation to fill with the Navy that summer, a four-week stint with an active-duty unit. There was only one tour that fit her internship calendar, and it would take her to the US Navy Base at Yokosuka, Japan, aboard the Aegis cruiser USS *Cowpens.*

Suddenly, just days removed from the subprime mortgage desk at Lehman, Danielle Thiriot was thrown into a massive, three-carrier group Navy exercise, simulating war in the South China Sea. She was assigned to watch duty, twelve hours on and twelve hours off.

Dramatic as it sounded, she spent those long hours staring at radar screens, and "just watching people do their jobs." When she wasn't on watch duty, she was posted to the bottom deck for general quarters drill during a simulated attack on the ship. It was dark, dank, and miserably hot. Thiriot was baking in her hazmat gear. And while it was a full-on military exercise, she found what she was doing downright dull. For a young woman who loved activity, this was hell. She could not imagine doing this year after year.

After one particularly dreary evening, when she had returned to the officer level of the ship, another officer peeked his head in. "Hey, we got a bootleg copy of the new *X-Men* movie and some snacks," he said, "and we're gonna go watch it in the ready room. Do you want to come?"

Thiriot was confused. *What kind of sailors are these? And why aren't they on watch duty?* The officer answered her question before she could say it out loud: "I'm a pilot, by the way."

The pilots! The ship had several helicopters on deck, but Thiriot hadn't thought much about them. Now here she was watching a movie with a bunch of the pilots. And before the movie had ended, there was another offer: "You want to come and fly tomorrow?"

There was no hesitation on her part, all the more so as the flight would be her excuse to get off watch duty. So at nine the next morning, just a week into her tour, Danielle Thiriot was strapped into the back of a helicopter and flown out into the Pacific, headed for the nearby aircraft carrier.

"We're flying around, raging at five hundred feet above the water," she said. "It was a beautiful morning, the rising sun hitting the bright-blue sea. . . . It was heaven."

The whole episode was strange and exhilarating—the trip out over the ocean, the helicopters landing, fighter jets launching, all of it. She also felt a connection to the pilots—young men who exuded a coolness under pressure, seemingly less uptight than the ship's sailors, despite the obvious challenges and dangers that came with flying for the Navy.

"It fit so much better with my personality," she said. "They were like the varsity athletes of the Navy, and I was like, *OK, I think I've found my people.*"

By the time the *Cowpens* was back on shore and her Asia tour was winding down, Danielle Thiriot had made up her mind. She got off the boat and called home.

"Mom," she said, "I'm gonna be a pilot." Her mother, Mary, didn't understand. Wasn't that a ten-year commitment?

It was. Thiriot told her mother she'd rather be a pilot for ten years than spend four years as a surface warfare officer.

When she arrived home, she found an offer letter from Dick Fuld, the CEO of Lehman Brothers. There was a job at the bank if she wanted it, and the invitation came with a $10,000 signing bonus. Fuld had even called their home and spoken to Thiriot's mother, who by then was fully behind whatever choice her daughter would make.

Danielle's answer to Fuld was, "No thanks." She had found her mission, her calling—and it wouldn't involve banking or subprime mortgages or anything else on Wall Street. Even if the CEO was asking, and dangling a bonus. She would be a Navy pilot.

Lehman Brothers imploded two years later, in the largest bankruptcy filing in US history, a catalyst for the global financial crisis.

Danielle Thiriot was commissioned as a US Navy ensign on June 6, 2007, on the steps of Memorial Church in Harvard Yard, a day before graduation. Next stop would be the Navy's Preflight Indoctrination in Pensacola, Florida.

It was one of many steps in a funnel process—a constant push to weed out the unqualified in a kind of throw-you-in-the-pool approach. Her first solo flight would be in a small single-engine plane to test whether she could handle the bare minimum basics. It would be under visual flight rules only, meaning she would have to see her way along the assigned route—flying to a distant airfield and back. She made her way to the airfield, but once she turned around, she was lost: "You're looking for landmarks on the ground. And I'm flying along on the way back, and I'm freaking out because I don't know where I am. I had missed the last turn point."

What she could see was a large military base in her flight path, and she knew enough to steer clear of that busy airfield. She also knew she needed to turn again at some point, but grew increasingly unsure of when to do it, or even in which direction. She needed help.

"I come up on the radio, and I say, 'Do you see me?' hoping for help from the military air traffic controller. And the controller answers, 'Yes. I do.'" The controller guided Thiriot back to her airfield. *"This nice person—thank you, whoever you are."* But it had taken her a lot longer than it should have.

"*Where have you been?*" the instructor asked. Thiriot was terrified—she figured they must know she'd lost her way, and that her career was over. *They're gonna fire me,* she thought.

As nervous as she was, she played it cool, never letting on she had to ask the controller for directions—but it was hardly an auspicious beginning. And for a moment at least, the episode dented her confidence. Danielle had already noticed that the few other female pilots—there were four in her cohort of eighty—lacked confidence too, while the men seemed to brim with it.

"The guys, they're in their fire-red Corvettes and aviator sunglasses, and they just can't wait," she said. "They're already Tom Cruise, in their brain. And the women, we get there and we're like, *There aren't a lot of us here. And I'm probably not very good at this quite yet.*" She felt a healthy dose of uncertainty. "The women had a much more realistic sense of their early skill level. If the guys felt the same, they didn't show it. These boys were all so sure of themselves, and so sure that being a fighter pilot was the only thing they ever wanted to do with their entire lives."

It helped to find women who had gone before her. Danielle saw a fighter pilot named Alex Dietrich on television and sent her a long email. Dietrich wrote back, and Thiriot wound up speaking with her and meeting other female aviators. It wasn't any one thing any of them said, just a feeling that she liked and respected these women. They were smart, brash, and funny. *My kind of people.*

She also credited her "on-wing" instructor, a Navy helicopter pilot named Napoleon DeVeaux, with steadying her nerves. On-wings were seasoned pilots who served as regular one-on-one trainers. Thiriot learned later that the on-wing could make or break your experience. In DeVeaux she found an instructor who was exacting but fair and never evinced the negative side of the "bro culture," as she saw it. Later she wondered whether he had approached the training of a young woman differently because of his own background as one of a relatively small number of Black pilots.

"He was just awesome, very smart and very measured and everything," Thiriot said. "And I think he knew that being one of only a few was hard and that I needed to be good. Not just average." She was more than good; Danielle Thiriot finished at the top of the class at primary flight school.

On May 14, 2010, Danielle Thiriot earned her Wings of Gold. She was now officially a US Navy Pilot. Whatever insecurities she had brought into her training had vanished through hard work and determination.

She'd met every test and challenge—carrier landings, refueling runs—and crushed them, for the most part, on the way to becoming a single-seat fighter jet pilot. For the next four years, she would train constantly for the combat missions ahead.

Thiriot was the only female trainee in her first fleet squadron when she met a TOPGUN instructor, a woman known as PINC—pronounced like the color pink, a call sign that stood for "politically incorrect," given her propensity for no-filter comments on just about any subject. To Thiriot, PINC was God's gift to fighter pilots, a great aviator and a charismatic, no-nonsense woman. Thiriot took to her immediately, following her around, and the guys in the squadron noticed and picked her call sign as a result.

"You're *Purple*," they proclaimed. As in, Purple, to go with "PINC." And it stuck. "The girls," Thiriot said, "would be 'Purple' and 'PINC.'"

In August 2014, Danielle Thiriot began her first overseas deployment aboard the USS *Carl Vinson*, the same carrier that had conducted the burial at sea of Osama bin Laden a little over three years before. The five thousand sailors and pilots traveling from San Diego to the Arabian Sea expected a relatively low-stress deployment, even though it would involve flights over Afghanistan. Combat flights were always difficult

Danielle Thiriot on deck of the USS Carl Vinson *before a combat flight in December 2014.*

and dangerous, but with a reduced US presence on the ground, the missions were not expected to be particularly kinetic.

Halfway across the Pacific, the crew had a terrible reminder of the dangers of their work. A young pilot and Naval Academy graduate named Nathan Poloski launched off the carrier, climbed rapidly, and, seconds later, collided in midair with another F-18 fighter jet. The other pilot ejected safely, but Lieutenant Poloski's jet plunged into the ocean. He was twenty-six years old.

The collision and Lieutenant Poloski's death were a gut punch for all on board the *Vinson*. It happened so close to the carrier that anyone on the deck saw the explosion and watched as only one parachute came down. Thiriot was in the ready room belowdecks, preparing to launch her own jet, when an alert blared over the radio: "River City, condition four"—which meant all outgoing communications from the ship were halted, a requirement when there is an accident or death so that word does not spread before families are notified. For a while it was unclear which one of the pilots was missing. "I can still remember all of it," Thiriot said. "It's a searing memory."

Days later when the carrier arrived in Singapore for a port call, the *Vinson* crew got a brief break—followed by another jolt. When Thiriot and the other pilots returned, the mood on the ship had changed dramatically: "We got back on the carrier and almost immediately, we knew that something was happening."

They were summoned for an urgent briefing, given by a team that had flown to the carrier for that purpose alone. The new arrivals gave a classified and highly detailed assessment, outlining the contours of a new mission, much of which involved a grave new threat to Iraq and Syria, and the extremist group that was behind it.

It was the first time Danielle Thiriot had heard the name ISIS. The Islamic State in Iraq and Syria. The briefers left the carrier and the *Vinson* headed west, with a new mission and new sense of urgency.

By then, Thiriot had garnered more than a thousand flight hours, as an instructor in the T-45 training jet, flying the F/A-18 Super Hornet fighter jet, and joining a strike fighter squadron based in Virginia Beach. But she had yet to mark her logbook with the green ink pilots used to record a combat flight.

There are plenty of pilots who go their whole career without green ink. It was clear on that day that Danielle Thiriot would not be one of them.

Over the next seven months, Purple would fly missions from the Persian Gulf across the sprawling desert sands of southern Iraq, along the spine of the Euphrates River, on past Baghdad, and up to Mosul in the north.

On some missions she flew close to the Iranian border, peering out at the Zagros Mountains that marked the frontier, much like the towering mountains that surrounded our hometown of Salt Lake City.

She was struck by how benign the landscape appeared. But there was nothing benign about the missions she was on. Or the consequences of failure.

The preparations for a combat flight were intense. The briefings ran early and long. Because she was new to combat, she was paired with a pilot who had done it before, although she would soon be leading the missions. They wore no patches, no name tape, nothing that might identify them in the event of capture. They carried a "blood chit," a waterproof card that included a message requesting assistance should the wearer be found in distress. The "blood chit" had a history dating back to World War I. In WWII Thiriot's grandfather had carried one when he was shot down just before D-Day and he'd been fortunate not to have to use it. He had hidden with members of the Belgian resistance before crossing Allied lines into France that September. Thiriot's blood chit included a pledge that the United States would help anyone who helped the bearer of the card. She was issued a sidearm for the mission—another addition for combat missions—for her to use in the event of an accident or shoot-down.

The pilots were given a special SERE briefing—a World War II–era protocol that was short for Survival, Evasion, Resistance, and Escape. The ISIS-specific version of the SERE was stark: The pilots were warned that in the event of capture "they are going to torture you, they are going to kill. . . . Don't expect that this is going to be like, the Red Cross–is-going-to-come-and-negotiate kind of thing." And for Thiriot and the few other female pilots in the squadron, an even more chilling warning. Multiple reports had described the rape and torture of women by ISIS forces, and the briefer made clear that if *female* American pilots were captured by ISIS fighters, they would face the worst of it.

"I remember him looking at me, and he was just like, '*Sorry*,'" Thiriot said. "It was very clear that the briefer was saying, '*Look, you can't get captured.*'"

By now, ISIS had taken swaths of territory in Iraq and Syria, where the group aimed to create a caliphate built upon the harshest and most extreme interpretations of Islam. ISIS was created in 2013, and by the summer of 2014 the terrorist group had won significant victories—blitzing through the northern Iraqi cities of Samarra, Mosul, and Tikrīt, home of Saddam Hussein, where the group boasted that it had slaughtered seventeen hundred people. In Syria, ISIS forces had captured the northern city of Raqqa, and on June 29, 2014, they declared Raqqa the capital of their new caliphate. Along the way they had enslaved men, raped women, and killed tens of thousands of civilians. By mid-2014, ISIS posed a serious threat to the governments in Syria and Iraq. Intelligence estimates suggested that the group controlled roughly a third of the territory in both countries.

The people of Iraq, who had seen flickers of calm and prosperity over the past few years, were now faced with a terrifying and immediate threat.

In one of her early flights from the *Carl Vinson*, Thiriot had flown over the Iraqi city of Hit. The name was familiar; she'd seen TV news reports about a mass killing of men in the city.

"I remember flying over that place," she said, "and thinking of the atrocities that they were committing, and murder and rape and all of this stuff that was just horrible."

The news of those atrocities, the carrier briefings, the details of the SERE warnings—they all pointed in the same direction. "ISIS," said Thiriot, "was an easy enemy to hate."

On an October night in 2014, Thiriot was in the air over northern Iraq, refueling her jet. "Getting her last drink," as she put it. Aerial refueling was considered safe over Iraq, but since she would be leaving Iraqi airspace, the KC-135 air tankers wouldn't be permitted to follow. Once she and her fellow pilot had filled their tanks, they made a sharp turn left, to the west. They were headed into Syria.

ISIS had been active in Syria from the start, but in mid-September the group upped their attacks, laying siege to the small but strategically important city of Kobani near the borders of both Turkey and Iraq. Some four thousand ISIS forces had gathered at the edge of the city. By October 2, the group was inside Kobani and had taken control of the entire region around it. Tens of thousands of Syrian Kurds were fleeing the surrounding villages and heading for the Turkish border. Reports from Kobani suggested a brutality that mirrored the experience of civilians in northern Iraq.

The city, east of the Euphrates, had grown up a century earlier around a train station that served as an important stop on the Berlin-to-Baghdad railway. More recently, Kobani had gained importance as a key city along a route marked by oil pipelines and refineries. If it succeeded in holding on to Kobani, ISIS would solidify its control of Syria's oil fields.

President Obama had by then announced a major expansion of the military campaign against ISIS, including—for the first time—American air strikes against Syria. Up to that point, the United States and its coalition partners had committed only to driving ISIS from Iraq. Syria would pose a different challenge; US intelligence was thinner there, and any major operation would require close cooperation with Syrian Kurdish forces, who shared a desire to keep ISIS out.

Suddenly Kobani was a front line the world was watching closely. It would be a pivotal battle against ISIS, and Danielle Thiriot would be part of that fight.

Danielle Thiriot crossed into Syrian airspace after refueling and flew toward Kobani. Another jet flew with her. She turned on the master arm switch in her aircraft—the mechanism that allowed the firing of ordnance.

The first thing she noticed, in those early moments over Syrian territory, was what was missing. "There was no light," she remembers. "It is so strange when you fly over civilization and there's no electricity at night. Syria was like another world." Even as they flew over Deir ez-Zur, the first real city in their path, there were hardly any lights. They tacked north, heading toward Turkey and the small city of Kobani.

From the moment they entered Syrian airspace they were in contact with the JTAC—the Joint Terminal Attack Controller—a kind of collection point of information and intelligence. Because it wasn't possible to have a JTAC on the ground in ISIS territory in Syria, the controller for this mission was based at Fort Bragg, in North Carolina. From that base the JTAC gathered inputs from various sources—drones flying far above the fighter jets, Kurdish forces on the ground, and other intelligence assets from the region—and relayed relevant information and directions to the pilots. Ultimately, the JTAC controllers would send pilots the coordinates for an air strike—a communication that would come in the form of a "nine line," a set of instructions that served as a detailed order for an attack. A nine line would include the precise target, the GPS coordinates, the timing, the type of munition required—everything to make sure the bomb would destroy no more, no less, than it was intended to. The JTAC would read the nine line; the pilot would enter the information into their aircraft's system, read it back, and clarify any questions. It all had to happen fast.

Thiriot had just had her first glimpse of Kobani when the call came from the JTAC. It began with "Judge," the call sign for the mission.

"Judge, two, one, standby for nine line."

Thiriot braced herself, thinking, *Here we go.*

The controller wanted a strike against a vehicle he had been tracking with a gun mounted on top that he had seen firing in the area. Thiriot could see it all for herself on the forward-looking infrared screen or FLIR in her cockpit.

There was the truck, and its mounted gun. She could even see the person in the vehicle. "The turret was still hot. I remember, you could see it in the FLIR," she said. "It was firing—there's a guy in the truck, and he's firing a gun backwards at some people."

She was watching it in real time—the house-to-house fighting in Kobani between ISIS and the Kurdish forces. The truck pulled into a garage in a three-story building, and she could see the turret of the gun sticking out of the garage.

She was still surveying the scene when the JTAC controller began reading out the nine line. He wanted her and the other pilot to drop five-hundred-pound bombs on the garage and the three-story building.

"*That's your target,*" came the order.

"He wanted the building down," Thiriot said. "There were people firing from the second and third floor of this building out into the street."

The target itself posed a challenge—what warriors refer to as an "urban canyon" situation. Kobani was hardly a teeming metropolis, but there were other buildings nearby.

"You want to be sure that you have a really high-impact angle on the weapon," Thiriot said, "so that it doesn't hit a different building."

The lead pilot went first. Thiriot saw his bombs impact, and then, less than one minute later, it was her turn. The coordinates and the rest of the data for the strike came up on her HUD, the cockpit's "Heads-Up Display," showing that she was now "in zone"—the target zone.

"Judge Two-One, in," Thiriot told the JTAC.

"*Judge Two-One, cleared hot,*" he replied.

That was the JTAC's two-word message that she had been cleared to drop her bombs.

Thiriot hit the red button to release her ordnance.

"Judge Two-One, one away," Thiriot said as she watched the ordnance head for the target.

"You feel it come off your plane. The whole wing sort of moves; you feel a *clunk* as it falls off."

It was a laser-guided bomb, and she could track the trajectory as it fell. She saw it strike the building's garage. A direct hit. But Thiriot was surprised by what she saw next.

The explosion had been powerful enough to flood her cockpit's high-definition imaging screen. For a few moments she had no idea what had happened. "It went white with the explosion," she said. "I remember the lead aircraft going, '*Whoa, whoa, Purple? What did you drop?*' Thinking that I had dropped a two-thousand-pound bomb."

The explosion was big—massive, in fact. "It was bigger than an explosion for a five-hundred-pound bomb. But it was my first bomb, so I didn't know any better," Thiriot said. It turned out she and the other pilot were watching secondary explosions. Her first bomb had not only hit its mark; it had ignited a hidden weapons storage facility.

The fight in Kobani continued to rage for months. When she returned on future missions, Thiriot and the other pilots worked with ground spotters and the JTAC teams to identify the ISIS fighters and distinguish them from the Kurdish forces on the ground—the friendlies, as the Americans called them. From the cockpit it was impossible to distinguish who was friend and who was foe without the help of other sources. Sometimes she saw groups of men digging—often a sign that they were ISIS fighters planting IEDs, but she would seek more certainty. She watched some battles that were so closely fought it wasn't possible to strike the ISIS fighters without risking hitting the friendlies. And over time she saw enough through her cockpit pod to gain a deep admiration for the bravery of the Kurdish fighters who were battling ISIS.

"I've never seen that type of resolve," she said. "They were incredible."

One combat mission over Kobani made that courage clear. It also presented Thiriot with a wrenching decision. She was flying that day with a junior pilot whose laser wasn't working, leaving him with a less-than-optimal system for targeting. Thiriot told him to forget about dropping bombs on this mission; she would handle that.

Then the JTAC targets came in, including an ask for two five-hundred-pound precision-guided JDAM (Joint Direct Attack Munitions) bombs on a house in Kobani. ISIS had been booby-trapping houses all over the city and the Kurds were fighting ferocious street battles to drive them out.

The house was small, little more than a mud structure. "We're not talking big concrete buildings," Thiriot said. "So that's a lot of firepower for kind of a small house."

The JTAC controllers wanted to "talk her on"—essentially, to visually guide her to the target from their vantage point.

"It's challenging, because that means I have to see what they see," she said. "This was an especially dense urban area; there's lots of buildings stacked close together. Everything looks the same. And so I was not comfortable with that."

While the JTAC controllers would identify targets and clear the pilots to strike them, the pilots themselves had the final authority to drop—or not drop—their bombs. To press that red button or not. Thiriot told the JTAC controller she wanted "mensurated coordinates," especially precise data which would confirm the exact location of the building with GPS, rather than just a visual talk on. She entered the information and prepped the attack.

"I checked the coordinates with my targeting pod and described what I saw to the JTAC," and he confirmed, "*That is your target*," but quickly added, "*Danger close*," meaning that friendly troops were in close proximity to the location. Inside the likely radius of a blast. The controller gave an estimate of 50 meters, roughly 150 feet.

That was *very* close. Too close, she worried. She had never heard of a "danger close" scenario that was this close—the risk of hitting the friendlies on the ground was high.

"*Five zero? Confirm five zero*," Thiriot asked.

"*Affirmative. Five zero.*"

Now she had the coordinates, had all the information she needed, but she kept thinking that she was being asked to drop a pair of five-hundred-pound bombs on a small house in a village with friendly forces taking cover just one house away. Fifty meters away.

The JTAC confirmed that yes, Kurdish forces were in the house. The friendlies. They were the reason for the JTAC's "*Danger close*" warning. The controller knew the risk to the Kurdish forces was extreme, and respected Thiriot's caution.

But then the JTAC added two words of clarification: "*They know*," meaning those Kurdish fighters, one house away, were well aware of what was coming. *They know.* They were the ones asking for it. They were calling for the bombs. Either the target was important enough to be worth the risk, or they themselves were in such imminent danger they saw no choice.

Thiriot knew she had no time for uncertainty. She would have to nail the target and hope that the blast damage wouldn't take the Kurds out too. Yet she also knew that the Kurds needed the bombs right away to even have a chance.

Thiriot dropped her bombs and waited. "The longest sixty seconds of my life," she said.

She had watched the impact on her screen, seen that the house had been destroyed, but she also saw three or four buildings nearby engulfed in the smoke of the aftermath. Not necessarily destroyed, but they might have been, for all she knew. She couldn't tell. She told the other pilot to get a good image of the scene. "I want you to take a wide-angle view of this," she said, "because we're going to need the footage. This is high-risk."

Then she came back on the radio and asked the JTAC controllers what they knew. They were trying to get back in communication with the Kurdish fighters who were next door.

"We waited and waited and waited," Thiriot said. It seemed like forever, but it was probably only a matter of minutes before she got the news she was hoping for.

"He said, finally, '*Good hits, good hits,*'" she remembers.

"*I have comms,*" the JTAC controller was saying. "*They're OK.*"

Thiriot kept trying to imagine the scene on the ground, the concussive effects of the blasts, what it must have been like for those Kurdish fighters in that nearby house.

"Because they were next door to this bomb that went off," she said. "But those people, they were fierce."

In March 2015, I saw for myself the impact of the missions Thiriot and her fellow pilots had flown. I traveled to the Turkish border with Syria, where I had a chance to both witness the trauma that had visited the people of Kobani and appreciate how the American air war and the courage of the Kurdish fighters on the ground had begun to make a difference. Even from a distance, it was easy to see that the city was nearly destroyed. Buildings that had once dominated the landscape were battered and barely standing. But in the Kobani region at least, ISIS was on the run. Streams of refugees had crossed the border into Turkey—people from Kobani and all those other towns and villages in the path of the ISIS assault—but the military operation had begun to drive ISIS forces away. By late April 2015, ISIS was gone from all those towns and villages, its fighters killed or scattered. The battle for Kobani had been won. It would later be considered a turning point in the campaign against ISIS. By December of 2018, the US-led coalition had declared victory over the terrorist group. By then ISIS controlled only a few scattered areas, having lost more than 95 percent of the territory it had captured in Iraq and Syria. Still dangerous, without question. But the dream of a caliphate that ISIS had imagined seemed for the time being . . . over. It was a positive coda to the long and fraught wars that followed 9/11, and it was unusual in that the battle had been waged largely from the air.

Lieutenant Commander Danielle Thiriot and her fellow pilots had helped turn the tide, helped end that ISIS reign of terror. Before her tour was over, she had flown more than twenty-five combat missions over Iraq and Syria. Her logbook was now filled with green ink. Most of those missions had been over Kobani.

Back stateside, Danielle Thiriot went to work as an instructor pilot at the VFA-106 Gladiators Squadron in Virginia Beach, training the next generation of Super Hornet pilots. It was during this time that she met Rosemary Mariner for the first time, at a Women in Aviation Conference. The conference was an annual get-together for thousands of women in commercial and military aviation.

Lieutenant Danielle Thiriot serving as an instructor pilot with strike fighter squadron VFA-106 in Virginia Beach, 2015.

Rosemary had recently received her cancer diagnosis, and she was frail, showing the effects of several rounds of chemotherapy. But she showed up in her full-dress uniform, as Thiriot remembered. The conference was honoring Rosemary and five other women—the Navy's first six female aviators.

"Everyone was like, 'Do you know who that is?'" Thiriot remembers. "And they were like, 'That's the woman who changed the combat exclusion law.'"

There were other trailblazers there, including some of the last of the surviving WASPs—the Women Airforce Service Pilots who flew service aircraft during WWII and many of Rosemary's contemporaries. Though Rosemary was ill during the conference, she took the time to engage constantly with the younger women. "She had some questions for all of us, about what we were doing and what squadrons we were in, and all this stuff," Thiriot said. "She had kind of an aura, for sure. It was just so cool to see and meet someone, to meet the woman who basically made it possible for us."

Thiriot and her fellow aviators, the other "lady lieutenants," as she called them, were blown away to be in the room with Rosemary and the other pioneers. They listened to the stories of the battles they'd fought, and they were happy to find that the older women wanted to hear their stories too, especially those of aviators like Thiriot who had flown combat missions—missions Rosemary's generation had never had the chance to fly. "I think it was really cool for them to see that we had all flown in combat." They had a million questions about the progress the women had made in the male-dominated profession.

Thiriot had suffered plenty of stings and slights during her career. When she flew in air shows in 2016–17, it was often in a two-seat aircraft, with a male weapon systems officer in the back. "People always figured the guy must be the pilot—every time," Thiriot said. "They just assumed that he was flying the plane, to the point where they would just be like, 'Wait, what?' They were confused that I could be flying the plane."

Along the way she has heard all kinds of absurd questions, hovering between silly and insulting, about being a female aviator.

"I have been asked everything under the sun," she says. "I've been asked if I can have children, if I can pull as many G's as men. Because clearly I shouldn't be able to. I mean, I'm a woman. How could you pull as many G's as a man?"

Someone told her once that she shouldn't fly upside down in air shows because her ovaries would dislodge—and that "we have to watch how many times we fly upside down in the air show. Like, what in the world? *This was 2017!*"

On the other side of the world, there was the man in a Bahrain bar who had inquired about buying her. "A Saudi who asked the other guys in the squadron how much I cost, because I was with a bunch of men in this Irish pub in Bahrain, and it became the joke," she said.

"Of course, it's not that funny, but most of the time you have to laugh." Whatever indignities she and the other pilots were experiencing, she knew it was nothing compared to what the older female pilots had been through.

When Rosemary Mariner died on January 24, 2019, Danielle Thiriot had just finished her junior officer tour as the Flag Aide to the Chief of Naval Operations, the Navy's highest-ranking officer. She got the news about Rosemary just a few days after leaving the job.

The idea of a flyover came quickly to Thiriot. She had done her share of air shows, including as lead tactical pilot for the Navy's 2017 air show season. Given Rosemary's life and record as an aviator, a flyover in her honor seemed like a no-brainer. After all, Danielle thought, "she's the reason we're all here."

She knew she'd have no problem finding enough women for the job—there were fifteen of them on base at Oceana, the Naval Air Station in Virginia Beach that was home to all East Coast strike fighter jet squadrons, and she only needed eight women for the flyover. "We can get the people to do it," she figured. But finding four jets became the problem.

She knew the Commodore at Oceana well, but that ask went nowhere at first.

"He's like, 'Ahh, Purple, I don't think we can do it. We don't have any jets here this weekend.'"

Thiriot didn't understand. "You guys, we do this every weekend," she said. "You guys go to football games on the weekend, and we make that happen. So don't tell me that this is hard. I know it's not hard."

She called the public affairs officer at the Chief of Naval Operations, where she had been working, and pitched what she figured would be a slam-dunk bit of great PR. "*Hey, you want a good news story, try this,*" she told her. Eight female combat pilots were going to honor the one who made it happen. *What a cool thing that would be.*

But that didn't work either. The officer was very supportive, but had no authority to approve the flyover. Slowly, and doggedly, Thiriot began chipping away at the hard "No." She sent a mass email to what she called a who's who of female aviators. She told a fellow pilot, "*Hey, let's scheme a little here.*"

It worked, finally, thanks mostly to what Thiriot called "the underground lady network," her female aviator friends. But Thiriot's' enthusiasm and persistence eventually spread to her male superiors—especially when some realized the flyover was for Captain Mariner. Before long, everyone was on board. They wound up corralling four two-seat jets, with spots in each for a pilot and WSO—the weapon systems officer in the back seat. That meant there would be eight top-class female aviators up in the skies over Tennessee, to honor Rosemary Mariner. Four of them had been Thiriot's students, when she'd been a flight instructor. More trailblazers, passing the torch.

"It was really just an amazing thing to be part of," said Jen Hesling, a Navy pilot who flew one of the jets that day. Hesling credited Danielle Thiriot not only for the aerial tribute but for building what she called a "band of sisterhood" among female pilots, past and present.

When Thiriot veered sharply up and away, breaking free from the formation and becoming the "missing lady," she heard her friend and fellow pilot Commander Stacy Uttecht bellow over the radio: "For Rosemary!"

Just weeks after that flyover for Rosemary Mariner, Danielle Thiriot was overseas again—deployed on a mission to the Mediterranean and Adriatic Seas, on board the carrier USS *Abraham Lincoln.*

Lieutenant Commander Danielle Thiriot with Martha Raddatz after flying in the first Navy all-female flyover to honor Captain Rosemary Mariner in Norris, Tennessee, February 2019.

She was in a position of leadership in her squadron now, a department head, on track to be a commanding officer. Months into the deployment, on a morning in early May, Thiriot and her squadron were part of a large air-to-air combat exercise with the Italian air force over Northern Italy. It was a spectacular day when she launched off the carrier, to begin the three-hour exercise. These practice runs with allies were complicated and had taken months of planning. So when Thiriot noticed her jet was having intermittent pressurization issues, she remained determined to complete the exercise. The gauges were showing quick fluctuations, which she deemed only a minor problem. In a fighter jet, the dynamic maneuvering and rapid change of altitude require air to be pumped quickly into the cockpit when the jet ascends and pumped out just as quickly when it descends. Thiriot completed the exercise successfully and returned to the ship, where she reported the issue to the mechanics.

The next morning, she was assured that the problem had been fixed by replacing a valve. She hopped back in the jet and launched off the carrier. To her great annoyance, the pressurization problem was still there. Again, Danielle Thiriot powered through. Three hours later, returning to the ship, she felt exhausted—unusually exhausted.

Once she was out of the jet, her wingman noticed that her speech was slow and slurred. Minutes later, when she tried to fill out her post-flight paperwork, she couldn't write her name. A drug and alcohol test followed. "The Navy's answer to everything," Thiriot said. "I was insulted." Then a session in a pressure chamber, with medical personnel concluding it must be something akin to the bends. But her condition was deteriorating quickly. She was grasping for words and was uncharacteristically emotional. The medics knew something was very wrong. Within forty-eight hours she was medevaced off the ship and returned to the United States.

Unbeknownst to Lieutenant Commander Danielle Thiriot, that trip off the aircraft carrier would be her last. The Navy's rising star and expert pilot would never fly a fighter jet again.

The diagnosis came at Walter Reed National Military Medical Center in Bethesda: a traumatic brain injury (TBI), the result of a massive pressurization failure in the cockpit of her fighter jet. Thousands of feet in the air, a world away from all those IEDs and anti-tank mines in a combat zone, the rapid and steep dip in air pressure had delivered a blast wave—a heavy concussive impact—and damaged her brain.

Thiriot suffered for several months—regular migraine headaches, short-term memory failings, and profoundly low levels of energy. Suddenly a woman who had always pushed herself hard had lost the ability to do so. A bad night's sleep, even something as simple as bright lights or loud noises, would set her back. In the early period of her recovery, she had more issues with speech, and she could sense that her processing of thought had slowed.

"I immediately went from someone who did not have sensory overload to someone who had it all the time," she said. "I had a hard time going to the grocery store."

That December, seven months after the incident, she entered an in-patient program at the Veterans Administration's Tampa Polytrauma Rehabilitation Center. By now the VA had—by necessity—become far better versed in the care of TBI patients. Thiriot joined a group that numbered in the tens of thousands of veterans of the wars in Iraq and Afghanistan who had suffered wounds to the brain.

Her career as a fighter pilot was over. More than that, she began to wonder when and whether she would feel better and regain her basic daily-life abilities—never mind the skills needed for aerial combat.

"It's very different than a physical injury," she said. "If you break your arm, you know what that is, and people can see it, and when your brain is not functioning properly, it's terrible. It's devastating."

Thiriot responded well to treatment. "I was one of the lucky ones, where my brain ended up being quite resilient," she said. "I was able to recover."

In January 2021, more than a year and a half after the air-pressure incident, she was cleared for normal activities. By then she had left active duty and entered the Navy Reserve. She found it hard to contemplate life after flying for the Navy—worrying about how she would cope with the "massive deceleration" from the high-octane life of a fighter pilot.

It was not long after she got the "all clear" that Danielle Thiriot was back in the air, flying 737s for a commercial airliner. It's not a fighter jet, but this is still a job she loves. She is back home in Utah, hiking, skiing, and mentoring others. Always mentoring.

Her experience as a female pilot in the Navy is still on her mind, seven years after her last mission. She remains profoundly grateful for the opportunities she was given—grateful to Rosemary Mariner, to those who flew before her, and to the many other women who helped her along the way. She does worry about the slow pace of progress for women since then. The bumps along the way. And the occasional setbacks.

"Things certainly continue to get better," she said. "But sometimes it's two steps forward, another step back." The flyover at Rosemary's funeral was a triumph—but also frustrating, given what it took to convince others to do it.

The 2025 gathering of Women in Aviation International—a group that "envisions a world where the sky is open to all"—was to feature fifty Navy aviators, all women. Thiriot loved the WAI events, the mingling with her peers, the younger pilots, hungry for stories. "It was just this really cool reunion of sorts every year; it was really awesome," she said. One year, a group of older women had rented a big hotel room and filled the bathtub with beer.

"It was hilarious," she said. "These old ladies know how to party.

First Navy all-female flyover. Martha Raddatz with six of the eight female Navy aviators who honored Captain Rosemary Mariner at her funeral. Lieutenant Commander Danielle Thiriot is third from left. With her (left to right) are Lieutenant Christy Talisse, Lieutenant Commander Jennifer Hesling, Lieutenant Amanda Lee, Commander Stacy Uttecht, and Lieutenant Emily Rixey.

They all wear their leather jackets and stuff, and it was sweet because they just wanted to host us. They just wanted to tell us their stories."

Thiriot said one enormous change from Rosemary's generation is how she and the other female pilots are treated by male pilots. "They never even think about it. I have seen nothing but support," said Thiriot. "It is a different generation of men; they had moms who worked and sisters who were athletes and went to college." The doors that Rosemary and others opened for women mean that there is nothing in Naval aviation they can't do, including being TOPGUN instructors. They have the same challenges, take the same risks.

Thiriot, who is now Commander Danielle Thiriot in the Navy Reserve, says she thinks often about Rosemary Mariner—and how far women have come. Among those eight women who performed the flyover, one is now a carrier air wing commander, one a squadron commander, another a Blue Angel pilot. Three were TOPGUN graduates and three have been commanding officers.

I think about Rosemary often as well. She was not only a remarkable professional but one of the most loyal friends I have ever had—and hands down the smartest. She was consumed by learning. After her retirement, she taught military history at the University of Tennessee and was a resident scholar at the Center for the Study of War and Society. I look at the last text message she sent me, during her final and excruciating chemo treatments. "The world is full of people who suffer much worse," she wrote. "I have had a good life and am blessed with a wonderful team of professionals, family and friends."

To me, Danielle Thiriot is a big part of Rosemary's legacy. She's a skilled pilot, with a towering intellect. She's also a fighter. A true professional, who has passed on her own legacy and her own fight to those who come next.

"Rosemary changed my life and so many others'," she told me. "She died knowing the doors she had opened for all of us. I take comfort in that. It was the honor of a lifetime to know her and to fly for her."

The Arsiaga siblings would all serve their country: (from top left) Robert, Angel, Gilbert, and, the youngest, Jeremy.

CHAPTER 8

A Gold Star Family

Sylvia, Robert, Angel, Gilbert, and Jeremy Arsiaga

IN THE MORNING HOURS OF APRIL 4, 2014, ANGEL MUÑOZ stood before a solemn crowd of soldiers and families at Fort Hood, Texas, home of the First Cavalry Division. Those who had gathered that morning, young and old, were still grieving the loss, years earlier, of the soldiers whose names were carved into the granite memorial behind her. It had been ten years to the day since Angel's brother Robert Arsiaga and seven other soldiers had been killed in Sadr City after a sudden ambush by armed insurgents. That Sunday, April 4, 2004, was the beginning of a yearlong deployment for the First Cavalry Division and it marked the division's largest loss of life since the Vietnam War. By the end of the deployment, another 162 soldiers were dead. Like the Arsiagas, their families were designated Gold Star Families, a tradition that began in World War I to honor the fallen and those they left behind.

This ten-year reunion was the first time Angel had summoned the courage to speak publicly about the day her brother was killed. It was a eulogy of sorts, both for the dead and for those who had lived and come home with the weight of what they had seen—and of having survived when so many of their friends had not. Some of the men had been there when twenty-five-year-old Robert Arsiaga had taken his last breath in the cab of an open Army truck.

Standing close to Angel as she spoke were her two other brothers, Gilbert and Jeremy. Her mother, Sylvia, was nearby. I had met most of the family years before, when I was writing a book about that April 4 battle, but I met Jeremy and Gilbert for the first time as we gathered on that day for the dedication of the memorial. All of the siblings—Angel, Gilbert, Jeremy—were military veterans. I watched tearfully as the brothers squeezed closer to their sister when her voice began to quaver.

"Ten years ago today, our hearts and lives changed forever," Angel said, looking skyward. "Not only for those who lost someone, but for those who returned home with memories they never asked for. I miss my brother each and every day and it breaks my heart, but in the midst of sorrow and heartbreak comes a ray of light, when we remember what these men were like in their short lives."

Angel spoke about each one of the soldiers who were lost that day, ending with a simple remembrance of Robert as "a loving man, a good friend, and my little brother." Looking directly at the crowd before her, she ended by saying, "We will never forget."

What Angel could not have imagined, what I did not imagine as she spoke of hope in the face of tragedy on that day, was that her family's pain was far from over. As she was wrapped in her brothers' embrace, no one knew that there was one more bullet coming for the Arsiaga family. And the second time, the pain would be even greater.

Angel, Robert, Gilbert, and Jeremy grew up in a small suburb of Midland, Texas, a city founded in 1885 as a railroad stop between Fort Worth and El Paso. Theirs was a proud, poor, fiercely patriotic family that had migrated many years earlier from Mexico. Their grandfather Modesto Muñoz and great-uncle, Maximo Muñoz, had both served in World War II.

Angel was the oldest and the first to enlist, signing up to join the Army while still in high school. For her it was a way out. It wasn't that she didn't like Midland, but she craved something more than Central Texas could give her. She wanted to *do* something that might make a difference. She knew that staying in Midland wasn't going to be it.

Growing up, Angel had never excelled at anything physical—she

US Army Private First Class Angel Muñoz.

almost failed PE class—so she figured this choice of hers would surprise some people and show them what she could accomplish.

Sylvia was indeed surprised, and not at all pleased. She could not imagine how her eighteen-year-old daughter, barely five feet tall, would manage in the military. "She was mad," Angel said. "I can't remember the words that she said. All I know is, she was mad. She really thought that it was going to be too hard for me. She was scared for me, because I was a young female going into a world where it was mostly men, and she was worried—not that I wasn't going to make it, but that it was going to be difficult for me."

Angel trained in South Carolina and Georgia before being sent to Korea and then to Fort Hood, the massive base back in Texas, about a five-hour drive from the family home. This was in 1998, before 9/11 and before the US wars in Iraq and Afghanistan, before military service became a very different experience. For Angel, the two years she spent in the Army helped teach her new skills, and gave her the chance to venture far from her small hometown and to serve her country. But then she wanted to come home and start a family.

Angel's military service seemed to spark something in the rest of her family. One by one, her younger brothers signed up. Gilbert enlisted in the Marine Corps in 1998, Robert joined the Army a year later, and then Jeremy became a Marine in 2002. Unlike Angel, the boys were still serving after 9/11, and all three brothers would head off to war.

"My mom liked to say I started it all," Angel says, "Those are her words—*'Angel started it all.'* Just like, *'Damn, Angel started it and it was like dominoes.'*"

Angel was closest to Robert, who was just a year younger than her. The three boys had a different father—hers was not a big part of her life and the boys' father had died in a car accident when they were young. The accident brought the boys closer to their mother and sister. Bubba,

Robert Arsiaga playing high school football in Midland, Texas.

as she called Robert, was a prankster with a faintly crooked smile and a scar on his lip from falling off a tire swing as a toddler. Jeremy, the youngest, could be a headache, pestering her but always knowing when to stop. Gilbert was the serious one, "the grown-up." In a house full of brothers, there were constant antics, but the siblings had a powerful bond. One that would become even tighter once they all had military experience.

"Not only were we super, super close as siblings, but becoming soldiers and Marines put a different spin to it, because we had a different appreciation for what the military stood for at that time," Angel says. "So it made us love each other a little bit deeper."

Robert Arsiaga graduated from Greenwood High School in 1998. He had planned on a drafting career with his brother Gilbert, but he deferred those dreams and joined the Army. Robert followed his sister in other ways—serving a tour in Korea, returning to Fort Hood, and then deciding that he, too, would leave the military earlier than expected, and for the same reason—he wanted to start a family. He had met Tracie Rodriguez years before through relatives. They were young and in love and married quickly in late 2003, when Tracie was only eighteen. It was because of his marriage to Tracie that Robert decided he would begin a new life back home, just as his sister had done.

Robert's plan was to leave the Army in August 2004. But it turned out that was not the Army's plan.

At the beginning of 2004, Specialist Robert Arsiaga was assigned to the Second Battalion, Fifth Cavalry Regiment, First Cavalry Division—the 2-5 was how they were known—based at Fort Hood. Gilbert had taken part in the initial invasion a year earlier. A swift and successful assault that was nothing like the action Robert would soon experience.

When it came time for Robert to deploy, in March 2004, the family gathered to bid him farewell—all except Angel, who was now a single mom to three boys under the age of seven and working at a day care, and Jeremy, who was doing Marine Corps training in San Diego. Angel's goodbye would have to be over the phone. She told Robert how proud she was of his service and how much she loved him. Robert called Jeremy too, but Jeremy missed the call.

The 2-5 arrived in Iraq on March 31, 2004. Five days later, Robert Arsiaga was dead.

He was on a rescue mission, one of sixteen soldiers hustled in the back of a two-and-a-half-ton cargo truck, sent to find a platoon that had been ambushed by hundreds of Iraqi insurgents. The truck was unarmored, a cab with an open back. The men sat in the back, with canvas draped over the metal benches, nothing more. The commanders were under no illusions; they knew it was unsafe. But the truck was there and available, and their fellow soldiers were in deep trouble.

Robert Arsiaga sat on a bench directly behind the cab of the truck, his gun propped between his legs, boxes of water bottles and plastic MREs stacked on the truck bed. None of the men in the truck had seen combat before. They had just turned onto a street they knew as Route Copper when they heard the snap of an AK-47 somewhere behind them.

US Army Specialist Robert Arsiaga.

Then, gunshots from the rooftops followed by a searing barrage of gunfire all around them. The Americans returned fire, and the convoy kept moving forward. Then came a rocket-propelled grenade that landed in the space between two vehicles, narrowly missing both. Another turn, and they found their way blocked by a makeshift barricade of car parts, refrigerators, metal bed frames, and burning tires.

The sixteen men in the back of that truck were shooting in every direction, with very little idea of what was going on. The sound of the incoming fire was deafening.

Robert Arsiaga was firing from his perch on the bench, scrunched up against the cab. The gunfire continued, with explosions and the *whoosh* of bullets all around. He was looking at Israel Garza, who was right across from him, when his friend took a round straight to the gut, just below his body armor. He let out a powerful scream and tried to stand. Arsiaga tried to help, but there was little he could do. In a matter of seconds, Garza fell backwards in the truck.

The gunfire kept coming, blanketing the truck with bullets. It was only a few minutes later that Arsiaga himself slumped in his seat, struck by a clean shot to the cheekbone, which left a lethal hole the size of a dime just under his eye. Every soldier in the back of that truck would be wounded by the time the firefight was over and the truck was turned around and heading back to base. Neither Arsiaga nor Garza would survive.

Back in Midland, Sylvia had been worrying about Robert all morning. She had seen a news story out of Iraq that a soldier had been killed in Sadr City, where Robert had been for the last few days. She called Gilbert to tell him how worried she was. "I am sure he is fine; don't worry," Gilbert told her. Gilbert was heading to a class at the local community college where he was studying drafting. As soon as he made it to the classroom he did his own online search for news from Iraq. His mother was wrong. There was not one soldier killed in Sadr City; there were eight. In those few minutes between his phone call with his mother and the time it took to search for news online, casualty assistance officers had arrived at Sylvia's house to inform her of her son's death. She collapsed on the floor. As soon as she could manage to speak, she reached for her phone to call Gilbert.

"You need to get home. There are soldiers here." It was all she could say. Gilbert rushed to the house, hoping that perhaps Robert was only injured, but fearing the worst.

When Angel Muñoz got her mother's call, she was in almost the exact spot she had been when Robert had called to say goodbye: changing a diaper at the day care center where she worked. Seeing who was calling, she was puzzled; her mother knew not to call her at work. Keeping one hand on the baby, she answered the phone.

"*Come home,*" was all her mother said. When Angel asked why, Sylvia did not have the strength to tell her about the soldiers in the house. She didn't say Robert was dead. She just cried, "*Come home. Now.*"

It was obvious to Angel that something terrible had happened, and in her mind she instantly thought it could only mean bad news about Robert. Angel looked at the baby on the changing table and called out urgently to a coworker, "Hey, get the baby, I have to go." She took off, running down a hallway to her boss's office. "*I gotta go,*" she said. *"Something's really wrong, and I think it's my brother. I hope it's not, but I think it's my brother."*

Just as Gilbert tried not to think of the worst as he approached his mother's home, so did Angel. But the siblings were both veterans.

"I got home. I see the government vehicle parked in the driveway, and I knew," Angel remembers. "I mean, *I knew*, because this is what we all know when we go to the military. We know what that means. But I was still hoping."

Opening the door slowly, she saw her mother and brother awash in tears and officers in their formal Class A uniforms. Any hope she had vanished. She began to scream as she folded herself into her mother's arms.

More than eight hundred miles away, on a training mission in the Arizona desert, twenty-year-old Marine Corporal Jeremy Arsiaga was oblivious to his brother's fate. Sylvia had tried to reach her youngest son but was unable to make contact. Married just six months, Jeremy's wife, Patricia, was alone at their home base in San Diego when Sylvia called, crying.

"You need to get ahold of Jeremy," she said. Patricia was young, just seventeen years old, and two months pregnant.

"I was totally naive about the military or war," she says. "So when Sylvia told me that she couldn't get hold of Jeremy and that he needed to know Robert was dead, I was just in shock."

Patricia tried to get through to Jeremy any way she could, but no one seemed to know where he was. Finally, hours later, the Marine Corps gave Jeremy the news and rushed him back to San Diego. Patricia and Jeremy held each other and sobbed. When he finally was able to speak, the first thing Jeremy said to his wife was, "If our baby is a boy, we are going to name him Robert."

For all the broader impact of the war and the loss of seven other soldiers on that day, the news from Iraq meant one thing for Robert Arsiaga's family: a sudden and shattering end for a much-loved, newly married young man who was supposed to be leaving the Army to start a family and a new life. Now he was coming home in a flag-draped coffin.

For Tracie Arsiaga, still a teenager at the time, it meant her marriage had lasted all of five months. After that knock on the door from Army officers, she knew there would be no future for the couple, no children with the man she loved.

And for Angel Muñoz, the sister who had been the family trailblazer, the one who enlisted first, it was a blow that would leave her profoundly depressed. She had been proud to serve, proud to have "started it all," as her mother had put it, inspiring her brothers to join the military. Now it had come to this: Robert wasn't coming home alive.

She was angry too—angry at God, for having allowed it to happen. It wasn't fair, Angel thought. Her brothers were angry too: *He will never be a father.*

Robert's death brought an outpouring of support from the community, visits from people they hardly knew, total strangers turning up at their door with food, flowers, and other gifts. From the terrible blur of that time, Angel remembers the profound realization that hers was now a Gold Star Family. An honor no family wants.

On April 11, 2004, just seven days after Robert was fatally wounded, the family gathered for his funeral. They were able to have an open casket despite the injury. Lying in the church in his dress uniform, Robert "looked perfect," Angel remembered. Bagpipes played "Amazing Grace" as mourners left the church service: "a sea of people in the bright sun."

At the cemetery, the solemn bellow of "Taps" was followed by a twenty-one-gun salute. The burst of sound, the guns blasting in the stillness, and all the mourners gathered—the wider family, the local sheriff, and so many people they didn't know—brought Angel to her knees. "It nearly broke me," she says.

But she also felt heartened by the love of the community, all those who came, and by something she learned when they brought Robert home. She had given her brother two things when he deployed—a Bible, inscribed with a note saying how proud she was to be his sister; and a small chain and pendant engraved with a verse from Joshua 1:9: "Have I not commanded you? Be strong and courageous. Do not be afraid; do not be discouraged, for the Lord your God will be with you wherever you go."

Among the personal effects the Army returned to Robert's family was the chain Angel had given him. He had been wearing it when he was shot.

As the weeks passed, each member of the family entered their own long, painful path of unrelenting grief. Angel was determined to summon every memory she could of her brother—his hugs, his sense of humor, his voice, even his smell. But the depression that engulfed her after his death clouded those memories.

Sylvia struggled to find joy in anything. She withdrew from friends and from her surviving sons. No one other than Angel would talk about Robert. "Because we didn't want to hurt each other," Sylvia says. Jeremy and Gilbert avoided mentioning Robert's name because they did not want to make their mother cry. For that reason, Sylvia's reliance on Angel became more pronounced as time went on. "She would let me cry," Sylvia says.

For Gilbert and Jeremy there was only anger and guilt. Gilbert would walk through town and feel nothing but envy when he saw happiness in others. All he saw was darkness. Robert was supposed to have joined him at the community college when he returned from Iraq to take drafting courses. Now Gilbert wasn't sure he could finish. He asked his teachers for time off, but when he returned, he would stare blankly at the computer, his motivation draining away as quickly as his career plans. He couldn't stop thinking about why he had survived a tour in Iraq and his older brother had not. It was a toxic mixture of depression, anxiety, and resentment.

Jeremy, at twenty the youngest when Robert died, had always been the quiet one among the siblings. He responded to his brother's death

US Marine Corps Sergeant Jeremy Arsiaga.

by growing quieter still, trying to bury the sadness and anger whenever it came—and it came often. Jeremy felt guilt over not having been able to say goodbye to Robert before he deployed, and missing that last call before he boarded the plane.

Jeremy's guilt was magnified by a decision the Marine Corps had made. His Marine unit was scheduled to deploy to Iraq in the months following Robert's death. Sylvia pleaded with the Marines to let her son stay back, given the loss of her oldest son. The Marines granted her request, but Jeremy was sick about it. He wanted to fulfill his duty to the country, especially since his brother had been killed doing the same. Instead, he was left stateside, teaching his fellow Marines how to use a rifle and then watching them go off to war.

Patricia, his wife, didn't know what to do. It seemed like they were fighting all the time. Over and over, he would sit and listen to patriotic music about service and sacrifice and weep. "He was angry that I didn't grieve in the same way he did," Patricia says. "He didn't think I cared enough."

Patricia was patient and gentle, apologizing for her lack of experience with war and death. But she couldn't reach the dark place her husband seemed to land each evening. Jeremy struggled even when their child arrived, the boy they named Robert, just as Jeremy had promised. *Maybe, maybe* if he could just get to Iraq everything would be better, he thought.

The opportunity to deploy came years later. On September 6, 2007, on the day of his twenty-fourth birthday, Jeremy Arsiaga received a notice from the Marine Corps. He had left the Corps earlier that year, but now he was told he could be reinstated for deployment to Iraq the next year. It was an optional deployment, one he could have avoided. But this was what Jeremy had been waiting for. Gilbert had gone to Iraq in that first wave of US troops, and Robert had died serving his country. Jeremy felt it was his duty to go, despite having a wife and three-year-old son at home, and an older son, Adam, from a previous relationship. He felt this was the opportunity that might assuage the guilt he had been feeling. The opportunity to move forward.

No one in the family wanted Jeremy to go to Iraq. The pain of Robert's death was still raw and the fear was real. Yet there was an understanding that Jeremy needed to show that he, too, could serve. Patricia understood it most of all. She believed that this deployment was exactly what Jeremy needed to heal. And she was determined to make the best of his time away. Her plan was to stay busy and go back to college while he was gone.

What she wasn't prepared for was Jeremy's instant regret. On July 4, 2008, just hours after Patricia and little Robert saw Jeremy off, he called her from a refueling stop on his way into Iraq.

"What have I done?" he asked Patricia. "What if I never make it back?" Patricia was gentle, reminding him that this was what he wanted, that he would be OK, and then telling her husband—the one avowed atheist among the Arsiaga children—that she was praying for him.

In the months that followed, Patricia and Jeremy were able to video chat almost every day over Skype. He told her little about what he was doing, and on the days he could not call he did not say why. All he said was that he was doing guard duty for long hours at the Al Asad air base in western Iraq.

Patricia talked eagerly in the beginning about college and working full-time at a furniture store. Little Robert was in day care. But she sensed that when she talked about her day, Jeremy would get homesick and get it in his head that she didn't need him anymore. They argued from time to time, and he would have the occasional crying jag, but she thought things would be OK.

Six months into his deployment, in the middle of a war zone, Jeremy had a major mental breakdown. A breakdown so profound that the Marine Corps sent him home. Jeremy called Patricia to tell her he simply couldn't handle the stress and had been given a medical waiver. He told no one else. Not his mother, not his siblings. He never explained to Patricia what triggered the breakdown, or what it entailed. He would carry the pain in private.

Days later, on his arrival back in Midland, Jeremy was met with a grand celebration. Unaware of his reason for returning, the entire family, along with forty Patriot Guard Riders, including many Vietnam veterans, came to greet him. Some thirty American flags waved in the desert wind.

The local paper, the *Midland Reporter-Telegram,* celebrated his return as well, assuming it meant he was finished with his deployment. "Descending the stairway Thursday night at Midland International Airport," the paper wrote, "Marine Corps Corporal Jeremy Arsiaga was one of the most composed people present, as he was welcomed home from Iraq with cheers, applause, flags and posters." The gratitude was "tripled," the paper said, because his brother Robert had been killed in Iraq. Gilbert was quoted as saying the family was "relieved and excited" that "they would experience no further war related tragedy."

But Jeremy Arsiaga was feeling nothing but shame, and the celebration surely made it worse. He had chosen to go to Iraq to honor his brother, and he had not been able to complete the deployment. His brothers had both fought in the war, but he could not take it. He returned to Patricia sleepless and plagued by nightmares. He was hearing noises constantly and would stay in the living room to protect Patricia and little Robert from threats that weren't there. He tried therapy but didn't like it, and medication didn't sit well with him either. Patricia could see more than ever now that losing his brother had left him with survivors' guilt.

"My brother was such a great person. He will never have a wife and child like I have," he would tell Patricia. Jeremy insisted on keeping a gun at his side on those sleepless nights. Patricia hated guns, after a young cousin had accidentally killed his little brother, and did not want them in the house, but Jeremy insisted he had to keep the family safe.

Patricia, just a teenager when they had married, stayed by his side. She saw resolve in her husband. He wanted to be a good father and a good husband.

Jeremy began talking about Robert constantly to keep his memories alive. He would tell stories of how Robert had teased him as a kid and how hard the death of their father had been on all of them so many years before. A good sign, she thought, hearing her husband talk about his lost brother and the feelings he had for him.

In 2010, Jeremy and Patricia welcomed a second son, Silas, and Jeremy's progress continued. He still had nightmares, but he had a good job in the oil fields and went back to school to become a firefighter. He also took another step that surprised Patricia. He started going to church, telling Patricia that if she was going, he would too. A friend of Patricia's from work formed a bond with Jeremy at Crestwood Baptist and answered the questions that had turned him away from religion.

Patricia was thrilled when her husband had found faith. "Jeremy finally let go and followed Jesus," she says. The Arsiagas were there at church every Sunday. Things were going well for Patricia and Jeremy.

With the ten-year anniversary of Robert's death approaching, it seemed all of the siblings and their mother were beginning to heal. Robert's young wife, Tracie, was in a new relationship and had two young children. She did not attend the memorial service at Fort Hood, but Angel, Sylvia, Gilbert, and Jeremy were all committed to attending. Jeremy even posted a much-belated message to his late brother days before the reunion on the obituary site Legacy.com:

> March 28, 2014 *I don't think that I have ever came around to putting this out in public like this but I want you to know brother that there is not a day that goes by that my heart doesn't break missing you. It still hurts like the first day I found out we lost you. I can't express my feelings very well so I push them deep inside so I don't have to deal with the pain of you being gone. How after all these years can I feel like I never spend [sic] enough time with you? I'm proud to call you my brother and I pray, god willing, that I will have the pleasure of being in your presence again.*

On the morning of April 4, 2014, the ten-year anniversary of the Sadr City battle, the word "family" was heard often at the Fort Hood

(From left) Gilbert Arsiaga, Jeremy Arsiaga, Angel Muñoz, and Martha Raddatz at the tenth reunion for veterans of the Black Sunday ambush in Sadr City, Iraq. Salado, Texas, April 2014.

Remembering those who gave their lives during the 2-5 Cavalry's deployment to Iraq at the tenth reunion. Salado, Texas, April 2014.

gathering—not just biological family, but the Army family, there at the base where it had all begun. The Army family that had suffered so much on that day in 2004 and over the year that followed. I felt very much a part of that family, since so many who were there for the anniversary had shared their stories with me and had become close.

For Sylvia, the day was complicated and difficult. The memory of her son was vivid, and yet the trauma of standing among those men who had served with him was painful in ways she had not expected. Hearing Robert's fellow soldiers tell stories about her son was gratifying, but she wanted to be sure that none of them felt shame or guilt over what had happened. "I got a lot of comments like, 'I wish it would have been me,'" she remembers. She told them, "No, it was the way it was supposed to be."

I have pictures from that day and from the BBQ that evening. In one, I am with Sylvia and Angel, who are both smiling and proud. In another, I am wedged between Jeremy and Patricia, who was standing quiet but strong.

Angel's speech, with her brothers by her side, sparked in her a new way to express her pain and move forward. In the spring of 2015, Angel's mother told her that the Army's Survivor Outreach Services was seeking written reflections to publish in advance of Memorial Day. Angel decided she would submit her thoughts remembering Robert and the broader meaning of the somber holiday:

> *I want everyone to know that Memorial Day is not just about the day off, BBQ's, and parties. I want them to know that it is about the men and women who wear the uniform of our great military, the ones who made the ultimate sacrifice, those who lost life protecting each other and the very freedom our country stands for. I would like for them to take time out of their busy days and go to a memorial wall or cemetery and take in the realization that so many have died to protect our very right to live and to live free.*

The Army published the piece on Memorial Day—May 25, 2015—and then invited Angel to come to Washington, DC, with a guest to commemorate the holiday. She brought her mother. They traveled to the Pentagon, where tens of thousands of motorcyclists had come to the city to pay tribute to those who died. They were there for Memorial Day speeches at Arlington National Cemetery, a cemetery Angel described to her Midland paper as a place "of sadness and beauty all mixed up in one." Most importantly, she would meet other Gold Star Families, forming what she said was an unbreakable bond between them.

It was during the summer months following Angel and Sylvia's trip to Washington that Patricia began to notice a change in Jeremy. And not a good one. He was clingy, insecure, and depressed. She didn't know what sparked the downhill slide. They had a third son, Iain, that year, and the three boys were thriving. Jeremy's job was going well, and the family was still attending church regularly. Jeremy understandably had moments when he was sad about Robert's death, but she thought he had learned to cope with them.

On the night of September 3, 2015, after putting their sons to sleep, Jeremy and Patricia sat together on their bed and talked about renewing their vows someday. Jeremy talked about playing their favorite songs about love and devotion. She felt close to him and encouraged by his optimism. It was three days before his thirty-second birthday.

The next morning, Patricia got up early to shower before seeing the boys off to school and heading to work. Jeremy followed her into the shower, which he had started doing in the last couple of weeks. He sat outside the shower stall on the toilet seat. She noticed a vacant look in his eyes. "Do you love me?" he asked.

It annoyed Patricia. She reminded him that just the night before they had talked about plans to renew their vows. "You don't love me," he responded. Patricia was getting ready for work and losing patience. "I don't want to argue," she said, reminding him again of their conversation and the many times she had told him how much she loved him. Jeremy stopped talking, stood up, looked his naked wife in the eyes, and headed for the bedroom across the hall.

"I am about to make your life easier," was all he said.

Panicked now, Patricia grabbed a towel and ran to the bedroom. The door was locked. The last thing she heard was Jeremy saying, "All I do is love you," and then a single gunshot. Patricia frantically banged on the door, finally managing to get it unlocked. Jeremy lay on the floor, barely breathing, with a shot to the temple.

She called 9-1-1 and her sons, aged ten, five, and eighteen months, woke up a few moments later. She gathered them together, took them into the living room, and said, "Daddy did something stupid. We need to stay in here for a while." Once the police arrived and Jeremy was pronounced dead, she asked the officers to drive her and the kids to the place she needed to go first: to Sylvia's.

The depth of pain that Syliva and Patricia experienced on that day was something beyond heartache. Patricia tried to stay strong for her young children, but Sylvia was inconsolable. And yet she, too, had to remain strong. She called Angel.

"You need to come home," Sylvia said to her daughter. Angel Muñoz had heard those very words before—eleven years earlier, after Robert was killed, when she had driven home to find the government vehicle in her mother's driveway. This time, she didn't wait to ask her mother why she had to come home. She wanted to know now.

"I wanted her to tell me," Angel remembers, and Sylvia did.

"Jeremy's gone. He killed himself," she said. Images of their lives as children flashed through Angel's head the moment she heard the news. Quick, happy memories of a little Jeremy in her arms pretending he could drive a car. Seconds later she blacked out.

Gilbert was driving by a Little League baseball field in Galveston when he got the call from his mother. "Jeremy killed himself," she said. Gilbert pulled over to absorb what his mother had just said, then stepped on the gas to head home.

Jeremy had called Gilbert just the day before to chat about football and the beginning of the NFL season. The Houston Texans were about to play, and both said they were going to watch the game. Gilbert said Jeremy was upbeat and gave no clues that he was considering suicide.

My husband and I were with my daughter and her little girls in

Middleburg, Virginia, walking through a broad green field, when I saw Angel's name appear on my phone. It was unusual for her to call, so I veered off the path to talk to her. Angel sobbed into the phone, wrenching sobs, telling me that Jeremy was dead. I sank down into the grass and cried along with her. It was unfathomable to me that this family, which had already seen such tragedy, had lost another son. Angel asked me to call Sylvia, which I did immediately. Sylvia was in a state of shock. She could barely speak. I told her I loved her and that her family would get through this. What I didn't say was that I had no idea how they would do it.

Jeremy had traveled a long, difficult, and largely under-the-radar journey to that moment in his bedroom. The loss of his brother, the feeling he had let him down, his failure to complete his own deployment all weighed on him. *How could anyone love a man like that?*

Looking back, the family recalled signs in the last few months. Patricia said he talked often about his mother and needing to help her. The couple was doing better financially, and he would say, "We need to take care of my mother." And in a few late-night conversations, he had said, "I feel like my time is coming."

Angel kept looking back at photos of her brother over the years and fixating on his eyes. "There is pain in those pictures, a vacant, hollow stare," she says. She saw that pain especially in the newspaper photograph from the day he returned from Iraq, greeted like a war hero. Haunting her further were those words that took Jeremy ten years to write on the online obituary for Robert, published just the previous year:

> *I can't express my feelings very well so I push them deep inside so I don't have to deal with the pain of you being gone.*

The scourge of suicide among veterans is well-known, but it wasn't as clearly understood then. Even now the statistics don't tell the whole story. Studies show that between 11 and 20 percent of veterans from the Iraq War suffered post-traumatic stress, and that those who served there were 41 percent more likely than the general population to die by suicide. A study done by Brown University's Costs of War project found that while more than 7,000 US military service members were killed in war operations in Iraq and Afghanistan, deaths by suicide among veterans of those wars were four times higher. When the study was published, in June 2021, an estimated 30,177 active-duty personnel and veterans of those post-9/11 wars had taken their own lives.

Angel and Gilbert knew the numbers were high, and they knew Robert's death had contributed to Jeremy's. So, on the day Jeremy died, they shared a promise: "*Don't you dare leave me,*" Angel told him. He was her one surviving brother. In return she made her pledge: "*I promise you we're gonna do what we can to stay.*"

For Angel Muñoz, the years following the twin traumas of her brothers' deaths challenged the adage that "time heals all wounds." It seemed to her that time wasn't healing anything. She was doing her best to raise her three children, but she was having constant feelings of guilt and occasionally anger over the war itself. Above all, she carried a deep sadness that showed no signs of lifting. Jeremy's death had sent her spiraling back to a dark place.

Gilbert said Jeremy's death made it hard for him to do anything. He lost the will to be better. His anger returned, his need to control anything he could, including his wife, Crystal. His marriage was strained, and his two children brought little joy. He was overwhelmed by feelings that life had been unfair to his family.

But no one suffered more than Sylvia, the Gold Star Mother. After eleven years, she had made peace with the death of Robert, and had promised herself she would live life in a more positive way. But when Jeremy took his own life it was unbelievable to her. She felt even worse than she had when Robert died, because she was filled with guilt. Again, she withdrew, pulling away from her children, her life, and her community.

It was Angel who first grasped the gravity of the depression she and her family were now experiencing. Desperate, and mindful of the promise she had made to Gilbert, Angel did something she had never done before. She contacted the Veterans Administration for help. She wasn't even sure what they might offer or what services, if any, she could seek. Angel had served during peacetime and left after only two years, nothing on a par with the experiences of most veterans of Iraq and Afghanistan, so she felt she didn't deserve the VA's services in the ways those soldiers did. But she reached out to the VA anyway and begged for mental health help. "I just knew if they didn't do something about this, something bad was going to happen with me," she says, "no matter what I promised my brother."

Angel says that the call to the VA saved her life. She came to understand that she was fighting hard—too hard—to push away her emotions. Were it not for what had happened to Jeremy and the promise she had made to Gilbert, she would never have made that phone call. All those things led her to seek help, to commit to psychotherapy, and to share her own story and that of her family. It would help other families, she reasoned, and it would be therapeutic for her. More starkly, she worried: *If I hold this in, I'll end up like the others.*

"I sat on it for a little bit," she says, referring to her own sadness after Robert's death. "And then we lost Jeremy. And then I knew that that's what I was supposed to do, to speak out and bring awareness about the issues that plague the guys that come back, and the men and women in uniform that struggle regularly with this stuff."

Angel went to work with the nonprofit HEART, an organization that helps people with PTSD. She became something of a public advocate, an achievement for a woman who had never given a public speech of any kind until that ten-year reunion of the 2-5 Cav Battalion in 2014. She spoke to VFW halls and Rotary Clubs, with two basic goals in mind: to speak the names of her brothers and share their stories and to hammer home the point that depression is a wound of war, every bit as dangerous as any bullet or bomb.

The public speaking helped her. As did writing—which she began doing regularly, at the suggestion of her mother and her therapist. It was both a form of therapy and one more way to spread the message.

"When Jeremy died, that was the first time I realized, *Oh, my God, we are not OK,*" she says. "You know, that was just a shield, just a wall I put up." She would slowly find her solace—very slowly, at first—in writing and speaking about the loss in her family. About how to spot the signs of depression and potential suicide that her family had seen. She would go to veterans' events and share anything she could that might help others. That was her purpose now. She felt strongly that despite the way Jeremy had died, she would make certain people knew something about him. "Jeremy was just as worthy of recognition and honor as my brother Robert," she says, "and so I wanted to make sure that happened."

On April 4, 2023, the nineteenth anniversary of Robert's death, she wrote an open letter on social media:

> *I used to think the grief of losing both you and Jeremy was going to kill me. I feel the loss in my gut, and the physical pain at times was hard to bear. I used to long for a sweet release so that I could be near you both. I love you both so much that this life was almost unbearable without you.*
>
> *But it didn't kill me. I'm still here and I'm not going anywhere. The long walk from tragedy and loss to acceptance and redemption is worth the fight.*

I spoke to the Arsiaga family during those years whenever I could. I saw Gilbert, Angel, and Sylvia a few years after Jeremy's death, and again in 2024 at the twenty-year reunion of Robert's Army unit. Slowly the family was emerging from the shadows.

Gilbert told me of the terrible road they had all walked—the recovery from one death and then the horror of another. "We struggled for a long time after we lost Robert, trying to understand it all," he said, "and actually coming to a point where we feel we're OK. And then getting knocked back down after losing Jeremy. Losing all that joy that we just refound."

He told me that small pleasures had helped him on the second road to recovery. He had remembered fishing with his brothers when they were young boys and realized after Jeremy's death that he hadn't touched his fishing poles in years—even though he had moved to Galveston, where finding spots to fish was easy. He took a job at a fishing pier, and the memories came. Good ones.

"I slowly saw it come back to me, the passion for it," he said. "And just one day I was like, 'I gotta get these poles back out.'" Which he did, on the fourth anniversary of Jeremy's death. He brought his old fishing poles down to the pier.

Gilbert watched two birds sitting on the pier. One of them flew off, and the other stayed. And right there with his fishing pole back in the water, thinking so much of Jeremy, Gilbert realized he was the one who needed to fly: *I just need to let this all go.*

There are setbacks, just as there are for those recovering from physical injuries. It remains a terrible burden to bear, and he knows the family will never be completely over the loss, but he searches for things to make it easier. Looking in the mirror has helped. He says he sees a man who had not allowed himself to be happy. Crystal, his wife of twenty-four years, insisted they go to marriage counseling. She would push and push and finally he felt he had no choice. The Veterans Administration helped with that as well. Gilbert says the couple "hit the jackpot with the therapist," saying he saved their marriage.

Sylvia has come a long way too. She says it happened suddenly, on a beautiful day in Midland years after Jeremy's death. A breeze was blowing through an open window, and Syliva felt something she had not felt in a long time. "I got this moment of peace," she says. She took a deep breath and at that moment realized that for years she had been trying to slowly kill herself, letting herself suffer, almost on purpose, to relieve the pain—physically, mentally letting herself die as if she deserved it. She was not leaving the house, not taking care of her health, pretending she wasn't home if there was a knock on the door.

But that morning, that breeze was an awakening. From that day forward she was determined to embrace the good part of her life, her family most of all. She has seen another generation born, and now has nine grandchildren and two great-grandchildren. Angel lives in a small house off a dusty highway in Midland and Sylvia has parked her RV in Angel's

Gilbert Arsiaga with his mother, Sylvia Macias.

driveway. She prefers it that way. It is tidy and bright inside. She loves being close to Angel but also cherishes her independence. And she has been working a part-time job at Chicken Salad Chick, a small restaurant owned by a family she describes as "kind and understanding." She has made friends there; she talks to the customers as she serves them food, enjoying the company of others the way she used to. There are moments of sadness, days when she cries, but she no longer stays in her blue moods for long.

Jeremy's wife, Patricia, now thirty-nine years old, and their three sons remain part of that tight-knit Arsiaga family as well. The first year after Jeremy died, Patricia was numb. She had suddenly become a single mother to three young children who were home when their father shot himself. The oldest, Robert, was ten at the time, and that morning he told his mother, "Dad should have listened to himself." An older boy at Robert's school had died by suicide earlier that year and Jeremy had told his son that it was no way to solve problems. Robert repeated what he had told his mother at his father's funeral: "Dad should have listened to himself."

But from that very first day, Patricia says she forgave her husband. There are days when she is angry, but she knows how much he suffered and that as hard as she tried, there seemed to be nothing she could do to change that. She says her comfort comes from her faith and knowing that Jeremy is reunited in heaven with his brother and his father. She and the children share only good memories of Jeremy and talk about him often.

"I have wanted positivity for my children since they lost their dad," she says, and she has found it. She works from home as an accountant, the same job she had when Jeremy died.

Robert is now at Trinity University in San Antonio, studying computer science. Silas, sixteen, plays baritone in the high school band, and Iain, at eleven, loves basketball. Adam, twenty-six, Jeremy's son from a previous relationship, is now living with Patricia as well. She has always

Angel Muñoz with her mother, Sylvia Macias.

been close to him, and even closer now that he is a father to five-year-old Luna. The family sees Angel and Gilbert often, and their cousins. Sylvia calls Patricia "Mija," a Spanish contraction for "my daughter."

Robert and Jeremy are buried in the same cemetery in Midland. Robert is near the back gate, in the veterans' section, and Jeremy near the front gate, because the cemetery ran out of room in the veterans' section. The family likes to think of the brothers as keeping watch over them. Angel often remembers what Jeremy said after Robert died: "It couldn't have happened to a better family."

What he meant by that is that their love for one another, their strength, and their will to keep memories alive would get them through. It was not enough for Jeremy, but for Angel, Gilbert, Patricia, and Sylvia, that family love is what got them through.

Sylvia had four children who served in the US military. Only two survived. Angel and Gilbert lost two brothers. To find the strength to carry on after that loss is an extraordinary feat. This is a family for whom life was never easy, even without the losses they have suffered. It has taken willpower, courage, and purpose to see a light. And despite the occasional setbacks, that light is shining bright now for Sylvia.

"I think my family is all I need now," she says. "I don't want anything else. I don't need anything else."

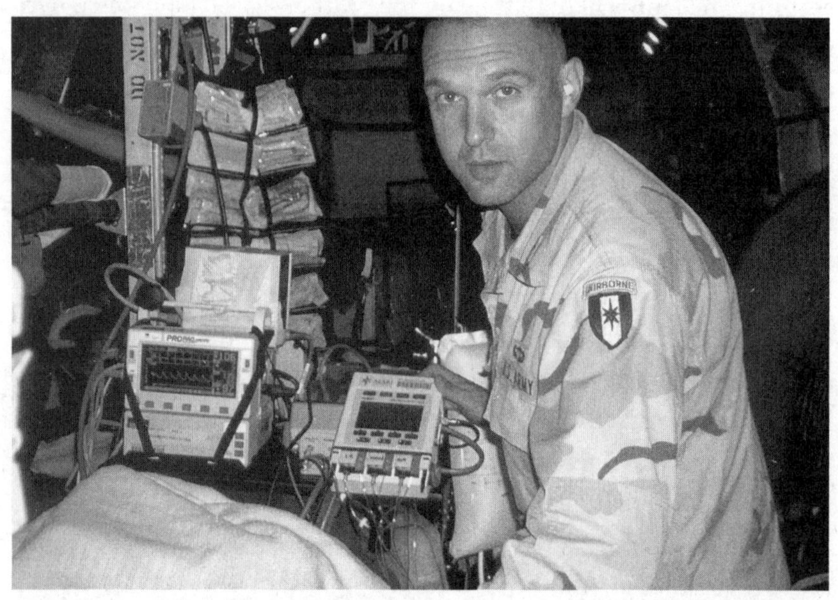

US Army neurosurgeon Dr. Rocco Armonda, with a critical patient aboard a C-17 medical transport flight from Iraq to Germany in December 2003.

CHAPTER 9

The Skull Cracker

Rocco Armonda

DR. ROCCO ARMONDA TALKS CONSTANTLY WHILE HE works. He barely takes a breath, pausing only for brief questions. Even with a mask tightly covering his nose and mouth, he is impossible to muzzle. Not that I would want to. What he is talking *about* is profoundly important. But it is not easy to listen to this man while he works.

Draped in sea-blue surgical scrubs, we are standing together over an open skull. Just inches beneath us, on an operating table, is a brain pulsing through a five- or six-inch opening where a bone saw carefully removed a portion of the skull. Dr. Armonda is gently and skillfully probing the glittering mass, searching for bits of shrapnel.

The man on the table, a severely wounded Ukrainian soldier in his twenties, was hit by Russian artillery earlier that day. I have seen many images of the human brain but never a real one up close. I was also keenly aware that the brain on the table belonged to someone's son or husband or father.

"This is definitely a long recovery," Dr. Armonda told us as he finished the operation. A bevy of Ukrainian doctors leaned in, hanging on his every word. Yet he was hopeful: "It's the frontal lobe, so his chances of recovery are much, much better."

Rocco Armonda was quick to credit Ukrainian doctors as the primary surgeons, but this soldier's chances of recovery were that much better because Armonda was there, and because of the lessons he and other doctors had learned in Iraq and Afghanistan.

We were at Mechnikov Hospital, in the eastern Ukrainian city of Dnipro, the closest major hospital to the front lines. Mechnikov handled over sixteen hundred patients daily, twice the volume seen at the largest trauma center in Washington, DC. The hospital's chief neurosurgeon, Andriy Sirko, later told me that since Russia had invaded Ukraine in February 2022, the hospital had performed thirteen hundred brain surgeries, amputated thirty-five hundred limbs, and transfused some fourteen tons of blood. When I was there, doctors were performing five to eight brain operations each day. The surgery I had watched Dr. Armonda perform was his fifth that day. Even for a war zone, it was a stunningly high number. No hospital anywhere in the world had more experience with penetrating brain injuries. It was not a record Dr. Sirko had sought to break; he just wanted me to know what they were up against.

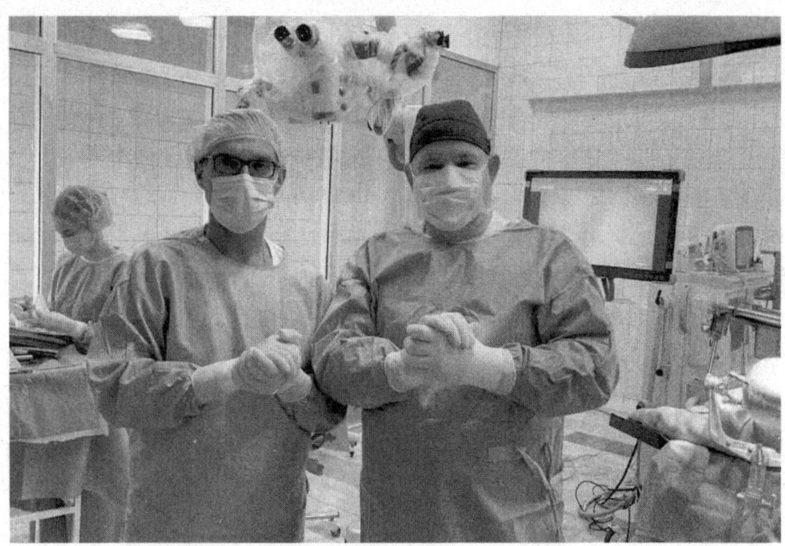

Volunteering in Ukraine. Dr. Rocco Armonda with Dr. Andriy Sirko, head of cerebral neurosurgery, in the main operating room of Mechnikov Hospital in Dnipro, Ukraine, May 2023.

Dr. Sirko also wanted to talk about the man who had come so far to help. "Without exaggeration," he said, "I can say that thanks to Rocco's help, thousands of wounded civilian and military lives have already been saved."

"Rocco" was a fifty-nine-year-old retired US Army neurosurgeon, avid cyclist, Ironman competitor, and director of Neuroendovascular Surgery and Neurotrauma at MedStar Washington Hospital Center and Georgetown University Hospital. He was also a regular volunteer physician in Ukrainian operating rooms.

Penetrating brain injuries have become commonplace in the recent wars, and experience in frontline treatment of these injuries has inspired important medical innovations. Neurosurgeons can now use minimally invasive endovascular surgery to repair arteries damaged by blast injuries with tiny devices delivered through a catheter. Dr. Armonda shared his surgical expertise with Ukrainian doctors, but he insisted he was also their student.

I met up with Dr. Armonda in Dnipro that February 2024, even though he had urged me not to come. "It's too dangerous," he said, "and I would feel terrible if something happened to you." But he knew me well enough to realize his efforts to wave me off would be futile. I've been to many combat support hospitals in war zones, and I too was a regular in Ukraine. I was there two years before, when Russian troops launched a barrage of missiles and rolled in ground troops. Some were predicting that Russian troops would overrun the country, and ABC had evacuation plans in place if that happened.

But the Ukrainians fought hard to stop the advance and have been fighting to keep as much land as possible ever since. Their losses have been staggering. When I reached the hospital, casualties were pouring in from Avdiivka, a small but critical town that had been captured by the Russians just a few days earlier. These battered troops were the latest in a procession of Ukrainians to come to the hospital—more than twenty-five thousand soldiers in just two years. And they have kept coming. By November 2025, the hospital had handled more than fifty thousand casualties, over one thousand per month.

Mechnikov Hospital is one of Ukraine's oldest and largest medical centers, a five-story facility in a city of more than one million. It has seen its share of trauma—centuries of it. Built in 1798, when Russian emperor Czar Paul I ruled Ukraine, its doctors had cared for wounded soldiers from the Crimean War and First and Second World Wars. The wounded streamed in again in 2014, when Russia invaded Crimea. Now, once again, the hospital was straining at the seams.

The day I visited was bitter cold. Arriving at the doors of the emergency room, I saw a line of ambulances waiting to unload patients. Only the most severely wounded were being seen with any degree of urgency. Sergii Ryzhenko, the hospital's director, told me that between thirty and fifty wounded soldiers were arriving daily from the front lines in the Donbas region, roughly one hundred miles to the east.

The hospital was treating brain injuries, penetrating neck injuries, chest injuries, and amputations. Men came with wounds caused by everything from old-style artillery shells to drones and cruise missiles.

When the war began, Dr. Armonda was in Washington, DC, treating stroke victims in Georgetown. Like many Americans, he was horrified by the images coming out of Ukraine. All he could think of was Germany's invasion of Poland in 1939. "It was a repeat of history, a sovereign country invaded," he told me. "People were dying, and the powerful US military could only watch. People did nothing."

Almost immediately, he started organizing shipments of high-end medical aid to Ukraine. A few months later, when asked if he would like to travel to the war-torn country, he said yes. He had a wife and six children, but they had long since come to terms with his sense of mission. His twenty-six-year-old daughter, Gabriella, who was five when he first deployed to Iraq in 2003, had written a letter to President George W. Bush asking: "When will my daddy come home?" When a staffer sent a card back thanking her for her interest in the White House, Gabriella immediately wrote back: "You didn't answer my question!!"

Heidi Armonda knew there was no stopping Rocco. "We are two very independent people, and we support each other in what we want to do," she told me. A neonatal nurse with years of experience in med-

Home. Dr. Rocco Armonda returning from deployment to Iraq and greeted by his daughter Gabriella in March 2004.

ical trauma, she understood that trying to talk Rocco out of going to Ukraine was a waste of time. "He is all about, 'I'll go wherever I need to go. I'll do whatever I need to do for whoever is in need,'" she said of her husband with quiet pride. A force in her own right, Heidi is a former trauma nurse, a fellow Ironman triathlete, and a consummate volunteer.

Rocco Armonda made his first trip to Dnipro in April 2023. He returned in February 2024, when I met him there, and again a year later. He was deeply inspired by Dr. Sirko and his colleagues and, despite his long career in military medicine, was floored by what he found. Patients lined up in hallways. Empty rooms turned into intensive care units. He estimated there was maybe one nurse for every five intubated ICU patients.

I saw the overflow myself. In one bed after another, critically injured soldiers and civilians were lying side by side. Double and triple amputees. Armonda's surgery schedule was far more intense than any surgeon would face at a hospital in the United States or in other war zones where he'd worked.

Rocco Armonda was no stranger to battlefield injuries. He had deployed with the first wave of US forces that rolled into Iraq in March 2003. Few Americans have any idea that the invasion force included a Neurosurgery Division—though "Division" was a generous term for the team attached to the Twenty-Eighth Combat Support Hospital operating out of Fort Bragg. The 207th Neurosurgery Division, whose code name was Skull Cracker, had eight medical team members, but only two were practicing neurosurgeons. The Pentagon hadn't seen a need for more, thinking that the war would be brief and that serious brain inju-

Skull Crackers. The 207th Neurosurgical Team at their base fifteen miles west of Baghdad, Iraq, June 2003. Dr. Armonda is second from left, rear row.

ries would be treated far from the battlefield. Both assumptions were way off the mark.

"We'll call you when we have casualties," Armonda was told. As it turned out, calls to his cell phone came often. The combat medevac teams around Baghdad began making evacuation plans for brain-injured soldiers based on the proximity of the 207th. They wanted to be close to the Skull Crackers.

"The injuries we saw in Iraq were something totally different than what we would see in civilian emergency rooms," Armonda recalled. "It's polytrauma, not just cranial or head and neck, but extremity injuries, with a multi-organ effect. And not just gunshot wounds, like you might see stateside, but significant blast and fragmentation injuries."

Armonda called his Iraq hospital the "Dark Side of the Moon." During the first few months of the war, even the most serious brain trauma injuries were treated under spartan conditions, with shortages of medical equipment and no internet connectivity. Logistical support and resupply runs were haphazard at best. The field hospital was in the middle of the desert, far from other facilities, with a large ammunition dump on one side and a refueling point on the other. "Danger on both sides," Armonda recalled, "and we were in the center of it."

One afternoon the ammo dump exploded or "cooked off," as Armonda put it. They were never sure whether insurgents had set it off or whether it was triggered by a mishap within their own unit. In any case, the secondary explosions had struck the hospital, and Armonda and his team had been forced to evacuate and create makeshift ORs in a few small garage spaces they found nearby. There were days when they ran out of oxygen or IV fluids or antibiotics. The location never made sense to the medical teams. It was one more indication, if any were needed, that there had been little attention paid by war planners to the injuries the war would produce. More than once Armonda wondered, *What the hell are we doing here? Why aren't we at an air base, where you could get logistics quickly and easily?*

Their worst day came on August 19, 2003, when the team was alerted to a mass-casualty incident in Baghdad. A suicide truck bomber had plowed into the United Nations headquarters with devastating force. Twenty-two people, including the UN High Commissioner for Human Rights, Sérgio Vieira de Mello, were killed, and more than one hundred others wounded. Armonda and his team treated many of them.

"We had civilian patients coming to us with the whole assortment of injuries," he said. "They had blunt trauma from the building falling on top of them. They had blast trauma from the explosion. They had penetrating trauma from the glass."

Two decades later, Rocco Armonda was back near the front lines of a global war. There was one advantage in Ukraine, however. The surgeons at Mechnikov were able to use advanced procedures that were impossible in the Iraqi desert, including those developed with the help of battle-tested neurosurgeons. But the injuries Dr. Armonda saw in Ukraine were far more serious than those he had seen in Iraq. For one thing, he said, there were so many more of them. "In Iraq, we had one-tenth the number I've seen here," he told me. "What we had, over twenty years of war in Iraq and Afghanistan, is basically what they've had here in just two years."

In Iraq, there had been powerful but crude explosive devices and gunshot wounds. In Ukraine, surgeons were confronted with the carnage caused by cluster bombs and thermobaric explosions. "Even with body armor and rapid medical evaluation," Armonda said, "these patients are very, very ill."

Key to the outcome was the speed with which a wounded soldier could be brought to the operating theater. On visits to Iraq and Afghanistan, I'd come to understand the importance of the "golden hour," the advantage that came when rapid and effective medevacs could bring wounded soldiers to a triage center within an hour. Armonda and his team had seen it time and again: Speed saves lives. But in eastern Ukraine in 2024, medevacs by air weren't possible, because it wasn't safe to fly. Armonda knew a Ukrainian helicopter pilot who had served with the United States in Afghanistan. The week before we visited Mechnikov Hospital, the pilot's helicopter was shot down as he was trying to ferry casualties in from Avdiivka. He was badly wounded, with multiple fractures, and his copilot was killed. Given such circumstances, the majority of Ukrainian casualties had to be brought in by road. That meant the "golden hour" in Ukraine was a fiction. A two-hour trip was considered a lightning-fast run.

"Sometimes it takes three hours," Armonda said. "Sometimes it takes twelve hours. Sometimes it takes a day to get the patients here." Moreover, medical personnel in Ukraine were often targeted in drone attacks, delaying casualty evacuations even more.

While he had been deeply impressed by the facility and by Dr. Sirko and his staff, Armonda worried the place was at risk of being overwhelmed. Beyond the heavy flow of wounded, the war had created profound staffing issues. Many Ukrainian doctors and other medical professionals left to protect their families when the Russians invaded. Almost all the hospital's nurses had nevertheless stayed. "Pretty remarkable," Armonda observed. "They're working day in and day out, not ever knowing what the end is." He noted that in his own military experience, medical teams had gone in for six- or twelve-month combat rotations, only occasionally extending to eighteen months. They had always been able to look forward to the date of their return home.

"Here, it *is* their home," Armonda told us. "It's their home that's under attack. I never had to worry about a missile or an artillery round coming and hitting my family while I'm at work. I never had to worry about my family scurrying down into a cellar or a basement for an air-raid siren, and then having your house destroyed or loved ones killed. They live that every single day. So every day they're showing up, going to work, dealing with all of these challenges—logistical challenges, patient care challenges—and doing it nonstop, not knowing when the end is and not knowing what the outcome will be. It's remarkable."

All Rocco Armonda had ever wanted was to be a military doctor. Growing up in Chicago, he had spoken from a young age about military service and medical care as twin callings. He had been inspired by his maternal grandfather, who served in the Italian Carabinieri and fled to

Chicago when Benito Mussolini came to power, and by his godfather, who served in the US military as an Army dentist after the Korean War.

Rocco's grandfather was a role model. He described him as "someone who was about the whole 'Officer and a Gentleman' type of military, where you're there to protect and serve others," Armonda said. "I always saw the military as embodying this amazing sense of purpose, of duty, of honor, of courage on behalf of serving other people and protecting other people. I saw it as basically a place where you can be part of something bigger than just yourself."

As a kid, Armonda was hooked on the TV series *M*A*S*H,* a hugely popular show of the 1970s and '80s that found both humor and pathos in a Korean War combat support hospital. He was inspired by "the idea of being a military surgeon and being able to take care of casualties and being in a place where you can make a difference, like the surgeons did on *M*A*S*H,* with that ability to serve two worlds, in military and then also in medicine."

Armonda grew up in something of a battle zone as well. His parents separated in 1970, when he was six years old, his sister seven, and his brother just a toddler. For Rocco, the separation came as a relief. He remembers his father as a "physical and verbally abusive person. He beat up my mom in front of us and hit us with golf clubs, plant stands, and pool sticks." Rocco remembers trying to take a swing at his father to protect his mother, "though I was just a little kid." Four years after the divorce was final, Rocco says his lawyer-father managed to get sole custody of the three children: "He was a lawyer and knew a lot of people. He lied and said my mother was using drugs and was irresponsible and cared only about her job." Rocco's father would later have his license to practice law temporarily suspended over accusations that he had cheated clients.

It was devastating for Rocco's mother, Diane, a Chicago public school teacher, and of course it was awful for Rocco and his siblings. Rocco said his father would not allow Diane to see the children. Even her frequent letters were hidden from them. So Diane moved to Southern California, partly out of fear, but also to chase a Hollywood dream. She changed her name to Micole Mercurio, and over the years she managed to secure roles in some eighty-two professional films and TV shows, including significant parts in *Flashdance, While You Were Sleeping, Hill Street Blues,* and *What Lies Beneath.*

Despite the distance, Rocco maintained a strong, loving relationship with his mother, whom he describes as "a wonderful human being." She saw in him qualities he had not seen in himself: "She saw good in me—an enthusiasm, empathy, and compassion, and she helped nurture that."

This was the opposite of what he felt for his father. Rocco was going to get as far away from him as possible and in no way owe him anything. Setting his sights on a military career for Rocco had the added bonus of rebelling against a father whom he saw as "anti-military." Rocco applied to the Naval Academy, the Air Force Academy, and the Military Acad-

West Point cadet Rocco Armonda, graduation day, May 1986.

emy at West Point. Because he wore glasses, the Air Force Academy required a waiver before it would admit him. But West Point readily accepted him. Armonda joked that in the post-Vietnam era "they would have taken anybody."

At seventeen, in the fall of 1982, Rocco Armonda began his "plebe" year at West Point. He recalled being one of the youngest there. He had never met a West Point graduate and had no idea what he was getting into, but he quickly realized it was where he belonged. The values and character traits that the academy promoted were precisely what he sought—teamwork, challenge, and "the whole idea that you can't just focus on one particular area. You must maintain fitness to fight, mental resilience, physical strength, emotional fortitude—along with academic and technical skills." Armonda had it all. His brother would follow in his footsteps, part of his own rebellion against their father.

In May 1986, the day after graduation, Rocco married a woman he had met his junior year at a West Point dance. Two daughters quickly followed. But it turned out, married life was not what she expected. Rocco was rarely home. He enrolled at the Uniformed Services University of the Health Sciences in Bethesda and then at Walter Reed Army Medical Center, where he quickly developed a reputation as a top-class student and resident neurosurgeon. But his marriage did not survive all his time away and his near-obsessive dedication to his profession, spending more than a hundred hours a week at the hospital. Later, after divorcing his first wife, he married Heidi. They briefly had met two years earlier while they were working at a shock trauma center in Maryland. He knew he had found the perfect match. Independent, strong-willed, a loving stepmother with her own experience in medicine, Heidi was a partner who understood Rocco's need to serve. It was not always easy, but this was the man at whose side she wanted to be for decades to come.

Ultimately, Rocco Armonda spent thirty-one years in the US Army. After 1990 he served as a physician, treating thousands of patients at Walter Reed and Bethesda Naval Hospital and in Iraq. When he left the military in 2013 and joined MedStar Washington Hospital Center, he continued his extraordinary work—but the longing to serve remained.

In the spring of 2022, just after Russia's invasion of Ukraine, two US veterans, former US military trauma surgeons who had gone to volunteer their services in the western Ukrainian city of Lviv, called him. "Roc, the neurosurgeons here could use your help," they told him. They needed help with logistics, but more importantly they needed guidance for some of the more complex procedures.

These weren't just any surgeons. John Holcomb was an Army physician who had multiple combat deployments, including in Mogadishu, Somalia, where he was a part of the surgical team that delivered nonstop care to soldiers for forty-eight hours during the battle that inspired *Black Hawk Down*. Warren Dorlac was an Air Force surgeon whom Rocco called "the trauma czar" in Afghanistan: "Warren and I had known each other for, gosh, twenty-five years. And I said, 'Well, what do you need?'" What they needed first was special equipment and supplies for the neurosurgery wards. Armonda began crowdsourcing equipment from companies and hospitals and soliciting donations from his own network.

"It started slow, and then more people wanted to help with the war," Heidi remembers. "And so more stuff kept happening. People just started showing up at the house and putting stuff in our garage. We'd just leave the door unlocked. So at any given time, somebody might pull in and throw a couple boxes in our garage and drive away."

"Initially, it was very small," Rocco said later. Storage tubs were filled with virtually everything neurosurgeons and anesthesiologists might need—stents, spirals, coils, flow diverters, and much more. Once the piles in the garage got too big, Rocco would rent a U-Haul truck, drive the containers to Newark Airport, and arrange with Ukrainian-American volunteers to take the stuff to Ukraine.

As the war dragged on and the bulk of the fighting shifted to eastern Ukraine, Armonda connected with an NGO called Razom—Ukrainian for "Together" or "Unity," which had been helping to arrange shipments of medical equipment to the front lines for the better part of a decade. In late 2022, one of the leaders of Razom, a woman whose husband was a neurosurgeon, linked Armonda to Andriy Sirko, the Mechnikov surgeon. They met first over Zoom.

"Every time, he asked what we need," Dr. Sirko told us. "Every time, we provided a list of what is needed, and Professor Rocco used all his strength, connections, contacts, acquaintances, colleagues, and friends to collect everything necessary, as quickly as possible." In a series of virtual meetings, he listened to Dr. Sirko and his team of doctors describe their conditions and their wish lists. Soon "Professor Rocco" began offering treatment advice as well; he could see that the Ukrainian doctors had been reading the literature and were acquainted with new developments in the field. In early 2023, Dr. Sirko invited him to Dnipro. Four weeks later, he was on the ground.

When Rocco first told Heidi that he was thinking of going to Ukraine, she questioned him, gently. At this stage of their lives, after all his deployments, was it really necessary to go back to a war zone? The couple had four children ranging in age from seventeen to twenty-five at the time. Rocco's two older daughters from his first marriage were in their thirties.

"The Ukrainian doctors invited him to come over," she remembers. "We're, like, 'Why? You don't actually have to go. You're already sending the equipment.'" But by then she knew that when her husband was inspired, he would be difficult to stop.

On that first visit to Mechnikov Hospital in 2023, he put on scrubs, joined the team, and began assisting the surgeons who were operating on Ukrainian soldiers with traumatic brain injuries. When I visited the hospital a year later, I asked him why he was so committed to coming back to a war where there were no US troops in battle.

"I'm committed because at West Point, we swore an oath to the Constitution to defend the United States against 'enemies foreign and domestic,'" he said. "This is a foreign enemy. Russia is an enemy against the United States, against democracy, against human rights, against all of civilization. And if there's ever a place and a time where America needs to lead, this is the place. It's hard to turn your back. It's so hard to see the sacrifices that these patients make, their families make. The number of soldiers and civilians who've been killed. The number of children who've been affected."

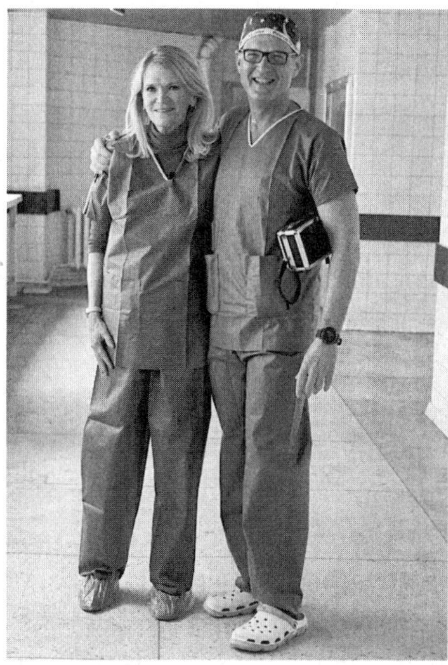

Martha Raddatz with Dr. Rocco Armonda after observing him operate on Ukrainians injured in the war with Russia. Mechnikov Hospital, Dnipro, Ukraine, February 2024.

If Rocco Armonda had been impressed and inspired by the Ukrainian cause, and by the doctors he worked alongside, the feeling was mutual. Sirko, the chief neurosurgeon, gushed, "Rocco has the most experience, not only in Ukraine but in the world."

He certainly didn't need to tell *me* that.

Andriy Sirko couldn't have known, but the fact was, I had known all about Rocco Armonda and his gifts as a surgeon and a human being for a long time. Eighteen years, to be exact. Since he helped save the life of a close colleague and dear friend.

Anyone who worked at ABC News in January 2006 will have a vivid memory of the last Sunday of the month, when we received devastating news. Most staffers woke up to a brief email from David Westin, the news division president, at 7:00 am:

> *Bob Woodruff and his cameraman, Doug Vogt, were injured in an IED attack near Taji, Iraq, today. They were embedded with the 4th Infantry Division, traveling with an Iraqi Army unit in an Iraqi mechanized vehicle. Bob and Doug are both in serious condition and are being treated at a military hospital in Iraq. At this point, we don't know much more than this. We'll keep you posted as we learn more. I know that all of us will keep Bob, Doug and their families in our thoughts and prayers.*

I had learned about the attack several hours earlier, when a frantic call from Bob Woodruff's producer in Iraq, Kate Felsen, awakened me before dawn. Kate had rushed to the combat support hospital as soon she heard about the IED attack, and between sobs, she was telling me what had happened. She told me Bob looked to be more seriously injured than Doug and pleaded for any information I could glean from my contacts in the military.

My first call was to General George Casey, the top US commander in Iraq, and Lieutenant General Peter Chiarelli, his deputy. Both sprang into action and vowed that Bob and Doug would get the same high level of care that the military afforded to those in the service. "*We'll treat them like our own,*" Chiarelli told me.

I'd spent a lot of time in Iraq with General Chiarelli and his men. He was one of the most compassionate and caring officers I'd ever met. He was also optimistic and—based on the information he was getting from the field—he seemed hopeful. Especially about Doug. The general was getting frequent updates from the hospital, all of which I was passing on to ABC, and to Kate.

Between calls, I got dressed and raced into our studios, in a kind of daze. I was scheduled to appear that morning on *This Week with George Stephanopoulos.* As I entered our small lobby in downtown Washington, my cell phone rang. It was General Chiarelli calling from Baghdad. He spoke slowly. When I think back on that call all these years later, I still get chills.

"I just got an update on Bob," the general told me. His voice was quieter than it had been earlier. I stopped in my tracks. "I am really sorry," he said. "I think the early reports were perhaps too encouraging." There was a long and agonizing pause. By now his voice was shaking. "It doesn't look good," he said. "I'm not sure he is going to make it."

I froze in place and closed my eyes, all my journalistic armor shattered. Tears came quickly. It took me a moment to compose myself enough to thank him and end the call.

Ten minutes later I was on the air with George, fighting to stay strong and steady, telling our audience what we knew—but certainly not *all* that I knew.

"Good morning, everyone," George began. "We have to begin today with some news that has hit close to home for all of us here at ABC. . . ."

As we were on air that morning, Bob was in surgery in Baghdad. He had already had more than a quarter of his skull removed to ease the pressure on his swelling brain. The surgeons removed rocks and shrapnel from his brain, but the injuries were profound. Doug had been far luckier. He'd had a shorter procedure and a much better prognosis.

For Bob, who had four young children at home, the future was unclear. He followed in the path of so many of our grievously wounded soldiers. From the blast scene, he was rushed to a field hospital, then to Landstuhl, Germany, and from there, once stable, to a military hospital in the DC area. On that day, Dr. Rocco Armonda happened to be on duty at the hospital.

He had returned from Iraq in February 2004 and had since been at the neurosurgery ward at Bethesda Naval Hospital. Because of his extensive experience in Iraq with traumatic brain injury (TBI) and his gifts as a surgeon, Armonda had become a go-to physician for American troops coming home from Iraq with significant brain injuries. They were coming in high numbers.

Rocco had no idea who Bob Woodruff was, only that he was a journalist who had taken shrapnel to the head and body after an IED blast.

But when the doctors in Landstuhl called to ask Armonda where Bob should go, he said, "To the same place our other severe brain injury patients go." That would be Bethesda Naval.

On January 31, 2006, just two days after the attack, Bob was transported to the Bethesda Naval Hospital from Landstuhl on a C-17 critical care flight, along with nearly a dozen wounded service members. Over Bob's head the nurses had placed a sign that read, "no bone flap," indicating part of his skull had been removed.

Bob's wife, Lee, had flown to Landstuhl and followed him back to Washington. Bob was in critical condition, connected to a tangle of tubes in a medically induced coma. Lee remembers Dr. Armonda entering the room in his white coat with a small box of Kleenex and taking a seat beside her. He gently explained how complex brain injury was and how uncertain recovery could be. So much is unknown, he said. Bob had a severe penetrating brain injury, resulting from the IED blast. Despite the rock and shrapnel, however, the important parts of his brain were intact. While Dr. Armonda never glossed over the harsh realities, he managed to see hope at nearly every turn. "He could have squashed any hope that I had, but he didn't," Lee recalled.

More than a hundred small rocks and countless fragments of metal had blasted into Bob's face, neck, shoulders, and extremities. The most serious threat was a grape-sized rock that had entered the left side of his throat, sheared off part of his jaw, ripped across his neck and lodged less than a millimeter from his carotid artery, just below his right ear. The rock had to be removed in one piece, unlike a tumor that could be picked apart. The surgery was delicate and would be decisive. Dr. Armonda and his team created a 3-D computer-assisted model of Bob's skull to help determine the best approach. Working with the other surgeons, Rocco Armonda wound up successfully completing what could have been life-altering or life-ending surgery in just ninety minutes.

After thirty-six long days, Bob finally emerged from his coma. In the months that followed, Armonda would perform the difficult cranioplasty procedure, replacing the part of Bob's skull that had been removed with a plastic replica. Remarkably, a year after the attack, Bob was back on the air at ABC News and traveling the world.

During those early days with members of Bob's family, I heard often about the confidence Dr. Armonda had inspired in them—his warmth, his sensitivity, and his "dream team" of doctors, as the family called them.

I watched as this compassionate doctor would enter Bob's room to check on his status and comfort his family. Our paths have crossed many times since, and I have seen Dr. Armonda's devotion to our veterans who suffered traumatic brain injuries.

Standing in Dnipro with the man who helped save my friend's life so many years before was surreal. When he went in to perform the surgery on Bob that day in 2006, Dr. Armonda did not know whether he would ever be a journalist again, but he was certain Bob could have a fulfilling life. That notion of a "fulfilling life"—what it means, and who was free to define it—had frustrated Armonda over the years. All too often in his early days in Iraq, and then at Walter Reed, he had contemplated more aggressive treatments for TBI patients and been told, sometimes implicitly, sometimes directly, "*Is it really worth it?*" It wasn't a callous question so much as an honest assessment of risks and rewards. *Are we certain that the inherent risk in a procedure and the resources involved are worth it, given that this person may never speak or walk or function independently again?*

As Armonda gained experience and saw more and more of these cases, he had a different question: *Who are we to judge?* By which he meant that it wasn't for him, or any doctor, to decide what would constitute a useful life. It irked him that many cases were seen as hopeless simply because the future looked so different from the present.

"In the civilian world," he told me, "there's a nihilistic approach to people who have penetrating brain trauma from gunshot wounds: 'It's not survivable. Don't even try.' But when we were taking these lessons back from Iraq and Afghanistan, we started thinking, 'You could actually change the outcomes of these patients if you took a much more aggressive approach.' If you don't take an aggressive approach, well, it becomes pretty much a guaranteed outcome. They will die."

The preservation of life was always the goal, Armonda said, "but also the preservation of function. Yes, it's different, and it's harder, and there are more challenges that they're going to face, but the fact that they're alive, that they can laugh, that they can interact with their family, that all counts."

I saw that up close with Bob Woodruff. A few weeks after he was discharged from the hospital, I went to Connecticut to visit Bob and his family. He had not yet had the large portion of his skull replaced, and I braced myself for the sight of my friend. I knew that since awakening from the coma, he was relearning how to speak. When I knocked on the door of the Woodruffs' home, it swung open quickly. And there was Bob, with something like a bicycle helmet covering his battered brain, scars visible across his body, an immense smile spread across his face. "Hey, girlfriend!" He beamed. For the next hour I marveled at his recovery. His gait was slow and his speech halting, but the funny, bright, and charismatic friend I knew and loved was still there.

Around 10 percent of Dr. Amonda's patients with severe brain injury never come out of their comas. But many more do. Most of these regain function over time and go back to school or work or both and begin new and meaningful lives. All of which brings us back to that tantalizing question: What is a "fulfilling life"? And who are we to judge?

Dr. Armonda has seen so many cases: "There'd be this young man in his twenties, totally disfigured and injured and in a comatose state, and what the family members see—and they'll pull out of their wallets—is this baby picture of this chubby little boy at swim lessons. That's what's in the mother's mind. It's not this horrifically injured young man. It's this memory—*this is who my son was*. Pictures of them throughout their whole life, and then their deployment—they'll put them up at the bedside, and you make this instant connection. This is not just an injury to a person; it's an injury to an entire family.

"They never give up," Armonda said. "So we should never give up."

This bedrock principle would be the catalyst for an innovation of

Rocco Armonda's that wound up saving hundreds, if not thousands, of men and women he never met.

That the battlefield can serve as a laboratory for innovation is not news. Soldiers and commanders must make do with whatever they bring to a war zone, just as Armonda and his small medical team had done back in Iraq in 2003, crafting makeshift catheter treatments or even entire ORs. But the 207th Neurosurgery Unit had done a lot more innovating than that.

Beginning in May 2003, Dr. Armonda and the doctors on his team began seeing serious head trauma—the kind that meant the soldiers would never have made it off the battlefield in earlier wars. He realized early on that many of these young men wouldn't make it off this battlefield either unless the doctors could find some way to deal quickly and effectively with the intense pressure on the brain.

The skull protects the brain, obviously, but after a traumatic injury, when the brain swells, it can become a problem. Expanding upward and out with nowhere to go, it pushes down on the brain stem, which acts as a control center for vital functions. Breathing, heartbeat, movement—even consciousness—are all regulated by the brain stem. Too much pressure can trigger a coma, paralysis, even death.

Ordinarily, surgeons dealing with a patient with severe brain trauma would perform a "craniotomy." A portion of the skull would be removed, the underlying blood clot would be treated, and the bone flap would then be replaced. Alternatively, a larger "craniectomy" could be performed, with the skull section left off temporarily to relieve the brain swelling. That procedure, however, was usually reserved for cases involving a stroke. In his desert hospital, Dr. Armonda found that the standard craniotomy wasn't doing the job, as the swelling would often not peak until three or four days later. "That would be the worst time period for these patients," Armonda explained, "just as they were being transported, not just out of Iraq, but from Germany back to the States."

Put simply and starkly: Soldiers injured in Iraq were dying on their way home or at Walter Reed from a cerebral hemorrhage or a stroke.

Dr. Armonda began to wrestle with a fundamental question: Could they perform the larger, more aggressive craniectomies early on without causing new dangers? Could they do better at relieving the pressure in the brain without killing the patient in the process? Could they identify and treat the blood vessel injuries in the brain that produced strokes?

Armonda believed his past work with stroke and brain aneurysm patients might offer a partial solution. At Walter Reed, he had performed large craniectomies to reduce brain swelling in stroke patients, but this was a highly controlled environment in a top-flight hospital. He came to believe that these more aggressive craniectomies might save the lives of brain-injured soldiers in Iraq. A standard craniectomy removed two to three inches of the skull. Now he expanded it in some cases to nearly six inches.

The results improved almost immediately, with higher survival rates and better retention of basic functions. "We just standardized that procedure for the majority of patients that were coming in with brain swelling or with penetrating brain trauma," Armonda said. He spoke matter-of-factly about a procedure, carried out in a field hospital in Iraq, that involved the removal of large portions of the skull.

"The tents were sterile," he noted, "as sterile as possible, with an air system set up for chemical warfare. Still, it was a tent." The tents were connected to three double-wide trailers that served as ORs. At best, they could each handle two surgeries at a time, meaning just six patients could be in surgery simultaneously. "So you can't take very long," Armonda said. "Your operations can't last six or seven hours. You have to be done, in and out, within an hour and a half, two hours, and you have to move very quickly." Moreover, there were no microsurgery tools, just headlights and magnifying loupe glasses for the surgeons. The key was to marry speed and skill. Armonda likened the work to the pit-stop precision at a racetrack.

"It got to the point where it's like a Formula One or NASCAR tire change," Armonda said. "You come in; you prep; you drape; you make your incision. Next step is hemorrhage control. Next step, expose the skull. Next step, put your burr holes in. And so on." Every now and then, there might be an anomaly. "So you had to be very adept in terms of adjusting things based on the kind of injuries."

The pit-stop analogy sounded apt. Armonda found that patients had the best chance of survival if an operation was done within one to four hours of an injury. He and his team would get a heads-up when a patient with a severe brain injury was coming in. Five or ten minutes later, they'd be in the OR. Two more hours, and the procedure would be finished.

Soon Team Skull Cracker was performing multiple craniectomies a month. Some of the injured were beyond saving, but for the most part Armonda worked from the premise that every one of these badly wounded soldiers could be helped. Once Armonda returned stateside, he was able to use endovascular surgery to repair damaged blood vessels in brain-injured patients and thus help prevent the brain hemorrhages and strokes that so often lead to death, though such procedures were never possible in Iraq.

US-based military doctors wondered whether such aggressive intervention was a good thing. "They didn't know what to do with them when they first got to Walter Reed," Armonda recalled. Even years later, when a new doctor showed up at the hospital and saw these patients, he recalled, some would question what he had done. "Why would you put a human being through this operation?" they would ask. "It's hard to explain to them," Armonda said, "because the conventional thinking is that you're saving a patient for a life not worth living. And we were worried about that as well, when we first started," he said. "Then, when we went back and looked at our patient population, we found it wasn't true. It was not just a higher survival that was higher; so was functional independence."

Ultimately, about 60 percent of Armonda's patients were able to regain that functional independence, as compared to around 10 percent of head trauma patients in the civilian world. It was a staggering difference. The Walter Reed neurosurgeons began taking note and sharing insights. Before long, Dr. Armonda's unconventional approach in Iraq had become the established approach at Walter Reed and Bethesda Naval Hospital. These experiences shaped the updated guidelines for penetrating brain injury, published in December 2025, with contributions by Dr. Armonda and other military and civilian neurosurgeons.

He has contributed to over a dozen scientific papers detailing the new techniques, in the hope that the world will benefit from these painful wartime lessons.

"We definitely realized as we left Iraq and Afghanistan that we had identified the best way to do this operation," Armonda said. In 2004, the number of craniectomies tripled to more than two hundred. More and more wounded soldiers were being saved, among them Bob Woodruff, who owes his survival to the large craniectomy performed on him in a field hospital in Iraq. Having introduced the use of large craniectomies in Iraq, Armonda arguably saved Bob's life a second time with his surgery in Bethesda. The techniques pioneered in Iraq became the standard for neurotrauma patients in war zones and for patients around the world who have experienced penetrating brain injuries.

Specialists at Walter Reed even developed a 3-D virtual trainer for the procedure, much like a flight simulator, for doctors to use before going into combat zones. "When they get deployed, we want them to feel very comfortable with craniectomies," Armonda said. "If you're a neurosurgeon in the military you are familiar with it. It's part of the general indoctrination for active-duty doctors."

In February 2025, with the third anniversary of the Russian invasion approaching, Rocco Armonda was again packing his tubs of donated medical gear and heading back to Ukraine. Once again, the family garage was overflowing. He ran through the inventory: "There's catheters and coils—coils that we use for aneurysms, catheters to allow us to do diagnostic angiography." Armonda told me the medical personnel in Ukraine had been reusing equipment that should have been disposable: "They were rewashing catheters. I'm, like, 'No. Please don't do that. I'll get you some new catheters.'" At the time, he was focused on the drills used in neurosurgery. "For us, drill bits are single-use items," he explained, "but for them, they use them again and again. So I'm trying to get them new drill bits as a way to help."

New souvenirs in his home spoke to recent trips. A *buława*—a ceremonial Ukrainian scepter—hung on a wall, along with a Ukrainian flag with signatures and messages from his colleagues at Mechnikov Hospital and an old red and black Ukrainian war flag dating from the Cossack wars in the 1600s. On another wall was a framed newspaper headline quoting Churchill's wartime speeches: "We Shall Never Surrender/Never Give Up!"

Armonda was due back at the end of the month, just days before the third anniversary of the invasion. After so many years of fighting and with a new administration arguing that money for Ukraine would be better spent at home, US support for the war effort was waning. But that only deepened Rocco Armonda's commitment. Heidi understood, but recent developments in Ukraine had her more concerned about her husband's plan to go back to the busy hospital so near the front lines.

The kids were more nervous this time too. He left flowers for his daughters before heading off, but the move may have backfired. "I think it spooked them," Heidi said. She loved Rocco's commitment and his sense of mission. She was proud that her husband was a doctor who put financial gain last and doing the right thing first. "He's not a businessman," she told me. "He's not about making money or anything like that. He is about buying the most expensive tub to get the equipment to Ukraine in the best condition that he can. He doesn't think about cost. None of that is ever on his radar."

Later that week, once he had safely arrived in Dnipro, Dr. Sirko was once again at his side. He credited Rocco with having inspired other American neurosurgeons—ten at last count—to visit Mechnikov. Dr. Sirko knows that the Ukrainian people have waged a heroic fight. But standing alongside those heroes is an American who will not give up on them. On February 19, when Sirko celebrated his fiftieth birthday, the man he calls his "blood brother" was there. Rocco's arrival, he said, "was the greatest and best gift for me."

Rocco Armonda believes there is nothing heroic about what he has done for Ukraine. "This is what I've been trained to do," he says. "This is what my oath as an officer is about. This is what your oath as a physician is about. It's not about prestige and it's not about power; it's about serving mankind, assisting those who are in the thick of it. It's about doing the best for humanity."

Lance Corporal Steven Schulz during his first deployment to Iraq in 2004.

US Marine Corps Sergeant Shurvon Phillip in Iraq, 2005.

CHAPTER 10

A Mother's Love

Debbie and Steven Schulz, Gail Ulerie and Shurvon Phillip

Friendswood, Texas
East Cleveland, Ohio

CARING FOR CHILDREN COMES NATURALLY TO DEBBIE Schulz. She has three of her own, and she's spent a good part of her life as a grade school special education teacher in Friendswood, Texas, a small town outside Houston. Kind and adventuresome, with a smile that belies her "Don't mess with Texas" roots, Debbie is the kind of friend who is always there for you. So when her son Steven would wake up at 6:00 am, Debbie was ready. She knew he'd need to get to the bathroom as soon as possible, if he hadn't already wet the bed. If he'd made it through the night, Debbie would help him pee in the toilet and then bring him into the kitchen with her to make breakfast. Steven could feed himself, but he was a sloppy eater who would shove the food into his mouth so quickly he would often choke. "Slow down, Steven; chew it; you don't have to hurry," Debbie would tell her brown-eyed boy as he mumbled a few words between bites. After breakfast, another trip to the bathroom so Debbie could help her son brush his teeth—another messy undertaking, so she would tie on a bib—and then she would slowly get him dressed in shorts and a tee shirt since they were the easiest to pull on. The socks and shoes were always a struggle for Steven, so Debbie handled that by herself.

These were the days when Steven was taking two naps a day. A short one in the morning, which allowed Debbie to take a quick shower and put in a load of laundry, and a longer one in the afternoon, when Steven was so exhausted he would tell his mother, "Tuck me in now." Debbie would fluff his favorite blanket, turn off the lights, bid him a sweet "Good night," and head for her own bed: "I took my nap whenever I could, just like when he was a baby. When he slept, I slept."

But Steven Kelly Schulz was not a baby when Debbie tucked him into bed on that November day in 2005. Steven was twenty one years old and nearly six feet tall. A US Marine who seven months earlier became wheelchair bound, partially blind, and badly brain damaged. Debbie Schulz, then forty-nine, had watched her boy go off to war as a grown man—and return as her child again.

Debbie and her husband, Steve (Dad was Steve, the son Steven), had never been keen on their son signing up for the military. Steven was the eldest of the three children. While his mother taught special education, his father worked as a national sales manager for a company that built support structures for construction projects. The kids were raised on the outskirts of Houston in Friendswood, a town of forty thousand people.

Steven was born in August 1984, a smart, happy "rascal" of a kid who did not like the confines of school. His sister, Elaine, says her big brother was adventurous and always getting into things, "or *us* into things." But he managed to grind his way through classes and graduate from the local high school, although he confessed that most of the time he was more interested in girls and partying. He had paid little attention to what would come next in life.

At his parents' urging, Steven enrolled at the community college in Austin, about three hours from Friendswood. It didn't last long. The books, the studying. None of that interested Steven. It seems the only thing he had really thought about while at school was the Marine Corps. When he came home for Thanksgiving break in November 2002, he told his parents he was done with school. "I'm not really liking college so much," Steven declared, before quickly announcing, "I'm thinking of joining the Marine Corps."

Steven was that rare teenager who recognized his own wild streak and was set on taming it. In another family, a mom or dad might have suggested the military to a son with Steven's habits; in this case it was his idea. And it wasn't just the structure he was after. He was a senior in high school when the Twin Towers fell. Anger and patriotism had swelled in him on that day and he never forgot the feeling. He wanted to fight for his country.

Debbie and Steve wanted to support their children's aspirations, but they found it difficult to get behind Steven's idea. There wasn't much military history in the Schulz family. Debbie's father had served in the Coast Guard during World War II and rarely said a word about it; Steve had been eligible to go to Vietnam but was never called.

It would be hard enough to swallow the thought of their son joining the Marines if the United States were in a period of peace, but Steven would be enlisting with the war on terror in high gear.

"*Oh, hell no*," Debbie told her son. "We've already got a war going in Afghanistan. Another one brewing in Iraq. This is a terrible time to get into the Marine Corps." If Steven really felt a need to serve, she suggested he follow in his grandfather's footsteps and join the Coast Guard.

"Marine Corps is the way I want to go," he told his mother. He needed the structure, he said, and thought the toughness would help him. And the Marines, he said, were the toughest. He was eighteen years old.

There was no changing his mind. By Christmas he had enlisted. Steven shipped out to the Marine base in San Diego in April 2003, one month after the first strikes on Iraq. Two months later, his parents traveled to his boot camp and already they found a changed young man. He had lost weight, turned muscular, and was almost unrecognizable with that close-cropped hair. Debbie also noticed a new demeanor—he was quieter and more polite, his speech punctuated with "yes, sir" and "yes, ma'am," his posture ever straight when they sat for meals.

"Where did this kid come from?" was all Debbie could think at the

Private First Class Steven Schulz with his parents, Steve and Debbie Schulz, at his graduation from Marine Corps boot camp in June 2003.

time. The answer to the bigger question, "Where is this kid going?," would come just one year later.

In April 2004, Lance Corporal Steven Schulz found himself in the hornet's nest of Fallujah, in Iraq's Anbar Province. It was a rough time for the United States in Anbar Province. In March of that year, four Blackwater contractors were ambushed and killed by insurgents in Fallujah. The photograph of their bodies lit on fire and hung from a bridge would become one of the most searing images of the war. The United States vowed retaliation.

The Schulz family paid close attention to the news while Steven was deployed, but heard from him only infrequently. There was no Skype or other platform for video calls, so they relied on emails mostly, and every now and then he would have access to a satellite phone. Even then, they got only terse updates on the deployment.

It would be seven months before Steven returned home. Debbie and Steve flew to San Diego to greet the returning Marines and were struck again by the difference. While they knew little about what Steven had experienced, he and the men he'd deployed with seemed noticeably changed.

As soon as Debbie saw the Marines get off the bus that day, she knew they were not the same young men. She could see the steel in their gaze and almost smell the grit of combat. As for Steven, the change was subtle but evident. Her boisterous boy was subdued. After just a little time spent with him that day, she worried he had been scarred by whatever he had seen and done. The easy demeanor and nonchalance were gone. That night and many that followed she found Steven sleeping on the floor.

Her nineteen-year-old son had witnessed Iraqis blown up by mortar shells, children wounded, and a Marine Corps sniper shot and killed during his time in Fallujah. Steven had watched as the sniper was pulled down from a one-hundred-foot tower, battered and bloodied. It was one of his most enduring memories of that deployment. But whatever anguish he needed to process after watching that Marine die, it would have to wait. He was called for a second deployment to Anbar Province just before Christmas. It wasn't long before he was back in Iraq. Steven was solemn when he spoke to Debbie, and adamant that he had to return. "I have the other Marines counting on me," he told her. "I have to go."

In those few months between deployments, the Marines had launched a major offensive in Fallujah. It was one of the fiercest house-to-house battles of the war. Hundreds of insurgents were killed and the city reduced to rubble; this was a volatile and unsettling period in Iraq, with Americans dying on a regular basis. It had become painfully clear that the insurgents were constantly mastering new crude Improvised Explosive Devices that were more difficult to detect with remote-controlled detonators. In 2005, more than half of the year's 158 combat deaths in Anbar Province were caused by IEDs or suicide bombers. Hundreds more were injured, and Steven Schulz was one of them.

On April 19, 2005, Steven Schulz was on patrol in Fallujah in an unarmored Humvee when a roadside bomb hidden in a curb was detonated by insurgents. The explosion pumped a sheet of shrapnel into the vehicle and one metal shard tore into Steven's face near his right eye and punctured his brain. Paralyzed on his left side, blinded in his right eye, and robbed of peripheral vision in his left, he was placed in a medically induced coma. The prognosis was grim. The four other Marines in the vehicle suffered broken bones, but nothing life altering.

Back in Friendswood, Debbie was in bed watching cable news when the phone rang in the Schulz home. Steve and their teenage son, Clay, were asleep. Their daughter, Elaine, was at college. It was just shy of 11:30 pm. Debbie figured it was Steven—he often called at odd hours. She didn't have her glasses on and couldn't quite make out the number, but she was certain it wasn't one she knew. That also suggested it was her son; he used different numbers, depending what phones he could access.

"Mrs. Schulz?"

A gruff male voice.

"Yes, this is Mrs. Schulz."

"Is Mr. Schulz home?"

The man gave his name, along with a military rank. He said he was calling from the Marine base in San Diego where Steven's unit was based.

"Can you get Mr. Schulz on the phone?"

"He's sleeping right now," Debbie said, feeling her anxiety rising. "What do you need?"

"I need you to sit down."

On high alert now, Debbie told the man on the phone, "*You tell me what you have to say.*"

"And he said, 'I need to read this verbatim to you, and you need to listen to all of it.'"

Debbie hustled out to the living room with phone in hand to awaken her husband, who had fallen asleep in front of the television. By then the man on the phone had begun reading: *"Steven Kelly Schulz has been . . ."*

To this day, Debbie Schulz cannot recall much more of the message, only that it was brief, and that he used a military acronym—"VSI," for "very seriously injured." She understood that her son was not dead—

the snippets she absorbed included "alive," "very sick," and "in surgery." And then: "severe brain injury."

That was it, in terms of information. Debbie had moved into the kitchen and picked up a notepad and pencil. Steve was awake now too. Struggling to stay composed, she asked the Marine on the phone to hold while she shared the information with her husband.

Grave as the news was, his reaction stunned her—and was the last thing she needed in this moment. Steve fell to his knees and began wailing, then howling wordlessly. Debbie remembered thinking, *Oh dear God.*

"I said, 'Come here, Steve. Sit down here. I didn't know *you'd* be the one that needed a chair.'" Debbie already suspected that the stress of Steven's deployment had sent her "sober alcoholic" husband back to the bottle after fifteen years without a drink. But she couldn't think about that now.

They asked the man on the phone for more details, but he had none. Just the basic message, with that terrible three-letter acronym: "VSI." He told Debbie and Steve to stay at home. The Marines would call when they had more information.

Debbie looked at her husband, collapsed in a heap on the floor, and as she struggled to pull him to his feet she thought, *Well, what do we do now?*

What they did was cry and hug and cry some more. After a while they turned to practical matters. Leaving messages for their respective places of work. They waited until the next day to tell Clay and Elaine.

Less than three weeks later, in another part of the country, Gail Ulerie would get similar news about her own son, who'd been fighting in the same part of Iraq. But in Gail's case, she'd already had a sense of what was to come. She was a health care aide, working a late shift in East Cleveland, Ohio, caring for a bedridden elderly man. Divorced when her four children were young, Gail worked multiple jobs—she was particularly tired that night, having done a day shift with another patient. At a little after midnight, she dozed off in a chair near the man's bed.

She describes what happened next with clarity and detail in the lilting English Creole of her native island home of Trinidad.

"I was sleeping, and it was like something shook me on my left shoulder and said, '*Get up and pray for Shurvon.*'" Shurvon was her youngest son, twenty-four years old. He'd been in Iraq for four months. "And when I opened my eyes, it was like an angel, white flowing hair, and a robe that was white," she remembers. "And I open my eyes, and I think, *Oh my goodness*"—a phrase she uses often. In this case it was laced with fear.

Flustered, and convinced she had received an omen or premonition, she did as the emissary in her brief dream had suggested she do—she started praying, repeating the Psalms. The 91st, 23rd, and 121st Psalms—"*Thou shalt not be afraid for the terror by night; nor for the arrow that flieth by day.*" Over and over, she prayed for her son Shurvon: *The Lord is my shepherd. The Lord shall preserve thee from all evil. He shall preserve thy soul.*

Gail hardly slept that night, thinking about her son, somewhere in Iraq, wondering what he was doing at that moment. She managed to work her day shift and came back to her apartment, exhausted and hungry and still distracted by her dream. She was looking in her refrigerator for something to eat when she heard a knock at the door.

"When I looked through the peephole, I saw people in Marine outfits. I couldn't remember how to open my door. And I finally opened the door and say, '*No, no.*'"

Gail remembers little about what happened next. Somehow, she got to a chair and just sat quietly. She struggled to remember her daughter's phone number or how to find it. For a time, it was just Gail and the Marines. To this day Gail has no idea how she reached her daughter Janelle, only that she must have, because soon Janelle was there with her, and then Janelle's husband too. Gail remembers only bits of her exchange with the men at the door.

"They told me that he got injured. And that he was still in Iraq. I said, 'He has his legs, he has his arms?' Yes. 'But so what is it then?'" The Marines told her there was "a blast" that had broken Shurvon's leg and several ribs. She recalls no mention of brain injury.

The rest was a blur. All Gail Ulerie knew was that her son had been wounded in Iraq. She understood that it was serious enough to bring some men in uniform to her door in East Cleveland, in a somber mood, saying they were sorry for her and for what had happened. And she knew that Shurvon was coming home. What she did not know was how grievous her son's injuries were or that what happened that day would change not only Shurvon's life but hers.

Shurvon Phillip had joined the Marine Reserve just after high school graduation, in 1998, to help pay for his tuition at community college and out of a sense of service to the country he loved, despite the fact that he was not even a citizen. He knew his devotion to the military would be tested after the 9/11 attacks, and that overseas deployments were likely. Gail simply prayed he would not get called. But in late 2004, at the

US Marine Corps Sergeant
Shurvon Phillip in Iraq, 2005.

same time Steven Schulz had been given his second deployment orders, Shurvon got his first. He was a Marine sergeant by then and his unit, the Third Battalion, Twenty-Fifth Regiment, Fourth Division—the 3/25 for short—was headed to Iraq. They would ship out in January.

When Shurvon told his mother he had to go, Gail tried her best to talk him out of it. But there was no way. He was a man now, about to turn twenty-four. Shurvon gently reminded his mother that this was what he had signed up for. "I have to go serve my country," he said.

Shurvon started going through his equipment, preparing for the deployment. He brought out his Kevlar helmet and vest and some of the other impressive-looking gear he'd been issued. As if to say, *Look at all this stuff. I'm going to be fine.* He was proud to be going. Proud to have been entrusted with the gear. Proud to be a United States Marine. Gail took heart in that. "I really had to support him," she said. "Being a mom, you just pray that he's going to be safe, and everything is going to be all right." Her faith was sorely tested only a few months later.

On May 7, 2005, while his mother wrestled with visions of doom back home in Ohio, Shurvon Phillip was patrolling the restive streets of Anbar Province, just as Steven Schulz had been doing a few weeks before. And just like Steven, he was riding with fellow Marines when their vehicle hit a bomb hidden by insurgents. All the Marines in the Humvee were wounded, but none as badly as Shurvon. The blast launched him from the vehicle, collapsing a lung, breaking his jaw, leg, and ribs, and, worst of all, acutely rattling his brain.

Shurvon Phillip and Steven Schulz, who never crossed paths in Iraq or in Bethesda, had suffered traumatic wounds in the same province at the same stage of the war. They would both survive. That was the miracle of it, for Gail and Debbie and the rest of their families. And "miracle" wasn't too strong a word, given the power of the explosives that had detonated under their vehicles and the damage the blasts had done. To some extent their survival involved good fortune—the trajectory of the blasts, the arteries missed—but mostly it had to do with advances in battlefield medicine and battlefield protection. It was another example of that small silver lining of the US wars in Iraq and Afghanistan—the protective gear, the on-site care, the caliber of the medics in American field hospitals. All of it meant that tens of thousands of men and women who would have died in prior wars were being saved. That was the good news. The bad news, of course, had to do with the nature of the injuries. Both young men had devastating brain injuries. And they were not alone.

The military doctors in the combat hospital in Iraq saw quickly that Steven Schulz had suffered severe trauma to the frontal lobe of his brain, and performed an immediate craniectomy, removing a portion of his skull to relieve pressure on the brain. While it would be some time before his physical and cognitive deficits became clear, frontal lobe injuries were known to produce changes in personality and behavior, loss of memory and speech, and damage to cognitive ability including planning and problem-solving. At that moment, the Schulz family wasn't thinking about any of that. They were focused only on packing up to get to their son's side. But even that was complicated and frustrating. Forty-eight hours after the call, Debbie and Steve were still in Texas, with no idea whether their son was in Baghdad or Bethesda or somewhere in between.

By then, their church had been made aware of Steven's injury and the family's situation. A parishioner named Missy called Steve and volunteered that she had connections in the Marine Corps, if there was anything they needed. To which Steve said quickly, "*What we need is information.*" Something more than "stay patient" and "we'll be in touch"—which was what they were getting from the military.

It turned out Missy knew someone who knew someone—they never did grasp the precise connection—high up in the Marine Corps. She gave Steve a number and some explicit instructions. He asked his wife to place the call. Steve knew that Debbie would be better at getting results and passed on the instructions from Missy. "Debbie, I need you to call this number," he said, "because you're much more composed. And talk to him like you need information *now*; talk to him like you're a Marine."

Which is what Debbie did. With Steve and her children at her side, she steeled herself and placed the call—not sure exactly who it was she was calling—and did her best rendition of what she called "tough Marine talk" when the man answered.

"I need to know where my son is. They haven't called us in forty-eight hours. We don't know if he's dead or alive. We don't know if he's in Bethesda."

"Well, ma'am, I don't know what I can do about it."

"I don't know what the fuck you can do about it, but I can tell you this right now. . . ."

Debbie started throwing F-bombs with her teenagers at her side, something they had never heard from their mother. But Debbie kept hurling the curse words, feeling that to get a Marine moving she had to curse like a Marine.

"Ma'am, you need to calm down."

"No, you need to fucking tell me where my son is. This is unacceptable."

More F-bombs followed. Finally, the Marine promised to get back to her—and to do so within the hour.

Debbie Schulz drew a deep breath. She thanked the man, and sure enough, he called back less than an hour later. Which was how they learned that their son would be going from Landstuhl, Germany, to Bethesda Naval Hospital. For Debbie it was a lesson in how to push—in this case, for more information. It was also the first of many battles she would fight on her son's behalf.

Another fight came the following day. They were preparing to travel to Bethesda, the four of them—she and Steve, and Elaine and Clay, who were desperate to see their brother. The military had said they would arrange to fly family members from Texas to Washington, DC, because Steven's condition was grave. And they said they would pay for three family members to go. No more.

Debbie told the liaison officer that there were four of them needing seats. She would be traveling with her husband and two teenagers. "He said, 'I'm sorry, ma'am. We can only allow three.' What the hell?" They wouldn't budge on the rule, and the limit. Debbie was furious. They found a way to get another ticket, but she never forgot the episode as she rounded up the family and headed to Bethesda Naval Hospital.

They packed for a brief trip—Debbie came with three changes of clothing. She never imagined that she wouldn't be back home for nearly seven months.

The family arrived at Bethesda Hospital just hours after Steven was transported. They found him attached to a tangle of tubes, bloated and comatose. Debbie stood at his side, stunned but stoic. The only sound in the room was the constant beeping from all the lifesaving machines to which Steven was tethered. With much of his forehead bone removed to make room for his swollen brain, he looked nothing like the young man who had gone off to war less than four months earlier. The only thing fifteen-year-old Clay Schulz could think of was Frankenstein, and he wondered how anyone could survive such catastrophic injuries. Elaine was worried not just about Steven, but also about her parents, who displayed utterly different reactions when they first saw their wounded son.

"My dad was grieving, like I think he thought Steven was going to die, and he was trying to prepare us for that," Elaine said. "And my mom was just sort of steadfast in the next step—like, 'OK, we're here now. Let's figure out, what are they doing for him next?'"

For the first few weeks, when Steven was undergoing multiple surgeries, Debbie rarely stepped out of the hospital, sleeping by Steven's side while the rest of the family slept at a nearby hotel. Three weeks after the injury, deep in the night, Steven was heavily sedated when she leaned over his bed and said, "*Son, if you can hear me, just squeeze my hand.*" She had said it before, many times. For those three long weeks there had been no response. But now, just before Mother's Day, in the dark room in the pre-dawn hour, she got a squeeze. And then she said, "*Can you squeeze it two times?*" And he squeezed twice. To Debbie, it was a miracle. A breakthrough. She had reached her son. That small moment, that sign that he was *there*, left her overjoyed. She leaned over her son and whispered, "*You're in Bethesda, you're safe, you have an injury, but you're fine. You're going to be just fine. Just keep squeezing my hand.*"

But that moment of joy was fleeting. Hours later, doctors discovered fresh bleeding in the brain. They would have to operate again. The news was almost too much for Debbie to bear—more questions to ask, more worries about the odds of survival.

By then, Elaine and Clay had returned to their respective college and high school (Elaine was a freshman at Texas State University, Clay a sophomore at Friendswood High School), so they were irregular visitors to Bethesda. But the day Steven's brain began to bleed again, they were by his side.

"We all huddled up," Debbie said. "We huddle up and go downstairs and we're praying outside. And it's spring, May in Bethesda, so the trees are blooming, and it's beautiful out there. And I say, we need to change our prayer."

She had always gone by the words of the Lord's Prayer—*"Thy will be done."* Now it had to change, she thought, and she said as much to her family. Because now, she reasoned, whatever God's will was, the message had to be simple: *We want Steven to live.*

Steven came through that surgery, but the costs of the multiple operations on his brain were high. Ninety percent of his right frontal lobe had been removed. He would remain in a coma for three more weeks at Bethesda before slowly emerging—after that first squeeze of his mother's hand.

Debbie and Steve heard a litany of dreary forecasts about their son's future. Steven was expected to recover the ability to walk and speak—but even in the best-case scenario, he would live with profound limitations and needs. A loss of inhibition was common, and a loss of emotion even more profound, with doctors predicting their once wisecracking son would lose his sense of humor along with the ability to cry. "There wasn't anything good," Debbie said about the prognosis.

As bad as things were for Steven Schulz, Shurvon Phillip's condition was worse. Weeks after Steven's arrival at Bethesda Naval Hospital, Shurvon joined him there. Gail had flown in from Ohio to meet Shurvon. Waiting outside his room to be escorted inside, still unclear what exactly had happened to her son, she overheard a nurse talking about what she understood to be a "brain test" for Shurvon. Gail stood, introduced herself, and asked the nurse what that meant. "*Why does my son need a 'brain test'?*" she asked with growing agitation. While the nurse tried to calm her down, Gail heard another attendant quietly say, "Oh, my God, they didn't tell the woman her son has a brain injury." But Gail would see this for herself soon enough.

Gail had always wanted to be a nurse. She loved medical dramas like *ER*, and although she was never able to complete a nursing degree, her job as a nursing assistant exposed her to a wide range of injuries and medical trauma. So standing there in that sterile hallway, feeling she was in her world, she thought she was ready to see her son. But nothing could have prepared her for the shock of seeing how badly he had been injured.

A large section of Shurvon's skull had been cut away to relieve the pressure of bone against his swelling brain. His head resembled a misshapen basketball, stomped and partially flattened. His leg was suspended in a sling. The number of IVs, tubes, and monitors keeping her son alive overwhelmed her too.

But what shocked Gail most of all was her son's face. His deep brown eyes, open wider than it seemed possible, gazed past her, up at the ceiling in a statue-like stare of terror. His mouth was frozen too, half open, as if ready to scream.

None of it stopped her from rushing to her child's side, and crying out, "Shurvon, Shurvie, Mommy here. Oh God. Shurvie, *Mommy right here.*"

If the initial visit from the Marines had hit Gail hard, this was the moment when she understood that everything would be different now. His life, her life. Life in general. *Everything.* That day, Gail told her daytime and nighttime clients they would need to find substitutes for a while. At first she said she'd be gone for a few days, but she quickly amended that. "I said, 'I'm not coming back. I am so sorry, but I have to take care of my child. I have to stay here and take care of him.'"

And yet for all the anguish of those terrible first days, the tears, the grief, Gail Ulerie was quick to turn to practical considerations—all part of a realization that came to her with force and great clarity: *This was what she would do now.* No more home-care clients, no more outings with friends and family, no more nursing assistant night shifts with anyone other than Shurvon. *God had given her a new patient.* This was the way she looked at it. From now on, all day and every day, 24-7 in the literal sense, she would be with her son.

"I was just praying," she said. *"Lord Jesus, just help my son."*

In many ways, Gail and Debbie couldn't have been more different. An immigrant from Trinidad living in Cleveland, and a sixth-generation American from a tiny town in Texas. A nursing assistant and single mom who cared for the elderly, and a teacher supported by her husband who worked with grade school kids. A Black woman and a white woman. And yet both now had one singular focus: helping their sons who had nearly died in the same year in the same province of Iraq. It wasn't just the circumstances that were similar; it was how they would deal with the trauma and steel themselves for the challenges ahead. Each woman felt she had been given a new mission, a fresh meaning and purpose: The fight they would wage to give care and hope to their sons and to eke out support from a Veterans Administration geared toward elderly or retired veterans. Both knew they were to be full-time caregivers now.

These two women, the nursing assistant and the teacher, marched forward with resolve, taking up the fight on behalf of their sons at every turn, in battles big and small, angling for better care. Forced to leave her home-care clients, Gail Ulerie came to this job—because that's what it was, a draining, all-consuming *job*—with certain advantages. She had a seemingly unending patience. She had stamina and resilience in great supply. She had her faith. And she had practical skills as well. Bedside work with seriously infirm patients, all the washing and changing and the IVs and catheters—none of it was new to her. Of course, she had never imagined that her skills as a nursing assistant would be put to use in this way, for her own adult son.

In the early days and weeks after Shurvon's injury, the news was unrelentingly bleak. One physician told Gail that given the extensive trauma to his brain, Shurvon probably wouldn't live more than a year or two, and would never budge from that rigid position.

From the beginning, despite his obvious trauma, Gail refused to accept the doom-and-gloom scenarios, even as she watched her son lie nearly motionless in his hospital bed. She was going to take things into her own hands. So on a beautiful warm morning in the summer of 2005, roughly three months into Shurvon's stay at the Bethesda hospital, Gail had an idea. She approached the ICU nurses.

"Shurvon has been inside for so long; can we please take him outside?" She told everyone, the doctors, nurses, the housekeeping staff, that she wanted to take him out, even if they had to wheel the bed to a hospital courtyard. There was hesitation, the staff was unsure they had the time or manpower, but Gail did not give up. "Well, show me the way," she said. "I push him myself."

Show me the way. I will do it. This was Gail's way. It would be her approach with everything now, for as long as Shurvon needed her help. She would be his nurse, mother, and advocate too.

Gail won over the staff that day, and together they moved Shurvon—moved him and the entire bed—to the small courtyard.

"When we finally got him outside, you should have seen the look on this child's face," she said. "You push him directly in the sun, and the wind was blowing on his face, and his head was up, and it was worth it, you know. And there were a couple of the staff people, they were like, 'Oh my gosh, I know he's enjoying this. What a blessing.'"

It was also the first time since the injury that she saw a glimmer in her son's eyes, some small sign that gave her hope. She didn't understand why the ICU nurses hadn't seen it too. Gail felt that while they took good care of Shurvon, to them he was just one of many Iraq blast victims, lying there propped up in his bed, staring out at a limited world in that vacant, frozen way. Gail was often frustrated by a belief that the medical teams didn't share her faith in her son's potential and hadn't seen or recognized those flickers of light that she was seeing. No one else seemed to believe he could be brought back to a life with any real agency, or cognitive ability.

But Gail *saw* things stirring in her son. She was sure of it. In her long hours spent by his side, Gail was convinced she saw tiny, almost imperceptible signs—the flutter of an eyelid, a soft touch of his hand. She was certain Shurvon knew what was going on. He would look at pictures of his nieces and nephews and Gail would narrate the scene. Even though he couldn't respond verbally, she believed firmly that her son was still somewhere deep inside wanting to communicate.

For Steven Schulz, the recovery was slow, but at least there was progress—encouraging signs as soon as his six weeks in the intensive care unit ended. Once he was fully awake from his coma and his intubation tube was removed, Steven began to talk, although he sounded nothing like he had before the injury. There was no emotion and no inflection. A steady, flat staccato, a metronome of requests or observations, telling his mother what he wanted to eat or watch on the small television by his bedside. But it was something. Some part of Steven had been brought back to his family, and they were certain there would be more.

By summer Steven was physically well enough to be moved to the VA hospital in Tampa, Florida. He would do his rehab there, at a facility known for its work with polytrauma patients. Debbie and Steve had been given a menu of options for VA rehab centers—Minnesota, Virginia, and California were on the list. They had been assured that the facility in Tampa was first-rate and had the added bonus of being in a warmer climate.

The family was relieved to have Steven placed in a good rehab center with Debbie there to support him. But in Tampa, Debbie found herself largely alone and without a strong support network nearby. Steve had to go home to Texas to get back to work. Without Debbie's income, the family had begun to dig into their retirement savings. Steve would come back on weekends to visit Steven and relieve Debbie a bit. The kids came when they could.

Debbie was lonely and tired but buoyed when she thought she saw glimpses of what she called "the original Steven" emerge. His sense of humor was slowly coming back, against all odds. One weekend when Elaine was visiting, they headed off for what Debbie guessed was Steven's fifteenth CT scan. He was slumped over in a wheelchair, exhausted, drooling into a towel. He perked up when he heard the words "CAT scan," and smirked. "CAT scan?" he asked his mother. "Where is this damn cat, and how many times are they going to look for it?'"

Debbie and Elaine looked at each other, stunned. And then Debbie turned to her son. "Was that a *joke,* Steven?" The neuropsychologist had told the Schulz family he would never have the ability to show any humor. Steven quickly answered, "Yeah."

Debbie and Elaine cracked up. "So, OK. He's got a sense of humor after all."

It was one more reminder, one more glimpse of "the original Steven." But during those early months the hope was almost always quashed by a dose of reality. Tampa was the place where the emotional pendulum swung "like a sledgehammer," as Debbie remembered. During a lengthy session with an occupational therapist, Steven was asked what his goals for his treatment were. He looked up and in his emotionless monotone recited three life goals: He was going to drive a car again, get married, and have children. He told the therapist he had already chosen names for his children: "There will be a girl called Coretta, and a boy named Wyatt."

It was one of the few times Debbie broke down. She gazed at her once muscular son, partially blind, partially paralyzed in his wheelchair, talking about marriage and kids and driving, and she began to weep. Offering a quick hug of encouragement from behind, she managed to hide her tears. She didn't want him to see her crying.

At an eye doctor's appointment following a surgery many months later, Steven specifically asked again about driving. The doctor waited a beat and then gently but firmly said, "Steven, I don't think that will ever be something you can do. Being blind in one eye and having only partial vision in the other, your vision is just too low."

Steven's expression hardly changed. He couldn't cry—he had lost the ability to shed a tear. But Debbie could. And she did. Again: "The tears were rolling down my face. I knew intuitively that Steven would not be able to do things he had done before, but it was that day I realized that my son would never be 'the original Steven.'" He would struggle to accomplish even the smallest goals: "It was hard to hear, very hard." But nothing stopped Debbie from trying to push forward.

The pattern of progress—two steps forward, three steps back—continued for Steven Schulz and his family. One operation after another, even an appendicitis emergency. But finally, at the end of seven months, Steven and Debbie would return home.

Back in Texas in the late autumn of 2005, Debbie threw herself into every corner of her son's recovery and his new life; the 24-7 home care—or, as she called it, full-time "child care." Steven would take over the primary bedroom, since it was on the main level of the house. His father would move upstairs, to Steven's old room, and Debbie moved

Turning twenty-one. Lance Corporal Steven Schulz celebrating his twenty-first birthday at the Houston VA hospital in August 2005, nearly four months after injury.

a twin bed into the primary bedroom to be near Steven. She would shower her buck-naked twenty-one-year-old son every evening. She would lift him out of bed in the morning and help him into his wheelchair and sit with him while he watched television. Steven favored commercials, constantly changing the channel so he could catch them all. He could not concentrate on anything that ran longer than a minute or two, so the commercials were a good fit. He had begun to mimic the pharmaceutical ads word for word, even attempting to sing the jingles.

The frontal lobe damage showed itself in different ways. Steven's thinking was slow and conversations difficult to sustain. He would stare strangely at people as he tried to angle them into vision in his left eye. "He might ask me four times, 'Who are you talking to? Where are we going?'" Debbie said. She would look Steven in the eye and say, "This is the third time I'm telling you, look at me and listen." It was back to a five-year-old's attention span.

In the afternoons, Debbie would roll Steven out for a walk in his wheelchair. Neighbors knew by now that his greetings might be profanity laced or sexual in nature. He had the impulses of a twenty-year-old, minus the filter. "He loved blondes," Debbie said, and made sure any blonde he passed knew it.

His stretching exercises would take up a good part of the day. Debbie would lift each of his limbs up and down to keep his circulation going. And in the afternoon, she would load her 160-pound son into the car for "an outing" to the local Walmart or grocery store. When Steve got home from work, he would take over, either watching Steven or cooking dinner. And then came the shower routine, before Steven was tucked into bed with his mother nearby. Debbie considered it a milestone when, as she put it, he was able to "train his bladder and brain to sleep through the night."

Steven was making steady, strong progress thanks to his mother's persistence. She found programs that would bring Marines to their home to spend time with her son. She arranged for him to have a service animal, a Labrador retriever named Sonny that Clay said "was a big turning point for his recovery, because he focused. He got to focus on something besides himself." Neighbors and family members all saw that Steven was doing much better after Sonny's arrival.

In 2007, nearly two years after Steven's injury, Debbie got bionics for her son that made it possible for him to walk by sending impulses causing his muscles to constrict. He needed a cane, and his gait was slow and labored, but it was a significant advance for both Steven and Debbie.

No one had told Debbie how to do any of these things. Information about programs and avenues for help seemed hard to come by. She had understood nothing, really, about home care. She and Steve, like tens of thousands of other caregivers of wounded warriors, initially had no clue how to navigate the different insurance options, and how the military and veterans' insurance networks were intertwined. Steve was holding down a job and managing his own considerable stress. Elaine was in college and Clay in high school—and Debbie was intent that her children's lives wouldn't be completely disrupted by what had happened to their older brother.

As the days and weeks and months passed, Debbie kept thinking about all the other caregivers out there, dealing with versions of the same issues with the same lack of a road map. For all these people there was the immediate impact—the emotional trauma—followed by a loss of income, depending on their professional circumstances. Beyond the loss of a regular paycheck, there were longer-term financial costs: lost payments into a retirement system, lost health insurance from a job, and the less tangible but critical matter of their own well-being. "Everybody always said, '*Take care of yourself.*' Well, how do we make that possible?" Debbie wondered. "Where do we find time for *that*?"

Both Debbie and Gail found champions for their sons in organizations that worked on behalf of badly wounded soldiers. For Debbie and Steve, the Wounded Warrior Project offered support—arranging for those Marines to visit and later for Debbie to travel to Washington to advocate on behalf of caregivers like herself. Gail Ulerie found passionate advocates too, including a military lawyer in the Navy reserve,

William Bailey, who was Shurvon's legal guardian and helped guide Gail through the maze of red tape.

Two years after his injury, Shurvon was accepted at the Rehabilitation Institute of Chicago—RIC for short. If Debbie was caring for Steven like a growing child again, for Gail Ulerie, it was more like caring for a newborn. And Gail was convinced that the baby she had welcomed to the world a quarter century before would make strides at the RIC.

The institute had deep experience in traumatic brain injury—though most of their cases involved victims of car accidents and violent crime. The RIC had a Brain Injury Rehabilitation program, and Gail found an ally in its medical director, a neurologist named Felise Zollman.

On the one hand, Dr. Zollman knew that for most patients with severe brain trauma, the window for restoring any real cognitive capacity was roughly eighteen months. The brain's neuroplasticity was such that beyond that time frame, even the best combination of medication and hands-on therapy was unlikely to effect change—and Shurvon had come to the RIC two years after his injury. But Zollman also saw what Gail Ulerie had seen—as she put it, "a guy with a little bit of a twinkle in his eye." And so, while she and the other RIC doctors quickly discovered the extensive atrophy in his brain—damage that could not be repaired—they also found signs of encouragement in Shurvon's responses to stimuli: a pursed lip or widening eyes when asked questions.

"The feeling was, this is a person who clearly possesses consciousness and clearly had the ability to interact with another person," Dr. Zollman said, "even if that interaction is limited by their inability to move or vocalize." The eye contact, the acknowledgment Shurvon gave in response to a question—it all suggested, as Gail had so often said, that he was *in there*. Zollman used the same language.

"Just that bit of exchange that says, this person is in there, and is acknowledging me, and is communicating that to me."

Zollman remembers something else about Shurvon Phillip's time at the RIC: a mother who never left her son's side. Gail Ulerie, she said, was never overbearing, never too pushy with the physicians or nurses, but always determined.

"Extremely dedicated," Zollman said. "My impressions of her were very positive. I felt like she was, you know, just a roll-your-sleeves-up-and-do-it kind of parent. 'This is where we are. This is what we're going to deal with.'"

And Gail had been right. There *was* a glimmer in her son, that "twinkle," that was worth all their time and effort.

And so Dr. Zollman and the others at the RIC refused to give up on Shurvon. She prescribed a series of intensive physical therapies and weaned him off brain-numbing narcotics that he had been given in his earlier treatments. Shurvon made slow but meaningful progress: His tracheostomy was removed as it became clear he could breathe on his own; the physical therapy helped loosen his arm and leg muscles enough so he could raise them; and that in turn gave him enough mobility to help his mother transfer him in and out of the wheelchair, and even to take a few short steps.

The RIC deserved credit, certainly. But Dr. Zollman believed Shurvon's mother deserved it too. "It's extremely important for a patient to have someone there who cares about them and is their advocate," she said. "It's important that someone is there, keeping an eye on what's going on, asking questions, understanding next steps, understanding what it takes to get from where this person may be while they are hospitalized to what it would take to return to living in a community setting again. So I think it helps on many levels."

From the time of his injury, Gail had made it clear that she wanted to care for her son at home. At the RIC, they had pushed hard to help Shurvon thrive, but at other facilities where he had been treated, the recommendation was that he be placed in a nursing home. His breathing had to be monitored, he was tube-fed, and he wore a catheter. His weakened immune system meant a risk of infection.

Gail had only one response: *"Over my dead body. He is not going to no nursing home."* The pushback from the various doctors and nurses was gentle yet firm. Her son needed to be in an institution because Gail would not be able to care for him on her own. Gail remained unconvinced: *"You know what? Train me. No nursing home for my son. Do you understand what I'm saying?"* She would remind them that she wasn't only Shurvon Phillip's mother, she was a trained and experienced nursing assistant, and she had effectively been caring for him anyhow in all the various facilities where he had spent the last two and a half years.

Speaking with a level of maternal ferocity that had grown since Shurvon's injury, Gail made her intentions crystal clear: *"I'm taking him home. I took care of Shurvon since in my stomach, nine months. I am his mother. There's nobody can give him the best care that I can give him. He's going home."*

There would be no dissuading her. Home they would go, back to the apartment in East Cleveland. Gail replaced Shurvon's old bed with a hospital bed and made room for an oxygen tank, his wheelchair, and other medical supplies. It would be a tight fit. So be it, Gail said. She told the woman who ran the building's services that her son was coming home, and that they would be moving these things in. That brief conversation produced a happy surprise when the paramedics arrived, bringing Shurvon Phillip with them.

On the twenty-fourth floor of Gail's apartment building, surrounded by nieces and nephews with balloons held aloft, Shurvon was wheeled across an actual red carpet as a cry of "Welcome home" was called out. She saw a tear in her son's eye as the paramedic leaned in to say, "Sarge, I can see you are happy to be home." It was the happiest Gail had seen her son since he had been wheeled into the Bethesda sunlight a few months after his injury.

The Veterans Administration had arranged for occasional home health aides, but on most days, it was Gail in the room, 24-7, as she had been in the various hospitals. She slept there in the cramped space, on a lounge chair at his side. During the night he would stir every two hours, like clockwork almost, apparently unsettled or anxious—"he just want me to stand there and comfort him," she explained. And comfort him she would, talking softly to her son, and then watching him drift back to sleep.

At six each morning, his tube feeding having run its course, she would disconnect it, flush it clean, and start it up again. It became a sunrise ritual. All the while Gail would talk to Shurvon, convinced he was hearing and understanding her every word. She'd get breaks when the health aides came—time she used to make coffee and prepare food for herself. Three times a week, she'd have a longer respite, when he was brought back to the Cleveland VA hospital for physical therapy.

She tried to see to it that at least once each day Shurvon would have a "trip" to the back of the apartment, where, from the living room, he could look out over Lake Erie. It was a ten-step walk for most people, but to bring Shurvon to that spot was a considerable operation. Gail

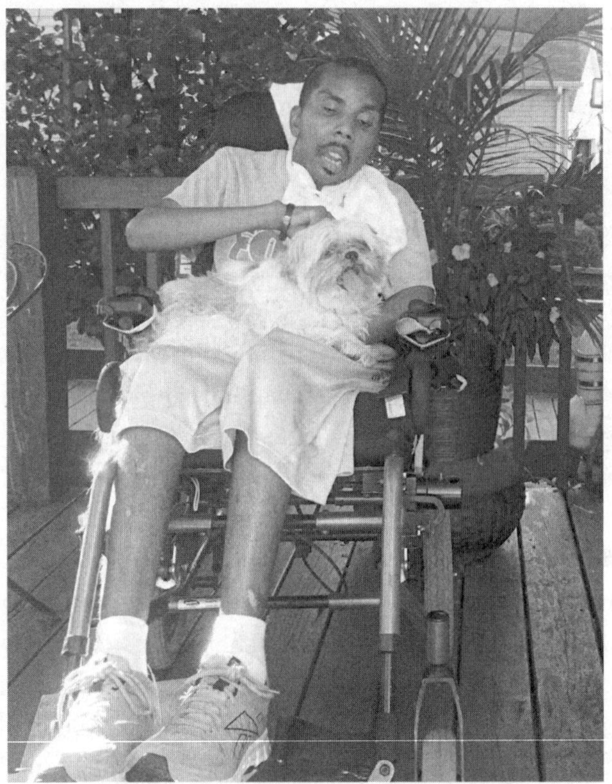

Shurvon Phillip with Polly, the family's shih tzu, in East Cleveland, Ohio.

would lift him to a sitting position, swing his legs over while holding up his head to transfer him to a dining-room chair, and then ease him into the adjacent wheelchair. She'd bring the feeding tube hookup and suction device to the window as well.

It was an arduous job and it took time, but one thing Gail and Shurvon had in ample supply was time. The "journey" to the back of the apartment afforded a change of pace, for mother and son alike. And a nice view of the lake to remind them of the bigger world beyond.

Shurvon and Gail would eventually get a new home with the help of William Bailey, the lawyer who had managed to get them into the RIC rehab facility. Bailey guided them through a long process with the Veterans Administration and local Marine Corps organization. These organizations would prove a godsend. Now Gail had more space for Shurvon, his sister Candace, and Candace's son. The boy played in and around his uncle's bed. Most important, Gail said, was the joy their presence gave her son: "I could see his face, how happy he was."

Gail bought a pair of stationary bikes from QVC, the home shopping network—a therapy bike that he could actually operate now, albeit at a snail's pace, and an exercise bike for her. She realized how little exercise she was getting in her care-for-Shurvon life, beyond moving around the home and various care centers. Now she set up their little bikes next to each other.

"We did it together, and I would play his reggae music, and see how alert he was," she said. "He loved reggae. And he loved his rap music." A VA occupational therapist came to the house with puzzles for Shurvon to piece together, and new hand exercises in the hope of improving his minimal range of motion. Shurvon still couldn't summon sounds beyond a kind of gurgling noise, but therapy at the VA had gotten him as far as a throaty "ah," which he could deliver on request. He had learned to listen to passages that were several paragraphs long and then answer multiple-choice questions about the text with that low-pitched "ah."

The Schulz family benefited from acts of generosity as well—and they, too, were given the hugely generous gift of a new home. It started when Steven had come home on weekend passes from the hospital, and they realized that the bathroom doors were too narrow for his wheelchair.

Debbie says her husband was always good about thinking about accommodations for their son. He heard about an outfit that was giving away fully customized homes to wounded veterans—it was called the Helping Our Heroes Foundation, based in Houston—and Steve filled out an application, with all the detail about their son's injury and condition. They got a call one day, meetings followed, and they were approved for one of the homes. "We had so many blessings along the way," Debbie said. "They were very generous and wonderful about building him a home that was totally accessible and flat and had all the things that we needed."

For Steven Schulz, the house made his life easier, but Debbie noticed that her son got a big boost from just telling his story. He would tell anyone who asked. And then tell it again. It was "the new Steven" who had embraced his disabilities.

"I'm half paralyzed, half blind. I was blown up in Iraq, in '05 second tour of duty. Spent six weeks in a coma. They said I'd never walk again. I've had twenty surgeries."

Rat-a-tat. No emotion. Just that same flat cadence and intonation.

"I dance every Monday. Ride a horse in Georgetown near me every Thursday. I do Zoom yoga, tai chi every Friday normally."

At times, Debbie said, especially in the early years after he regained his speech, Steven would overcommunicate, and overshare—consequences of the frontal lobe damage and what it had done to his sense of inhibition. Now the filter was back, even if the odd speech patterns remained. Debbie said her son had made great strides in being socially appropriate. No more bursts at random strangers, no more of what she called "the filthy talk," which had filled his earlier days after the injury.

On the physical side, while there were marked improvements—he walked several miles each week—he still moved slowly. Debbie and his other caregivers all started to feel he had plateaued. On their walks,

Debbie said, "it's one speed, about a forty-minute half mile," and he tires easily. But he loved counting his steps.

It was during these years of progress that Debbie and Steven Schulz would meet Gail Ulerie and Shurvon. This was when I met them as well. It was 2009 in New York City at what had become the annual Bob Woodruff Foundation Stand Up for Heroes celebration. A star-studded fundraiser for our nations' wounded and those who care for them. Steven and Shurvon were there in their Marine Corps dress uniforms. Shurvon in his wheelchair on the red carpet, Steven with a cane. Shurvon's face, once frozen in apparent fear, had evolved into a mask of seemingly permanent joy. His eyes had brightened and his

Debbie and Steven Schulz in New York City for the annual Stand Up for Heroes benefit in November 2016.

"That uniform made him sit up straight." Gail Ulerie with her son Shurvon Phillip and Martha Raddatz at Stand Up for Heroes in November 2013.

mouth was now more smile than anything else. And Steven wore a sweet smirk of pride. Flirty and yes, funny. "Do you have any daughters?" he asked me with a smile. The mothers dressed up for the occasion, giving each other a knowing glance. They spoke about the "complicated grief" they had endured. The sons they loved beyond all measure.

My own son, Jake, was a teenager at the time, and when I saw these mothers with their damaged sons I wondered how they did it. How they had watched these young men go off to war and return permanently altered. But deep down I knew the answer: Unconditional love, that is what it was. A love coupled with the most selfless sacrifice I have ever witnessed. These women told me their sons were the heroes, and indeed they were. But these mothers? Every year I saw them at the Woodruff event proudly touting whatever progress their sons had made, I admired them more. Their sons had changed, they had changed, but the love between them had only grown stronger. Yet out of the spotlight, away from the warmth of friends and the embrace of the veterans' community, their challenges were never-ending.

In 2011, the Schulz family suffered a blow that seemed too cruel, too much to bear. While Debbie's son was recovering, slowly but surely, her husband was slipping. Slipping fast.

By then, as Debbie had feared, her husband was drinking regularly. He had been sober for fifteen years prior to Steven's second and last deployment, but with Steven off in Iraq he started secretly drinking again. The injury accelerated the problem. Now, as the new house took shape, Debbie said her husband "was openly drinking heavily and very depressed and not doing very well, and not wanting to go to rehab." Their marriage grew strained.

He stayed at the old house after Debbie moved with Steven to the new one. The build had taken about two years, and in that time Debbie and Steve had spoken often about their next steps. "We had had many discussions about what Steve needed to do to get well again," she said, "and he wasn't ready. Those were his words."

In March 2011, Debbie was in Snowmass, Colorado, with Steven, at a Winter Sports Clinic for veterans. She got a call from someone at her husband's company saying that Steve hadn't come to work.

As rough as things had gotten, and erratic as his behavior had been, the call was a shock. Not showing up for work, with no explanation—that wasn't like him at all. She knew something was not right.

Steve had gone missing. Days passed. Weeks. The family agonized over his disappearance, as Debbie once again bore the burden of keeping the family on an even keel.

Six months later, Steve Schulz's remains were identified in a wooded area near Friendswood, Texas. He had died of a gunshot wound. He had hunted in those woods, but when he had disappeared it wasn't hunting season. No gun was ever found.

"We really can't say definitively what happened, except that we know it was a gunshot wound to the head," Debbie said. She assumes he died by suicide. Perhaps the gun had been found and taken by someone later. Debbie calls Steve's death "another casualty of war."

Their son's reaction was blunted—in the way all of his emotions had been since the injury. "Steven will tell you it's very frustrating because he can't cry," Debbie said. "And so he was very aware that he was sad, but also very frustrated that he couldn't cry."

After Steve's death, Debbie tried to make the best of it, seizing every opportunity to travel with her son and widen his world. Clay and Elaine would join when they could. Debbie arranged most of the adventures—though there were also trips sponsored by various veterans' support groups. Whoever else was along for the trip, Steven always traveled with his mother. Today, in his trademark rat-a-tat fashion, he can rattle off many of the places he has been since his injury:

"I went to Hawaii, Alaska, and New York City . . . Boston Cape Cod Martha's Vineyard. A few years back, it was pretty nice. Clam chowder.

"We went to Michigan last year, to Mackinac and Traverse City. It was very nice. Mackinac they have no roads. You take a horse and buggy everywhere. Making five thousand pounds a fudge a day for the tourists. It was pretty cool. They don't have roads; you take a horse and buggy everywhere."

"The new Steven" also talked about his war wounds. "He loves telling his story," Debbie said. "So many military people don't want to talk about their service or their injury, but that's his new identity, and he doesn't have that filter that says, 'I shouldn't talk about it'—so he does."

Gail Ulerie made sure Shurvon got out as well—not just out of doors, but on journeys far from home. Despite the major challenges she faced transporting him, the trips delighted them both. She had photos to document each journey. A trip to Washington, DC, to see the changing of the guard at the Marine Barracks. And another to Colorado. That trip had been arranged by the Wounded Warrior Project. It was meant to provide wounded vets and their relatives a break, and a form of therapy. "The highlight of that trip was Shurvon horseback riding," Gail remembered. He had needed a lot of help to mount the horse, but he did it with a guide behind him, Shurvon holding the reins.

Her best trip with Shurvon, though, was back to their native land of Trinidad. Gail sighed, recalling their first journey home: *"Oh, my goodness . . ."* It became an annual visit, made most years in conjunction with the celebrations of Carnival and festival of J'ouvert, a tradition born in Trinidad in the 1780s. Nearly two and a half centuries later, a young American Marine was coming back from Ohio for J'ouvert, in a wheelchair, year after year.

When they made the trip in 2016, her son flashed a rare sign of upset as they packed for the post-J'ouvert trip home. "Shurvon did not want to leave," Gail recalled.

In October 2016, back in Cleveland, Shurvon spiked a fever. Nothing unusual; he had suffered regular bouts of infections, nearly all of which had begun that way, with a fever that required antibiotics and close observation. Gail did as she had done before and brought her son to the Cleveland VA hospital. But this time would be different. The fever never ebbed. The infection was too strong, or his immune system too weak. Most likely it was a combination of both. Shurvon Phillip died four days later, on October 30, 2016, with his beloved mother by his side.

It was a sudden end to what had been a story of resilience and hope. Shurvon's journey had taken him from badly wounded Marine, bedridden, catatonic, and seemingly with no hope of anything different, to a young man who could move about and who had regained the ability to communicate. Most important—and most remarkable, given the early prognoses—Shurvon had progressed to the point where he had begun to enjoy many aspects of his life.

Gail Ulerie was shattered. But as the time passed, she came to marvel at how her son had beaten the odds. Shurvon had nearly died before even landing at Bethesda Naval Hospital, and doctors had given him a year or two of life at best. No one had imagined a "life" with anything like joy. No one, that is, other than his mom.

Shurvon was twenty-four years old when that explosion blew through his Humvee in Anbar Province. When he died he was thirty-five, defying all odds and predictions. Gail Ulerie deserves much of the credit for that.

Nearly a decade has passed since Shurvon's death, and Gail never tires of speaking about her son. When I saw her at the last Stand Up for Heroes event, which she still attended after Shurvon's death, she delighted in talking about Shurvon to those who had come to know him. Those joyful "Oh my goodness!" exclamations still spill out, often with tears, but there is evident pride in the stories she tells.

Some might have looked at Shurvon Phillip during those post-Iraq years—the early ones especially, as he lay there, mute and immobile—and thought, *That's not living.* But that was never how Gail Ulerie saw her son. There was something undeniably moving in Shurvon's own struggle and in his mother's fortitude and faith. While Shurvon Phillip never did regain the ability to speak, by the time of his death he had come a long way in his ability to communicate—and to convey joy. When he was asked whether he would have joined the Marine Corps if he had known what would happen to him, Gail said he raised his eyebrow, clearly and without hesitation, to indicate "Yes."

Steven Schulz gave a similar answer, when asked about his time in combat. Going to Iraq was the hardest thing he'd ever done, but he quickly

Gail Ulerie built a memorial for her son Shurvon outside their home in East Cleveland. Shown here on Memorial Day 2025.

added, in his rapid-fire, punctuation-free speech: *"Couldn't ask for better and would do it all again."*

Steven marked the twentieth anniversary of the day he was injured, his "Alive Day," with a family trip to San Diego. They visited Balboa Park and explored the Spanish quarters before a big family meal. Debbie put together a video of his long journey, showing the young Marine, "the original Steven," proud, fit, and full of fire—and his transition to "the new Steven." Debbie was an active forty-nine-year-old wife, mother, and teacher when Steven was injured. She turned sixty-nine just before the celebration, a proud grandmother to Elaine's two young children and still the full-time caregiver to Steven. More than twenty years of her life has been devoted to her disabled son, longer than the time she shared with him before his injury.

When Debbie looks at those images of her son before his injury, she does not hesitate: "My love for Steven is just the same." Yet she also tears up at thoughts of what was lost. "That smile, that 'go get 'em' is not the same. It took a long while to get over that loss. I still get that feeling sometimes. This anniversary brought home twenty long years of hard work for our whole family. That was part of my husband's deep sadness. That loss for not only Steven, but the family life." And yet Debbie quickly recovers: "I am so thankful he is here and has memories of his childhood and family and is happy ninety-nine percent of the time. That is when my gratitude kicks in."

Debbie knows she will not always be there for Steven. She has a plan for that as well—for when she is gone, or unable to care for him anymore. She has given Elaine and Clay "carte blanche" to help Steven in whatever way they see best.

Debbie credits her faith with helping her get through these two decades—the injury, the struggles, her husband's sudden death, the caring for Steven and her two other children.

"My faith, but also realizing everybody has life difficulties," she said. "I met a lot of families, military, that had a brain injury. But then there was a local brain injury group near Friendswood, and they were all civilian brain injuries from car wrecks, motorcycle wrecks. And I realized, these things happen everywhere, all the time, and we can't live in fear. We have to go forward, trusting that life is going to take us where we need to be."

The family has kept a photograph taken of Steven when he was first in the hospital. The "Frankenstein-esque" photo, as Clay describes it. No one seems to know who took the photograph. Clay recalls that Elaine used it for a school project about what had happened to their brother. "We were all like, we don't want to take pictures of this, but somebody did, and it's on Steven's wall of projects and awards."

When guests come, Clay says, Steven likes to share the photo with them. To help tell his own story.

"I think it's just incredible he's still here," Clay said. "I told him a long time ago, he's the strongest person I've ever known, and I still hold that true. Just the ability to not let it drag you down is something that I don't understand. He has something within him that few would ever know."

Twenty years later, Clay says he has come to better understand and appreciate the "tooth-and-nail, uphill climb" his mother made at every turn—to get her son's stipends and disability payments and sort out all the insurance issues. He appreciates deeply how hard she worked to shield him and his sister from the pain of the early years: "My mom tried to let me keep a sort of normal life. I don't think she wanted me to know. She didn't really tell me how hard it was."

In that sense, Clay feels the way I do about Debbie, and about Gail Ulerie as well: that they are the heroes in their sons' stories—the key to Steven thriving and surviving, and Shurvon living the best life he could. Neither mother ever became jaded or angry.

As for Steven himself, when I ask him about his mother's devotion, her care over these more than twenty years, I know he speaks for Shurvon as well. And I know that if Steven *did* have the capacity for tears, they would certainly flow when he gives his answer—because even in that same dry monotone you can feel the emotion, the depth of love in his big, proud heart:

"She is my guardian angel. Her strength helped me get through what I couldn't get through. They told her they should probably put me in a nursing home for the rest of my life. She said, 'Not my son.' Yeah she's the best. She is an inspiration. The best. I tell her I love her every day."

And that is the power of a mother's love.

Epilogue

IN MARCH OF 2025, NEARLY FIFTEEN YEARS AFTER I walked the beaches of Normandy with Medal of Honor recipient Sal Giunta, we met again in a brightly lit ballroom in Arlington, Virginia. I was the emcee for a Congressional Medal of Honor Society event recognizing citizens who exemplified "courage, sacrifice, integrity, commitment, citizenship and patriotism."

We were honoring Bryan Stern of Tampa, a combat veteran who has dedicated his life to rescuing Americans and their allies from conflict and disaster zones around the world. And teenager Jakob Thompson, who risked his life to save a woman being pulled out to sea from one of the most dangerous inlets in South Florida. Dan Marburger, the principal at Perry High School in Iowa, was honored posthumously for having confronted a shooter in the school's hallways—an intervention that allowed many staff and students to escape. Shot four times, he continued to distract the shooter, saving countless lives before losing his own.

Sal and some of his fellow Medal of Honor recipients presented the Citizen Honor Awards. Heroes honoring heroes. It was a fitting place for a reunion. A gathering of humble individuals, none of them wanting credit for what they had done, none of them accepting that their actions were anything out of the ordinary.

When Sal and I spotted each other before the program began, the years since our last encounter disappeared. We smiled, embraced, and remembered. We cherish our shared memories of that day at the cemetery in France. The salute from the Korean War veteran. The setting sun over the hallowed ground. Sal, still very much a young man at forty, was now a proud father of three young children. He showed me pictures and gave me an update on where life had taken him. I watched with emotion as people crowded around to shake his hand, young soldiers and cadets among them. His humility still defined him, and yet he had learned to embrace his own history.

Sal lost twenty-six friends in battle, including his best friend, Sergeant Josh Brennan. He now speaks for them. About them. Their memory inspires him every day, and they are the reason he has found new purpose inspiring others.

"I am about as average as they come," Sal tells people. "I am a five-nine dude from Iowa and if I can stand up here and be on the greatest team in the world so can you. In fact, you don't want to strive for what I am doing; you want to strive for better."

They were young and old, looking for encouragement and purpose, and there he was, telling each one of them who greeted him to find that direction and get it done. To face fear, to face challenges.

When I first approached the subjects of this book and told them why I was returning to their stories after so many years, they reacted in different ways, but every one of them made the same point in one way or another: *I was just doing my job. It wasn't just me alone.* Josh Webster wanted it known that everyone in his helicopter and the ground troops on that jagged mountainside had performed magnificently. Derek Herrera never stopped heaping praise on his team for carrying out a flawless rescue on that terrible morning in the Helmand Valley. Mark Little felt guilt for losing his legs and leaving his teammates back in Iraq. And Gail Ulerie and Debbie Schulz each said in her own way: What else would a mother do?

But I keep thinking back to Normandy, to the "Greatest Generation"—the moniker bestowed on the troops who fought the one war in our history that won near-unanimous approval from the American people. Tom Brokaw's book honored that generation in its twilight—and memorable films were made by Steven Spielberg and many other artists about its heroes. And rightly so.

But one of the reasons I wrote this book is that I am convinced we ought to honor the veterans of Fallujah and Tora Bora as we honor those who fought at Normandy and Iwo Jima. This generation of warriors and the families who support them are no less great. We should learn the lessons of the "forgotten" war in Korea and the shameful treatment of our Vietnam veterans. Yes, WWII had a moral clarity that other wars since have not had. But the warriors themselves showed courage, commitment, and patriotism.

Every one of these people, different as they are, whatever the battles they have fought, shares a passion for service that has outlasted the wars in which they fought. It's that sense of purpose, the search for mission and meaning, that feeling of *I am not done yet* that drove Derek Herrera to produce his groundbreaking innovation and Mark Little to create Warrior 360. It's why Debbie Schulz has worked tirelessly not just for her injured son, but on behalf of parents and spouses and other caregivers of the gravely wounded. You could rest on your laurels, if you were Kevin Shaeffer or Rocco Armonda or Charles Wickware, collect your military pension, and retreat from the challenge.

But none of these people have left it there. They've looked to do more—peered over the proverbial mountain, climbed it, and found the next mission. And that inspires me as well. I have known some of these heroes for so many years and I am a better person for knowing them. Their primary emotion is gratitude, for having made it home, and for the opportunities that a next chapter brought. And just as they have wanted to remind me of the other "heroes" in their stories, they remind me often of those they knew who didn't come home.

Whenever I visit with Eric Bourquin and the other members of that Brotherhood, there's a moment—often many moments—spent remembering and honoring the men who fell on April 4, 2004. Eddie Chen, Israel Garza, Robert Arsiaga, and the others. For all the trauma and pain Bourquin himself has borne, he considers himself a lucky man.

There will be more wars for our nation. Different wars with new technology. More unmanned aircraft and hopefully better protection for our men and women. But there will always be courageous warriors like those profiled in this book who put their lives on the line for the mission and for those fighting alongside them.

They have been a gift to me—these men and women, their stories and their friendship. When I have a day that feels challenging, personally or professionally, I think of them and what they have faced, and it becomes my own inspiration. Few among us will face anything like their challenges—a mid-firefight mountain rescue, a perilous bombing mission over Syria, or years spent at the bedside of a wounded child—but whatever challenges our own lives bring, we can all learn from their courage and resilience.

What's important to me is to try to be a good person and do my job well, and, beyond my family, the people who matter most to me are people like the ones whose stories I've shared in this book. Authentic. Bighearted. People who—at the risk of turning to an overused phrase—will always "have your back."

It may be too much to imagine that their stories will help build the bridges I mentioned in the introduction and remedy our divisions. But I have to believe this much: that whether you are from the right or left, a national security hawk or a fervent isolationist, you will absorb these stories and come to some common understanding. It can only help to be reminded that there are many among us who hold their love of country so dear—whatever their politics—that they are willing to fight and to die for it. Those people deserve our respect and gratitude; and maybe they will remind us that we all can do better—if we think in terms of our own "missions," the small and large ways we might work to better our communities, our fellow citizens, and our country. And in this moment, as our nation marks 250 years since the adoption of the Declaration of Independence, bridge-building and having lofty ambitions for a nation united seems a good way to go.

Respect and Remember.

Acknowledgments

I want to thank the people whose stories make up this book for their time, patience, and trust. Kevin Shaeffer, Steve Workman, Josh Webster, Kevin Mott Jr., Ben Hayhurst, Eric Bourquin, Carl Wild, Aaron Fowler, Mark Little, Charles Wickware, Danielle Thiriot, Gilbert Arsiaga, Angel Muñoz, Sylvia Macias, Rocco Armonda, Debbie and Steven Schulz, Shurvon Phillip, and Gail Ulerie are true heroes who, along with their families, deserve all the credit for this book. I cannot thank them enough for letting me into their lives and sharing some of their hardest moments with such grace and courage. It is an honor to know them.

I benefitted greatly from the expert help provided by Lieutenant Commander John "Chimpo" O'Neill, a Navy pilot, LSO, and friend who answered all my carrier piloting questions, and Steve Ganyard, a former Marine Corps fighter pilot and an ABC News contributor. Tommy Mariner generously shared memories of his wife Rosemary and gave his own unique insights into her life. General John F. Campbell, who commanded international forces in Afghanistan from 2014 to 2016, included me on many trips with him and was always generous with his assistance in my reporting. I know that he cares deeply about our servicemen and -women.

I could not have told the story of the rescue of Kevin Mott without the guidance of retired Army Master Sergeant Brent Schneider, former pararescueman Larry Hiyakumoto, and Lieutenant Colonel Thad Ronnau, all of whom participated in the rescue mission. Lieutenant Colonel Ronnau, the helicopter pilot, talked me through the mission using patio chairs to simulate the canyon through which he had to fly. What he did that day was extraordinary.

Thanks also to three of my favorite former soldiers—Josh York, Justin Bellamy, and Shane Coleman. They are all part of the Brotherhood and some of the finest people I know. Special thanks to Cory York for hosting me on my quick visit to her home state of Alaska.

A shout-out also to former Army Specialist Heriberto "Eddie" Arambula, a loyal friend over the years. After serving eleven years in the US Army and Coast Guard, he earned a PhD at Texas State University, focusing on veteran trauma and social reintegration. I am so proud of what he has done. I am also grateful to all the men and women of the 2-5 CAV who served in Sadr City, along with their families.

I am indebted to the CIA public affairs office for allowing Kevin Shaeffer to tell me his story. Tammy Thorp, Walter Trosin, and Dee Watson all recognized the power of Kevin's words. Walter and Dee first interviewed Kevin for *The Langley Files* podcast and generously shared their thoughts. I also relied on interviews Kevin did with the Naval Historical Center in 2002, while he was still recovering from his wounds.

This book could not have been written without the help of Tom Nagorski and Ely Brown. I have known Tom since his days as foreign editor at ABC News, and he has been both a mentor and a friend. Tom was instrumental in shaping my vision for this book, and he helped me see it through to the end. He is a careful and dedicated editor, and he was determined to help me make this the best book possible.

Ely has been by my side in conflict zones around the world for decades. A brilliant producer who feels as strongly about the people in this book as I do, her research and help with interviews were invaluable. ABC News is lucky to have her, and I am even luckier to have had her help on this book. She is as good a person as you will ever find.

I am also grateful to ABC colleagues and former colleagues who have been with me on some of the toughest assignments. Photographers Nicky de Blois, Scott Munro, Kuba Kaminski, Pat O'Gara, Nate Luna, Shadi Foley, Thorsten Hoefle, Bartley Price, and Doug Vogt are the best in the business, as are producers Cindy Smith, Richard Coolidge, Brian Hartman, Clark Bentson, Conor Finnegan, Aleem Agha, Habibullah Khan, Bruno Nota, Dana Savir, Bruno Roeber, and Nasser Atta. In recent years, I have also traveled with a new group of young producers who have eagerly embraced each assignment. It has been a pleasure to work with Sam Sweeney, Meghan Mistry, and Julia Cherner. Meghan provided some early research on the book as well.

Luis Martinez, who has been covering the Pentagon for ABC News for more than two decades, is one of the kindest and most honorable journalists I know. He has been a constant source of knowledge and expertise. Chris Donovan lent his sharp editing eye to a draft of this book. I also want to thank Anne Flaherty, Mae Joo, Imtiyaz Delawala, Mitch Alva, Kendall Heath, Quinn Scanlan, Chris Boccia, Eric Fayeulle, Andrea Owen, Jason Ratke, Van Scott, Brooks Lancaster, Perita Carpenter, Mary Bruce, Rachel Scott, Rebecca Jarvis, Linsey Davis, Elizabeth Schulze, Jonathan Karl, and Rick Klein for their support as well as Stephenie Ramos, our own ABC News Army veteran and correspondent.

Sabina Ghebremedhin managed to show love and support this past year despite the loss of her beautiful, brave daughter Natasha Allen to cancer. Sabina and Natasha are both heroes to me. And a special thanks to Marc Burstein, who retired in 2025. I miss his wisdom, humor, and depth every single day at ABC News. He will forever remain a friend. The keen minds of Kerry Smith, David Peterkin, and Karen Leo keep all of us on our toes.

Many thanks also to Chris Dinan, the executive producer of *World News Tonight*, and Simone Swink, the executive producer of *Good Morning America*, as well as Brian Reiferson, Chris Godburn, Pete Austin, Eric Noll, and Esther Castillejo. Thank you for caring about the beat I cover and for understanding the power of the stories I have been able to tell, as well as the people behind them.

Karen Travers, who has been an ace White House reporter at ABC News, escorted Mark Little to a White House Christmas party on my behalf when I was called off on an assignment. Just months after he was injured, Mark was able to meet President George W. Bush, thanks to Karen.

David Muir is a shining example to all of us at ABC and the most thoughtful colleague and leader anyone could wish for. As the daughter of a Tuskegee Airman, Robin Roberts knows the power of stories about unheralded heroes, and she is a continuing inspiration. I am immensely grateful to the incomparable Diane Sawyer for her mentorship, generosity, and inspiration since the moment I arrived at ABC News. Her career and her continued passion for storytelling are unmatched. I am in constant awe.

I could not have done any of this without the support of the leadership of ABC News. Bob Iger, Dana Walden, Debra O'Connell, and Almin Karamehmedovic have championed my work always. I am so lucky to work for such extraordinary people. Ben Sherwood and David Westin set that example. As the former president of ABC News, David was one of my greatest supporters over the many years I covered the wars in Iraq and Afghanistan, as were our former Washington bureau chiefs, Robin Sproul and Jonathan Greenberger.

Our Senior Vice President of Global News Gathering Katie Den Daas and our Director of International News Kirit Radia have supported me with incredible opportunities, and so have Joe Simonetti and Dimitrije Stejic.

I met several of the heroes in this book through the Bob Woodruff Foundation. Bob and Lee Woodruff deserve thanks from all of us for the extraordinary work they have done for veterans. They, too, are heroes. I am proud to be a member of the Foundation board and feel privileged to work with Dave Woodruff and Anne Marie Dougherty.

At Avid Reader Press, it was clear from the moment I first talked to Jofie Ferrari-Adler and Joy de Menil that they were passionate about this project. Their respect for the US military and the people whose stories make up this book was evident from the beginning. Joy's steady hand and commitment to the stories guided me every step of the way. Her dedication and skill are evident on every page. Thanks also to Avid's Alexandra Silvas for her patience and professionalism.

My agent, Gail Ross, at William Morris Endeavor, is the best in the business. She is the single reason this book got written. She knew I had more stories to tell, and she was determined to make that happen.

There is no one like her, and anyone lucky enough to call her their agent knows that.

I have been so fortunate to have the companionship of Brigadier General Troy Denomy and his wife, Gina, both dear friends, along with George and Sheila Casey and Matt Sherman. Mike and Irena Medavoy are the most gracious and generous friends imaginable. They are always there for me when I need a respite, and their support and love is unending. I met Jon and Hannah Beavers almost a decade ago and could not be more grateful for their friendship and love. Our joint trips around the world have provided a lifetime of memories. Thanks also to Mike and Caitlin Engelberg, Nate Fick and Margaret Angell, Susan Wornick, Viki Naisbitt, Patty and Clay Jensen, and Scott Williams.

There is no one I am more thankful for than my family. My husband, Tom Gjelten, is the most loving, caring, and supportive partner imaginable. A phenomenal journalist and author himself, he is an incredible editor and is also the world's best stepfather and grandfather.

My daughter, Greta, is brilliant and beautiful and a phenomenal mother to Magnolia and Morgan. She inspires me every day both professionally and personally. Greta has done remarkable work as a lawyer—work that matters. I could not possibly be prouder of her or love her more.

My son, Jake, is now a husband and a father of two adorable little boys, Eric and Gus. A high school football coach who mentors the kids who are lucky enough to cross his path and is a caring, kind human being, he could not have a better partner than his phenomenal wife, Karen, a child psychologist. Seeing her with Jake and their boys is pure joy.

Thanks also to my sister, Barbara Anderson, and her husband, Bob, who have provided nothing but encouragement and love.

We should all be grateful for the example that the men and women whose remarkable courage and resilience are chronicled in this book provide, and to all those who continue to serve the nation every day. I know I am.

Image Credits

Page / Credit

14 Courtesy of War.gov/Photograph by Gerry Gilmore

40 Photograph by Martha Raddatz

42 Photograph by Martha Raddatz

53 Courtesy of Kevin Mott

67 Photograph by Thorsten Hoefle

77 Courtesy of Kevin Mott

79 Photograph by Martha Raddatz

82 Photograph by Eric Bourquin

89 Photograph by Carl Wild

90 Courtesy of Carl Wild

92 Photograph by Carl Wild

93 Photograph by Carl Wild

96 Courtesy of Carl Wild

98 Photograph by Carl Wild

110 Photograph by Ben Hayhurst

113 Photograph by Ben Hayhurst

114 Courtesy of Martha Raddatz

116 Courtesy of Mark Little

119 Courtesy of Mark Little

134 Courtesy of Mark Little

139 Courtesy of Mark Little

141 Courtesy of Mark Little

146 Courtesy of Derek Herrera

153 Courtesy of Derek Herrera

162 Courtesy of Derek Herrera

166 Courtesy of US Marine Corps/Photograph by Sergeant Scott Achtemeier

172 Photograph by Brian Quach

174 Courtesy of the Herrera Family

178 Courtesy of Charles Wickware

181 Courtesy of Margaret Noble

183 Photograph by Margaret Noble

190 Photograph by Charles Wickware

191 Photograph by Jared Wickware

192 Courtesy of Charles Wickware

196 Courtesy of Martha Raddatz

205 Photograph by Charles Wickware

206 Courtesy of Danielle Thiriot

209 Courtesy of US Navy

217 Courtesy of Danielle Thiriot

227 Courtesy of Danielle Thiriot

231 Courtesy of Martha Raddatz

234 Courtesy of Martha Raddatz
236 Courtesy of Angel Muñoz
239 Courtesy of US Army
240 Courtesy of Angel Muñoz
242 Courtesy of First Calvary Division
247 Courtesy of US Marine Corps
252 Photograph by Lou Goodrum
252 Photograph by Lou Goodrum
261 Courtesy of Angel Muñoz
262 Photograph by Angel Muñoz
264 Courtesy of Rocco Armonda
266 Courtesy of Rocco Armonda
269 Courtesy of Rocco Armonda
270 Courtesy of Rocco Armonda
275 Courtesy of Rocco Armonda
279 Courtesy of Martha Raddatz
290 Courtesy of Steven Schulz
290 Courtesy of family of Shurvon Phillip
294 Courtesy of Debbie Schulz
299 Courtesy of the family of Shurvon Phillip
310 Photograph by Debbie Schulz
316 Photograph by Gail Ulerie
319 Courtesy of Debbie Schulz
320 Courtesy of Gail Ulerie
324 Courtesy of Gail Ulerie

Index

Page numbers in *italics* refer to images.

About the Author

MARTHA RADDATZ has been covering America's wars for ABC since September 11, as chief global affairs correspondent and co-anchor of *This Week*. She is the author of *The Long Road Home*, a *New York Times* bestseller made into a National Geographic miniseries. Raddatz was part of the team that won a Peabody Award for coverage of September 11 and an Emmy for coverage of the killing of Osama bin Laden. She has won seven Emmys. She was also awarded the George C. Marshall Medal for sustained commitment to the men and women of America's armed forces.